D0015831

THE BURNING HOUSE

THE BURNING HOUSE

Jim Crow and the Making of Modern America

ANDERS WALKER

Yale
UNIVERSITY PRESS
New Haven and London

Published with assistance from the income of the
Frederick John Kingsbury Memorial Fund.

Yale University Press books may be purchased in quantity for educational, business, or promotional use. For information, please e-mail sales.press@yale.edu (U.S. office) or sales@yaleup.co.uk (U.K. office).

Set in Janson type by Integrated Publishing Solutions,
Grand Rapids, Michigan.
Printed in the United States of America.

Library of Congress Control Number: 2017954709
ISBN 978-0-300-22398-9 (hardcover : alk. paper)

A catalogue record for this book is available from the British Library.

This paper meets the requirements of ANSI/NISO Z39.48-1992
(Permanence of Paper).

10 9 8 7 6 5 4 3 2 1

For Katharine

Contents

Acknowledgments

THIS BOOK FOCUSES ON intellectuals, mainly writers, who debated whether racial segregation contributed to cultural pluralism, a view that emerged in a variety of places and in a variety of forms throughout the Jim Crow era and into the 1970s and 1980s. My insights into this debate rely heavily on primary sources, including materials drawn from archives at Vanderbilt University, the University of Virginia, Emory University, Washington and Lee University, the University of Florida, the Southern Historical Collection at the University of North Carolina at Chapel Hill, the Library of Congress, and the Beinecke Library at Yale University. Many of the writers discussed in this book possessed a sense that even though Jim Crow was repressive, it also fostered racial diversity, a view that found its way back into law thanks to Supreme Court justice and Richmond native Lewis F. Powell, Jr. My recovery of Powell's views would not have been possible without the help of John Jacob at the Lewis F. Powell, Jr., Archives at Washington and Lee University School of Law.

In addition to Washington and Lee, which graciously invited me to present a chapter at its law school's workshop series, I am also indebted to the Florida State University College of Law, the University of Colorado Law School, Washington University in St Louis Law School, and Saint Louis University (SLU). I could imagine few home institutions more supportive of a project on law and culture than SLU, in part because of its longstanding Jesuit commitment to cultural understanding, a commitment that expressed itself not simply at the law school but also the Department of History and the Saint Louis University Center for Intercultural Studies, which provided early research support. Center director and history professor Michal Rozbicki deserves thanks, as do Torrie Hester, Silvana Siddali, Matthew Mancini, Lorri Glover, Joel Goldstein, Sam Jordan, Matthew Bodie, Eric Miller, Justin Hansford, Michael Korybut, and Jonathan Smith.

Just as SLU provided a supportive environment for this project, so too has Yale University Press been a joy to work with. I would like to thank my agent, Wendy Strothman, for brokering the deal with Yale; Steve Wasserman (now at Heyday) for providing early comments and advice; and Jennifer Banks for steering the project to completion. Jennifer's comments and advice helped sharpen my argument and bring out some of the book's relevance to current debates about race and diversity in America. I would also like to thank Heather Gold for helping get the manuscript and permissions in order and Margaret Hogan for a monumental job on the copyediting. All mistakes are my own.

Because the book relies heavily on unpublished sources, I am grateful to the following for granting permission to quote letters, drafts, and unpublished interviews. Excerpts from Eudora Welty's letters to Robert Penn Warren are reprinted by the permission of Russell & Volkening, Inc., as agents for the author, copyright © 1965 by Eudora Welty. Excerpts from Ezra Pound's letters to James Jackson Kilpatrick are reprinted by the permission of New Directions Publishing Corporation acting as agent, copyright ©2017 by Mary de Rachewiltz and the Estate of Omar S. Pound. Excerpts from the unpublished manuscript of Robert Penn Warren's book *Segregation: The Inner Conflict* on file at the Beinecke Library at Yale University are reprinted by the permission of the Literary Estate of Robert Penn Warren, c/o John Burt, Department of English, Brandeis University, Waltham, MA 02454. Unpublished writings of Lewis F. Powell, Jr., are reprinted by the permission of John Jacob, Lewis F. Powell, Jr., Papers, Washington and Lee University School of Law, Lewis F. Powell, Jr., Archives, Lexington, VA 24450.

Many scholars have weighed in on the project along the way, including David J. Garrow, Werner Sollors, Fitzhugh Brundage, James Cobb, John Burt, Glenda Gilmore, Daniel Sharfstein, David

Konig, Matthew Frye Jacobson, Jane Dailey, Christopher Schmidt, Jonathan Holloway, Brad Snyder, Deborah Dinner, Karen Tani, Sophia Lee, and Suzette Malveux. I would also like to thank the Georgetown, Columbia, USC, UCLA, and Stanford Law and Humanities Junior Scholars Workshop, and especially Ariela Gross, Naomi Mezey, Nomi Stolzenberg, Katharine Franke, Michelle McKinley, and Martha Umphrey.

Finally, I would like to thank my family for their support. This includes my parents for moving to Thomasville, Georgia, in 1979 and my wife, Jennifer, for encouraging me to return.

THE BURNING HOUSE

Introduction

In November 1962, James Baldwin disavowed the idea of racial integration, calling white America a "burning house." "I do not know many Negroes who are eager to be 'accepted' by white people," exclaimed Baldwin in the *New Yorker*, for whites "had robbed black people of their liberty," "profited" from their crime, and corrupted America in the process. They were "criminal," Baldwin charged, "terrified of sensuality," and could not, "in the generality, be taken as models of how to live." By contrast, African Americans possessed a more humane set of "standards," along with "other sources of vitality" that whites would do well to adopt. "The only way" that America could advance, argued Baldwin, was if whites agreed to "become black" and "to become part of that suffering and dancing country that [they] now watch wistfully from the heights of [their] lonely power."[1]

It was a startling assertion, not least because it challenged the prevailing view that African Americans wanted desperately to integrate into mainstream, white American society. This was the position taken by the National Association for the Advancement of Colored People (NAACP) in 1950, and it was adopted by the Supreme Court of the United States in 1954, in a landmark ruling styled *Brown v. Board of Education*, that declared integration the solution to America's racial "dilemma."[2]

Baldwin objected.

And he was not alone. In an early version of his novel *Absalom,*

Absalom! William Faulkner referred to the plantation owned by his main character, Thomas Sutpen, as a "burning house," a vainglorious ruin forged out of equal parts ambition and oppression, a symbol not simply of the Old South but perhaps America itself. Although Baldwin would criticize Faulkner's defense of southern moderates in 1956, both authors agreed that there were serious problems with mainstream American society, and that integration into that society was not necessarily a categorical good. Others joined, including Robert Penn Warren, who sat down with Baldwin in 1964 to discuss the implications of integration for the region. He took Baldwin's point that whites and blacks possessed different cultural traditions and that federally mandated integration aimed for a world where "everything is exactly alike and everybody is exactly alike," a monocultural dystopia that eliminated diversity and ordered whites and blacks into the same burning house.[3]

This yielded a paradox. How could racial justice be served without racial integration? And had the southern system of segregation fostered perceptions and/or manifestations of racial difference that were somehow worth preserving? Had the Jim Crow South, in other words, fostered diversity? Such questions occupied a cadre of prominent intellectuals, mainly writers, in the 1950s and 1960s, all of whom possessed close ties to the eleven former Confederate states. They included Robert Penn Warren, James Baldwin, William Faulkner, Richard Wright, Eudora Welty, Ralph Ellison, Zora Neale Hurston, Flannery O'Connor, Harper Lee, and Alice Walker.[4] This book recovers their exchanges and, in so doing, provides a dramatic rereading of Jim Crow's career. Although most historians emphasize Jim Crow as a system characterized by racial humiliation, violence, and terror, which it certainly was, many of the authors featured in this book added nuance to that story by balancing southern violence with southern art and suggesting that the segregated South, terrifying as it was, also proved fertile soil for artistic innovation and cultural production, a region that had escaped the homogenizing effects of northern industrialism and mass culture, and whose very system of racial segregation had fostered cultural development.[5] For such voices—white and black—ending segregation was less important than providing opportunities and jobs from within a framework that also respected racial traditions, racial identities, and loosely defined notions of racial culture. Such debates constituted an important, if counterintuitive chorus to the epic saga of civil rights at the time, which focused on desegregating public accommodations and schools.[6]

Why remember this now? The critiques of integration mounted by the writers in this book invite us to reconsider the Supreme Court's landmark decision integrating southern schools in 1954, suggesting that it may have hinged on a false assumption. Hailed as one of the Court's greatest opinions, *Brown v. Board of Education* cited a sociological study that declared black traditions, institutions, and culture "pathological," an indictment that left Baldwin, Ellison, and Hurston outraged.[7] "I regard the U.S. Supreme Court as insulting rather than honoring my race," noted Hurston, balking at the presumption that African Americans wanted to junk their history for the opportunity to rub shoulders with whites.[8] Ellison agreed, noting that there was much of great "value" and "richness" to black cultural traditions, even as there were deep problems with mainstream white society. "Lynching and Hollywood, faddism and radio advertising are products of the 'higher' [white] culture," argued Ellison. "Why, if my culture is pathological, must I exchange it for these?"[9]

Ellison's question raised a point that warrants debate, even today. As black journalist Ta-Nehisi Coates noted in his acclaimed 2015 book *Between the World and Me*, the "heritage" of white America may be one of such "enslavement," "rape," and "crime" that the "dream" of integration is itself undesirable. "I would not have you live like them," Coates enjoined his son in the book, for whites live in a state of "ignorance" that blacks, by their very "vulnerability," do not, a tragic condition that nevertheless places African Americans "closer to the meaning of life." Quite intentionally, Coates modeled his work after one of Baldwin's 1962 essays, leaving one to wonder whether white America remains a burning house, and whether the integration of blacks into mainstream white society may be less of a priority, even today, than the construction of a radical critique of that society, one that is "closer to the meaning of life," even if that means foregoing liberal, integrationist efforts at reform.[10]

Several writers featured in this book tended to think yes, even whites. For example, William Faulkner, Flannery O'Connor, Eudora Welty, Harper Lee, and Robert Penn Warren all believed that the push for racial integration stood in tension with the preservation of diversity, or "pluralism," for integration implied that everyone would be made the same (same wealth, same culture, even the same ideas). Zora Neale Hurston, Ralph Ellison, James Baldwin, Richard Wright, and Alice Walker agreed, maintaining that the pains African Americans had been forced to endure under Jim Crow's harsh, violent regime had actually made African Americans morally and spiritually superior, not inferior, to their violent, racist white peers.

This leads to a final reason for focusing on critiques of integration in the 1950s and 1960s now. As this book demonstrates, the worldview articulated by southern writers at that time helps to explain much about America today. For example, *Brown*'s emphasis on integration is generally viewed as a precursor to our current interest in diversity and to the Supreme Court's elevation of diversity as a constitutional ideal. However, the architect of that ideal was a Supreme Court justice from Virginia named Lewis F. Powell, Jr., who happened to frame diversity in the same way that many of the southern writers in this book did, as a bulwark against big government, a preservative of local particularity, and a guarantor of cultural innovation and growth. In case after case, Powell invoked pluralism as a rationale for tolerating lingering inequality—not equality—in the United States, a move that historians have overlooked, and that this book terms "southern pluralism." Once we place Powell's opinions in the context of southern letters at the time, we begin to see a legal landscape very different from the one charted in *Brown*, a constitutional legacy that prizes diversity over equality, that celebrates black perspectives but shies from big-state solutions to social problems, and that links diversity not to affirmative action but to other goals, including institutional freedom and pluralism, both more permanent than the Court's current emphasis on racial equality, which it has capped at twenty-five years.[11]

Powell's opinions are woven into this book, as are the opinions of another Supreme Court justice who hailed from the South: Clarence Thomas. Born in Pin Point, Georgia, in 1948, Thomas grew up reading Richard Wright and Ralph Ellison, agreeing with them that there was nothing inherently inferior about black institutions. And he, like Zora Neale Hurston, came to believe that *Brown*'s emphasis on segregation and psychological harm was misplaced, a dismissal of black achievement and an endorsement of white supremacy that prompted him to endorse a form of southern pluralism even more radical than that espoused by Lewis Powell.[12]

Using literature to shed light on a forgotten strand of southern thought, this book provides a radically new perspective on the struggle for civil rights by showing how southern intellectuals invoked the values of diversity and pluralism to critique integration. It concentrates on a prominent but also discrete cast of characters, mainly writers, who interacted in compelling, sometimes surprising ways, and in so doing asks fresh questions. How, for example, did cosmopolitan southerners—not violent extremists like George Wallace—but intellectuals and writers like Eudora Welty, Robert Penn Warren, William Faulkner, and Flannery O'Connor explain Jim Crow? Why did they insist on writing novels, short stories, poems, and memoirs that skirted emphatic support for civil rights and softened, instead, the story of segregation, downplaying its violence and extolling its tendency to encourage pluralism, two cultures—one white and one black—each with its own institutions, traditions, even identities? Why did they celebrate these identities, even arguing that they were threatened by the Supreme Court's order to desegregate southern schools in *Brown v. Board of Education*? And how did prominent black writers like James Baldwin, Ralph Ellison, Richard Wright, and Zora Neale Hurston participate in this debate, at times disputing but also, more often than one might expect, agreeing with their white counterparts? Was *Brown*'s insistence on assimilation a form of cultural imperialism? Was there a link between defending segregation and promoting diversity? Was integration really a burning house?[13]

CHAPTER ONE

The Briar Patch

AMIDST THE LUSH LAWNS, grey spires, and boggy canals of Oxford University strode a young, copper-headed man, sleight, with a chiseled face and an unsettling, unmoving glass eye. He was from Kentucky, and his name was Robert Warren. He would later add his mother's maiden name, Penn, but to Oxford he was simply Warren, a forgettable American from a forgettable town on the Kentucky/Tennessee border, one of many rural Americans who probably did not deserve a place at England's most prestigious university. Or at least that was the view of a growing number of Oxford professors, who lobbied the Rhodes Trust to amend its practice of sending one scholar from each American state to England, especially when many of those scholars were young men from southern and Midwestern states who happened to be unsophisticated, uneducated, and intellectually inferior, at least by British standards.[1]

Not Warren. The young southerner, then twenty-five, had entered Vanderbilt University at sixteen and so impressed prominent professors on the English faculty that they had invited him to join them at social gatherings to hear his views on poetry and literature. Warren, they all agreed, was a prodigy, a natural talent who graduated with honors, picked up a Masters at the University of California, landed a position at Yale, and then scored a prestigious Rhodes scholarship that took him from New England to New College, one of the most storied divisions of Oxford University.[2]

While many Rhodes scholars expressed a sense of awe and intimidation at England's great medieval university, Warren affectionately deemed the place a "dump," a vestige of a once great Britain, an imperialist power that had been rightly trounced by a ragtag bunch of sharpshooters and squirrel hunters from the North American backcountry, men not entirely unlike himself. Warren took this backwoods irreverence with him to New College in 1928, ignoring the cultural pretensions of the school's upper-class, boat-rowing elite and opting instead for poker, cocktails, and the company of women, a vice that almost got him expelled in 1929. All the while he was drafting a biography of violent, gun-toting American abolitionist John Brown.[3]

Warren had hatched the idea of a project on Brown at Vanderbilt, a southern school named for Yankee railroad magnate Cornelius Vanderbilt, who incidentally never set foot in the South but hoped to uplift the region by founding a college there. The plan failed. By the 1920s, Vanderbilt had become an operating base for a lost battalion of Confederate poets who decried the North, extolled the South, and dreamt of an America made up not of industry and railroads but small towns, rolling farms, and close-knit communities where black and white worked together side by side in Platonic harmony, composing folksongs, reciting folklore, and generating regional literature like blackberries on barbwire.

Warren called it a briar patch. He came up with the title after one of his former professors at Vanderbilt, a young poet named Donald Davidson, asked him to compose an essay defending the South's system of racial segregation, Jim Crow. Davidson, along with fellow Vanderbilt professor John Crowe Ransom, belonged to an informal literary group called the Fugitives, who fancied themselves fleeing from northern industrialism and "mass culture," both of which they feared were undermining tradition, religion, leisure, and the arts. By the 1930s, they had assumed another name: the "Agrarians," more assured, less defensive, more committed to a holistic—almost utopian—vision of the South. As they made clear in an anthology that featured Warren's Oxford essay, Jim Crow was not a dungeon of dehumanization and repression so much as a hub of slow-paced, leisurely living where individuals worked according to the relaxed cycles of harvest and planting, meanwhile retaining considerable time for social interaction and creative self-expression. "The South has been rich in the folk arts," wrote Davidson, "and is still rich in them, in ballads, country songs and dances, in hymns and spirituals, in folk tales, in the folk crafts of weaving, quilting, furniture-making," all practices that distinguished the region from the rapidly industrializing North. Part of the reason for the South's rich culture, argued Davidson, was its slow pace of life, a languid mode of living that was shared by both races and, perhaps ironically, exemplified by blacks. "If you paid the Negro twice the normal wage for a day's work," argued Davidson, "the Negro simply and ingenuously worked only half as many days or hours as before—and spent the rest of the time in following his conception of the good life: in hunting, dancing, singing, social conversation, eating, religion and love." Clearly prejudiced in his portrayal of African Americans as lazy and unenterprising, Davidson nevertheless took it as an article of faith that blacks embraced a particularly laudable manifestation of "southern principles." Blacks "had not been corrupted into heresy by modern education," explained Davidson, but rather remained "the most traditional of Southerners, the mirror which faithfully and lovingly reflected the traits that Southerners once all but unanimously professed." Although inferior, in other words, African Americans were also exemplars of the South's attention to culture, community, and creative self-expression, harbingers of its pluralism.[4]

Warren agreed, choosing not to describe racial segregation as a repressive legal regime so much as a place where African Americans could thrive free from the corrupting influences of status-conscious, work-addicted whites. To make his point, Warren borrowed an image from a black folktale about a rabbit who outsmarts a fox. In the story, Brother, or "Brer," Rabbit is captured by the fox and begs not to be cast into a tangle of prickly scrambling shrubs, a "briar patch." Of course, Brer Rabbit refuses to confess that he, like other rabbits, grew up in precisely such an environment and could easily negotiate the thorns and escape. For Warren, the motif described Jim Crow. Just as Brer Rabbit considered the briar patch a place of safety, so too did Warren liken racial segregation to a haven, a legal refuge that allowed African Americans to develop their own traditions, culture, and creative practices apart from whites.[5]

Warren even went so far as to lobby for a completely autonomous black society. "There are strong theoretical arguments in favor of higher education for the negro," argued Warren, "but those arguments are badly damaged if at the same time a separate negro community or group is not built up which is capable of absorbing and profiting from those members who have received this higher education." If the races integrated, he posited, competition and violence would ensue, leading to riots such as those in northern cities like Youngstown, Ohio, in 1919 and East St. Louis, Illinois, in 1917. Mobs of whites had rampaged through the streets of East St. Louis attacking blacks, many of whom had recently moved from the South, looking for work. "It is an old situation in the North," noted Warren, "where the negro, cut off from the protection of the unions in time of peace, made an ideal scab in time of trouble. This fact and the related fact of the negro's lower standard of living have been largely responsible for the race riots which have occurred in the north since the days of the [Civil] war." There was some truth to this: black migrations northward following the war had antagonized relations with white, unionized labor, particularly as manufacturers hired African Americans to break strikes.[6]

Warren's invocation of labor violence in the North enabled him to link the cause of segregation to southern arguments that Jim Crow promoted racial harmony and peace, in part by creating two separate societies, one white and one black, each capable of "tak[ing] care of all the needs and wants of [their] members." This was not a new idea but rather a notion that had been popular in the South since Warren's boyhood. As North Carolina governor Charles Brantley Aycock explained in 1901, four years before Warren was born, whites endorsed the production of black "literature" and "art" so long as it did not involve "social intermingling." That African Americans might develop their own art and literature reflected an emerging view of race common at the turn of the century, a sense that the races were better off in separate spheres, divided to an extent they had not been under slavery. During slavery, for example, southerners tended to argue that bondage improved black life by assimilating slaves into Anglo-American culture, Christianizing them and stamping out their pagan, African past. Further, slave owners did not, as a group, endorse racial segregation. Not only did they live and work in close proximity to their slaves, but a not insignificant number fathered children and formed entire families with their slaves. Even though most southern states prohibited interracial marriage, in other words, many slave owners assumed that their property rights included the right to engage in coercive sex with black women, particularly women they owned, resulting in an illicit, but all too common, form of integration.[7]

After the war, this changed. Interracial sex assumed a particularly controversial cast as an emerging generation of white leaders argued that "race-mixing" threatened white supremacy, leading to an obsession with racial purity that had not existed under slavery. Terms like "miscegenation" emerged to describe social chaos and collapse, as a new generation of southern leaders stoked fears of interracial sex and black-on-white rape to rally white middle- and lower-class voters into joining them in common cause against Republicans, Readjusters, Populists, and anyone else who might endorse black rights. Meanwhile, a rising generation of New South boosters led by figures like *Atlanta Constitution* editor Henry W. Grady argued that African Americans no longer needed to be absorbed into Anglo-Saxon culture but rather should be left free to develop their own culture, their own institutions, and their own identity.[8]

Religion provided an example. According to Grady, efforts by white religious leaders like Methodist Episcopal bishop Gilbert Haven to join white and black congregations failed because African Americans preferred to worship alone. "After the first month" of integrated services, noted Grady in 1885, Haven's congregation was "decimated." Not only did blacks and whites not want to worship together, but "blacks left it in squads." Instead, African Americans opted for "their own churches, congregations, pastors, conferences, and bishops," a mutually agreeable arrangement that became a model for Jim Crow. "There is not the slightest antagonism between them and the white churches of the same denomination," maintained Grady, nor should there be; separate institutions bred harmony.[9]

Even historian C. Vann Woodward conceded that churches were

segregated long before Jim Crow laws required it, a counterpoint to his argument that whites and blacks were coming together after the war. Also separate were "militia companies, schools, state and private welfare institutions, and a wide range of activities." When formal laws restricting interracial contact were finally passed in the 1890s, many simply codified older patterns "deeply ingrained in southern life." As Henry Grady observed in 1885, black southerners "have their own social and benevolent societies, their own military companies, their own orders of Masons and Odd-fellows." The forces that sustained such organizations were not "centrifugal" but "centripetal," argued Grady, meaning that they came from within, not without, the black community.[10]

Of course, the forging of separate institutions did not always happen centripetally, or peacefully. In some parts of the South, like Colfax, Louisiana, and Wilmington, North Carolina, whites took up arms and drove African Americans from courthouses, polling places, and even homes. But proponents of Jim Crow like Grady downplayed such violence, arguing that tensions exploded only when blacks challenged white authority, not when they remained in their own spheres. Indeed, the maintenance of separate racial spheres, argued New South boosters, provided the best chance of maintaining interracial peace.[11]

Separate spheres served other goals as well. According to Grady, blacks enjoyed "more freedom" and "more chance[s] for leadership" than if they had been forced into "association with the whites." The same held true, Grady maintained, for schools. "Far from feeling debased by the separate-school system," argued Grady, African Americans "insist that the separation shall be carried further, and the few white teachers yet presiding over negro schools [be] supplanted by negro teachers."[12]

While Henry Grady harbored his own self-interested reasons for claiming that African Americans balked at sending their children to school with whites, he was right to assume that blacks bore no special love for their former masters. Not an insignificant number of southern blacks "longed for vengeance" against their white countrymen, even dreaming of a "race war" to "wipe [whites] out of existence" during and after Reconstruction. Others "resent[ed]" whites quietly, working with their Anglo-Saxon "enemies" so that they could "survive and advance." Rather than come together after slavery, in other words, the races grew even "farther apart," leading some to deem the odds of a voluntary rapprochement between black and white unlikely. "Things Southern whites and blacks said about one another at the turn of the century" reached "extreme" levels of "bitterness, hatred, and confusion," argued historian Edward Ayers, raising the possibility that progressives like Grady really did believe that southern "negroes" were "satisfied" with segregation.[13]

Although many blacks came to detest both Jim Crow and the whites who sponsored it, some prominent African American leaders came out in favor of the arrangement. "In all things that are purely social, we can be as separate as the fingers," declared Booker T. Washington in 1895 in Atlanta, "yet one as the hand in all things essential to mutual progress." Mutual progress, argued Washington, hinged on developing a skilled black labor force that could command a decent wage in the open market, gradually accumulating black property and wealth. Even black leaders like W. E. B. Du Bois, who publicly decried white efforts to legislate African Americans out of politics in the 1890s, endorsed the notion that black "destiny" did not lie in an "absorption by white Americans" nor in a "servile imitation of Anglo-Saxon culture." Instead, Du Bois advocated "the creation of "self-sustaining" black institutions and a "cooperative" black economy as "antidotes to white supremacy." Such self-reliant strategies exemplified the kind of pluralism that progressives like Grady endorsed, even pushing whites in the South to celebrate Jim Crow as an incubator of African American culture. "Where is the mother college" that produced "negro culture," asked the Atlanta Chamber of Commerce newsletter in 1917. "Is it Africa or Asia? No it has grown on Atlanta soil."[14]

Ironically, even as white southerners celebrated racial pluralism, northern voices stressed assimilation. Some criticized black churches, decrying black modes of worship as "too emotional, too primitive and wild, and too lacking in moral directive." Others declared African Americans incapable of managing their own institutions, on account of the fact that slavery had "dulled the minds of its victims," "destroyed their self-respect, and rendered them incapable of taking care of themselves." Convinced that their way of doing things was irrefutably correct, northerners "could not connect the right to be free with the right to be different."[15] White southerners, by contrast, had no problem with the notion that blacks were different; in fact, they presumed it. Even if they were racists, they were not necessarily, to borrow a term from James M. McPherson, "culturalists," meaning individuals who insisted on the imposition of one, monolithic culture across the South. According to President Woodrow Wilson, a Virginian, segregation encouraged the "comfort and the best interests of both races," avoided interracial "friction," and facilitated the "independent development" of the races.[16]

Robert Penn Warren shared Wilson's view and spent his time at Oxford criticizing northerners who wanted to eradicate black culture, none more notorious than white abolitionist John Brown. In his biography of Brown, Warren demonstrated how Brown had been a failed businessman who suffered repeated bankruptcies during his lifetime, leading him to forgo material gain and attach himself to higher causes, including evangelical Christianity and antislavery, both of which inspired him to lead a raid against proslavery settlers near Lawrence, Kansas, in 1856. While inspired by high ideals, Brown ended up killing five civilians—an act of savagery that intrigued Warren—who made a point of linking Brown's antislavery idealism to his proclivity for violence, ultimately leading to his death at the gallows for plotting a slave uprising in Harpers Ferry, Virginia. Although held up as a hero by many, Brown struck Warren as a fanatic who cared less for the plight of slaves in the South than his own self-aggrandizement, an individual whose "egotism" eventually convinced him that "his own will and the divine will were one."[17]

Oddly indifferent to Brown's noble aspirations, Warren focused instead on Brown's dismissive attitudes toward African Americans. For example, Warren attacked a "pamphlet" that Brown wrote in 1848 called *Sambo's Mistakes* in which Brown presumptuously categorized black "failings," including a tendency to spend money on leisure rather than benefiting "the suffering members" of their own race, meanwhile squandering literacy by reading "silly novels and other miserable trash." Of course, these were the very traits that the Fugitives admired about African Americans, a stereotypical aversion to work and a passion for leisurely pursuits. Warren underscored this, casting Brown as a heartless Yankee who secretly reviled blacks, complaining that they "wasted" their time joining organizations like the "Free Masons, Odd Fellows, Sons of Temperance, and a score of other secret societies" when they could have been "seeking the company of intelligent, wise, and good men." To Warren, such indictments were condescending dismissals of black institutions, traditions, and cultural practices, all of which were worth preserving.[18]

Naturally, Warren was prejudiced. But his prejudice, oddly, made him a pluralist. Warren underscored his appreciation for black institutions by celebrating Booker T. Washington in his Oxford essay, praising Washington's emphasis on vocational training for African Americans. "An emphasis on vocational education for the negro," argued Warren, was not "a piece of white man's snobbery" but a practical solution to the legacy of slavery. Only when sufficient numbers of black workers emerged to support a robust black economy, he suggested, could African Americans afford to support "intellectual aristocrats." Here, Warren challenged Du Bois, who had lobbied for the creation of a black elite, or "talented tenth," to uplift the race. Warren thought this backward. "There are strong theoretical arguments in favor of higher education for the negro," noted Warren, "but those arguments are badly damaged if at the same time a separate negro community or group is not built up which is capable of absorbing and profiting from those members who have received this higher education."[19]

Although he extolled practical training for African Americans, in other words, Warren did not envision a black society entirely made up of serfs. Instead, he pictured an African American elite existing in a parallel universe to white elites, both supported by laboring classes. To his mind, the creation of a talented tenth was not a bad idea; it just needed to come after the South produced a lower class capable of supporting it, lest they depart for better opportunities in the North. "If the negroes in the South cannot support their more talented and better equipped individuals," argued Warren, "the educated negro will leave the South to seek his fortune elsewhere."[20]

Unsurprisingly, this is precisely what happened. Even as Warren banged out his essay on Jim Crow in England, blacks were leaving the South in staggering numbers, seeking jobs and opportunities unavailable in Dixie. Repelled by white violence and drawn by the promise of industrial work, nearly 1 million African Americans emigrated from places like Birmingham and Atlanta to seek opportunity in northern cities like Chicago and New York during the early decades of the twentieth century. Such outmigration undermined the Fugitives' claims about the advantages of rural southern living, particularly arguments about the mutual agreeability of segregation. Warren and his fellow Agrarians felt "saddened" by such departures, hoping instead for a biracial South where whites and blacks could live and work productively in their separate spheres, busily dedicated to the "development" of their respective cultures and "art."[21]

Instead, black art moved to Harlem. Southern-born writers like James Weldon Johnson traveled north to New York, where they proceeded to write eloquently about black life under Jim Crow—forming a type of ex-patriot community that rivaled, if not eclipsed, the Fugitives. Even black artists not born in the Deep South like Langston Hughes from Missouri and Jean Toomer from Washington, D.C., focused heavily on southern themes, at once underscoring Warren's conviction that the South provided cultural inspiration, even if it drove the inspired away.[22]

Disappointed that so many black writers had *not* taken a stand in Dixie, Warren acknowledged that certain aspects of the South's legal order needed reform. "The negro frequently fails to get justice" from the courts, he confessed, prompting him to support "equal right before the law." Yet, what Warren termed "equal right" did not mean ending black poverty or promoting integration. Rather, it referred to procedural justice, the notion that blacks deserved the same due-process protections as whites. "It will be a happy day for the South," he argued, "when no court discriminates in its dealings between the negro and the white man." Such discrimination did not, of course, mean ending segregation, which Warren deemed a positive arrangement. In fact, anyone who believed that abandoning segregation might promote the cause of racial justice, argued Warren, suffered from a "subtle and confused" logic rooted in an unwarranted "desiring" of another "man's art." The races, he implied, should develop their own art, and their own culture. "The Southern white man," noted Warren, "may conceive of his own culture as finally rooted in the soil, and he may desire, through time and necessary vicissitude, to preserve it." Such a move toward cultural preservation benefited African Americans as well, he suggested, for Jim Crow provided "the readiest and probably the surest way, for the greater number of the negroes to establish themselves."[23] Blind to Jim Crow's discriminatory aspect, Warren recast racial segregation as an unlikely source of black cultural freedom, the fabled briar patch where Brer Rabbit could thrive.[24]

Published in an anthology with the provocative title *I'll Take My Stand: The South and the Agrarian Tradition*, Warren's "Briar Patch" essay provoked little reaction, most critics taking issue not with the Fugitives' defense of segregation so much as their "poetic and passionate attack upon mass production, the machine, the industrial way of life, and its ideals of service and progress." Here, they disagreed with Henry Grady, who promoted economic development, and Grady's followers, a cadre of whom worked at the University of North Carolina in Chapel Hill (UNC) and published their own anthology of essays responding to Warren and company entitled *Culture in the South* in 1934.[25]

Sponsored by a young editor named William Terry Couch, *Culture in the South* aimed to present the region in a positive light, not by maligning the North for building factories but rather by discussing "all of the important phases of culture in the southern states," including "the daily routine" of average southerners—black and white—their "folk songs," "speech patterns," "humor," and "handicrafts." Like Warren and the Agrarians, Couch and company celebrated black cultural practices, adopting an anthropological definition of culture that documented patterns of life as practiced by ordinary people, not elites. Earlier definitions of culture had focused almost exclusively on upper-class customs, highly "conscious and rational" practices like ballet, opera, and orchestral music, all aimed at expressing the "highest stage of evolutionary progress yet attained." That such highbrow practices constituted the only legitimate manifestation of culture drew formal criticism around 1900, however, when an anthropologist named Franz Boas advanced the idea that the customs and practices of common folk also qualified as culture, and that every culture possessed its own intrinsic worth, a notion that would come to be called "cultural relativism." To demonstrate, Boas advocated the intensive study of folklore, including traditional practices of storytelling, music, and crafts.[26]

The Chapel Hillians loved it. One of Boas's students, a UNC

professor named Howard W. Odum, was a friend and colleague of Couch. Odum had published an essay in 1915 arguing that racial characteristics were subject to "movement," "progress," and "development," an idea that coincided with the notion that the races, and their cultures, evolved over time. Odum explored these themes further in a 1926 book called *Negro Workaday Songs*, which rooted black cultural practice not in biology or heredity but in the segregated labor conditions of the Deep South. Fascinated by the link between segregation and culture, Odum stressed the importance of studying the "environment" in which African Americans lived, including ways that said environment implicated whites. To illustrate, he endorsed the improvement of black housing conditions because "good homes for whites and good homes for the negroes are closely related," not least because "bad housing" for blacks could lead to "disease," "poor health," and "insanitary surroundings," all of which might compromise the "health conditions" of whites. To prevent white children from being exposed to ailing black domestics, Odum recommended that whites work to improve conditions in black communities. "Conditions of housing and health," he argued, are "not the problem of one race, but of two."[27]

Meanwhile, Odum cautioned against integration, arguing that challenges to segregation might lead to disaster. "Wherever law is broken," he warned, "there ensues civic tragedy." One such tragedy was lynching, often triggered by perceived violations of the code of segregation, a practice that Odum believed spread "devastating fear," cheapened "human life," and "violate[d] all the better traditions of southern honor and ideals." To his mind, lynching should be eradicated, even if it stemmed from deep-seated racist customs, or "folkways," embraced by large numbers of southern whites. Such folkways could be tempered, believed Odum, through "the principles and practices of Christianity," along with the continued maintenance of segregation, a legalist arrangement that allowed for mutual development and peace.[28]

It was a noble but naive, idea. While Odum envisioned a segregated South without lynching, it was unclear that violence could actually be separated from Jim Crow. At its core, the system relied on violence to survive. Despite aspirational claims that segregation promoted cultural development, which it did, it also demanded a level of deference from blacks that could not have been maintained without the omnipresent threat of violence. At every turn, African Americans faced threats of recrimination if they crossed racial lines, even minor ones. This was not a point that intellectuals like Odum and Warren liked to admit, but it formed an intrinsic part of the system nevertheless. In many ways, it hemmed the briar patch, leaving African Americans with little choice but to develop their own cultural practices and traditions, lest they face the noose.[29]

Odum suggested as much in 1931. Speaking to a group of sociologists, he invoked the idea of "folkways" to describe unwritten customs that guided human conduct, independent of written law or "stateways." Stateways, argued Odum, lacked authority, but folkways did not. "There was a folk society for both white and black" in the South, he claimed, each with its own "folklore, folk song, and more primitive folkways." White folkways, warned Odum, included a deep commitment to racial supremacy, sanctioning violence if racial norms were breached. Black folkways, by contrast, incorporated rich oral and musical traditions that Odum heralded as "genuine poetry," arguably superior to "what the white man calls 'culture.'" Further, black folkways evolved in part as a means or dealing with white violence, a coping mechanism that allowed African Americans to survive Jim Crow.[30]

Odum's paean to black folkways raised complex questions about cultural evolution, syncretism, and origination in the American South. To what extent, for example, could there actually be said to exist quantifiably different racial cultures in the region? And, if there were separate cultures, did black culture originate in the material conditions of the American South or did it hail from other places? To what extent, if any, did it derive from white, European traditions? To what extent did it derive from Africa or the Caribbean? Such questions became a topic of debate in the 1930s, prompting early students of black culture like Melville J. Herskovits to warn that endorsements of black culture might also yield defenses of segregation. White southerners "who urge social and economic segregation for the American Negro," argued Herskovits in 1937, "vindicate their position by contemplating the Africanisms retained in American Negro life. Is this not evidence, they say, of the inability of the Negro to assimilate white culture to any workable degree, and should not Negroes therefore be encouraged to develop their own peculiar 'racial' gifts—always, that is, within the bounds of the Negro's 'place.'"[31]

This, in a way, was what Warren was doing: defending segregation by celebrating black culture. Yet, white interest in black culture was not simply a ruse for reactionary politics. Some took a genuine interest in African American artistic expression. In the winter of 1926, for example, one of the contributors to Terry Couch's *Culture in the South*, a UNC professor named Guy B. Johnson traveled to New York City to meet with black intellectual and civil rights leader James Weldon Johnson on the topic of black vernacular music. Much like the black elites that Warren argued might leave the South, James Weldon Johnson had done just that, relocating from Florida to New York after establishing himself as a lawyer, educator, journalist, author, and—finally—composer in Jacksonville. By the time he left Florida in 1901, Johnson already enjoyed national acclaim for composing a popular tune entitled "Under the Bamboo Tree" and a more serious song called "Lift Every Voice and Sing," later celebrated as black America's "national anthem." Even though his music drew on southern themes, he preferred the "cosmopolitan" atmosphere of Harlem to Dixie, eventually rising to executive secretary of the NAACP in New York. There, Johnson merged art and politics by dedicating himself to the political and cultural dismantling of negative racial stereotypes, including negative cultural portrayals of African Americans in literature and film. For example, he attacked the film *Birth of a Nation* in 1915, noting that the movie's romantic portrayal of the Ku Klux Klan did African Americans "incalculable harm." Seven years later, he stated explicitly that "nothing" would do more to reform the "mental attitude" of whites than "a demonstration of intellectual parity" through "the production of literature and art." Johnson's interest in the political salience of art pushed him not only to develop his own work but also to recover extant black folk traditions, including poetry and music in the South, a move that would become central to the Harlem Renaissance.[32]

Needless to say, gathering black southern folklore in New York proved a challenge. To aid him in this project, James Weldon Johnson enlisted the expertise of Chapel Hill scholars Howard Odum and Guy Johnson, the very same experts who had defended segregation on cultural grounds at UNC. On January 29, 1926, James Weldon Johnson wrote Guy Johnson a letter noting that he was working on a book recovering southern black music and that the white North Carolinian's familiarity and proximity to the material would greatly help his project. Flattered, Guy Johnson traveled to New York with a collection of black music that he had transcribed in North Carolina. James's brother transcribed the melodies and sent Guy back to procure more, inadvertently making him—a white southerner who believed in segregation—an agent of the Harlem Renaissance.[33]

That Guy B. Johnson aided James Weldon Johnson in the recovery of black folklore in the 1920s was remarkable. On the one hand, the North Carolinian's assistance clearly bore political implications, particularly given James's interest in dismantling negative racial stereotypes. On the other hand, Guy's contribution underscored the potentially countervailing point that the races were in fact culturally different, a core belief of segregationists. Yet, even as he stressed the differences between black and white, Guy Johnson seemed to indicate that black culture was also equal to white, in some cases superior. He reflected on this precise subject in *Culture in the South*, arguing that even "people who believe that the Negro is little more than a brute and that his presence here is a horrible menace to white civilization" have nevertheless been "fairly unanimous in their praise of his musical achievements." Black musical achievement, he continued, represented one of the South's great cultural assets, stemming not only from "borrow[ed]" white music but also from original black music "as good as, or better than, anything" whites had produced. In fact, he elevated indigenous black folksongs above the "monstrosities of Broadway," citing directly to black scholars like James Weldon Johnson, who had documented black folksongs in the South in his compilation *The Book of American Negro Spirituals*.[34]

Guy Johnson's reference to Broadway's "monstrosities" proved ironic, not least because many of New York's most accomplished composers at the time took regular inspiration from southern themes—even songwriters who lacked personal knowledge of the region. For example, Brooklyn-born songwriter George Gershwin scored a hit in 1919 with a song about banjos, mammies, and Georgia's Suwanee, or "Swanee," River as he called it, while Brooklyn-born composer Walter Donaldson impressed audiences in 1921 with a tune simply entitled "My Mammy" and another in 1922 called "Morning in Carolina." Although James Weldon Johnson had himself been a successful Broadway composer, penning tunes like "The Congo Love Song" and "Hello Ma Lulu," the dramatic rise of white, northern "imitators" and "adulterators" as Johnson put it, may have explained his subsequent interest in southern folklore collectors like Guy Johnson. While Guy possessed little interest in black rights, he too believed in promoting southern culture—including black culture—something that both James Weldon Johnson and NAACP secretary Walter White thanked him for. In fact, both White and James Weldon Johnson spent the 1920s engaged heavily in promoting black writers and artists, a campaign that would contribute to what the New York *Herald Tribune* declared in 1925 to be a "renaissance" of black art, music, and letters in Harlem. However, much of that renaissance had its roots in the South, in places like UNC.[35]

Other leaders of the Harlem Renaissance hailed from Dixie as well. In addition to James Weldon Johnson, there was Georgia native Walter White, who joined Johnson at the top of the NAACP in the 1920s, and a third, arguably even more "important" architect of the renaissance: black Virginian Charles S. Johnson, who spotlighted new talent and procured financial support for working artists through a journal called *Opportunity*. Like James Weldon Johnson and White, Charles S. Johnson had also left the South for the North. However, he joined Robert Penn Warren in recognizing that even if blacks faced insurmountable political odds in Dixie, "no exclusionary rules had been laid down regarding a place [for blacks] in the arts." Culture, in other words, presented itself as a place of relative freedom for African Americans living in the briar patch of Jim Crow.[36]

If Robert Penn Warren lamented the departure of black elites from the South in 1929, the convergence of those elites in places like Harlem lent credence to Warren's notion that Jim Crow had in fact coincided with the development of a distinctively black "art." Even black Harlemites who did not hail from the South became interested in southern themes. For example, African American scholar Alain Locke, a native of Philadelphia, encouraged northern interest in southern black culture when he published an anthology of black poetry, prose, and social commentary entitled *The New Negro* in 1925. While rooted in Yankee soil, Locke and his contributors drew much of their inspiration from "resources in African American folklore," a task that, ironically, Guy Johnson had assisted with. On October 10, 1928, Locke wrote to Johnson at UNC, thanking him for assisting in the collection of black music in the South.[37]

Yet even as Johnson helped Locke, he did not, at the end of the day, believe that whites and blacks were equal. This became clear when he volunteered to help a Swedish social scientist named Gunnar Myrdal study race and racism in the United States in 1939. Invited by the prestigious Carnegie Corporation, Myrdal arrived in America in 1938 and promptly began assembling a massive team of researchers to investigate all aspects of black life, including religion, schools, culture, and economics. The study drew inspiration from former mayor of Cleveland and Carnegie Corporation trustee Newton D. Baker, who cautioned in 1935 that "neglect" of black conditions in America had led to "tragic episodes" like "the Springfield and East St. Louis riots" and warranted further study. While Robert Penn Warren had of course invoked both Springfield and East St. Louis to explain why segregation was normatively good, Baker took it to be bad, calling for a more critical inquiry into black conditions, North and South.[38]

Carnegie President Frederick Keppel chose Myrdal in part because he came from Sweden, a country that boasted a "nonimperialistic" history and was therefore capable of approaching American race relations with a "fresh mind." This Myrdal did, foisting many of his own views about assimilation and progress onto black America. For example, even as he did an excellent job documenting the violence and discrimination that stalked African Americans in the Jim Crow South, he also concluded that African American culture was "pathological," at best an impoverished version of white culture with inferior schools, churches, and voluntary associations that only exacerbated a host of "social pathologies" endemic to black communities, including "broken families, crime, disease, [and] prostitution."[39]

For all his research on black folklore, Guy Johnson did little to stem Myrdal's critique of other aspects of black life, at times even contributing to it. For example, from 1939 to 1944, Johnson advised Myrdal on recruiting researchers and designing a course of study, agreeing to draft a section of Myrdal's final report on black religion. In that report, Johnson indicated that even if black music might have been superior, other aspects of black life were not. "The Negro church," he wrote, suffered from "backwardness," and he complained that black churches "indulged in emotional ecstasy" while eschewing politics for an "otherworldly outlook."[40]

Other contributors proved even less sympathetic. Arnold Rose, a University of Chicago graduate student, penned a controversial chapter on "the Negro community" that openly declared black culture "pathological." To Rose's mind, cultural "assimilation" comprised a "central element" of the "American creed," a point underscored by the "melting pot" ideal in which "diverse ethnic groups" emigrate to the United States and "abandon" their "cultural particularities." Excluded from this process, argued Rose, were African Americans, who had not been "allowed to assimilate" but rather had been kept apart by prohibitions against intermarriage and laws that "segregated" the races. Shut out of the American melting pot, blacks had "developed" their own "separate institutions" including their own "American Negro culture." However, that culture did not—to Rose's mind—possess its own inherent value or worth but rather represented a "distorted" or "pathological" version of the "general American culture." To bolster this claim, Rose referenced a series of factors, including a study of the black family by African American sociologist E. Franklin Frazier, noting that "family disorganization" was high in black communities, as evidenced by the fact that "Negroes have about eight times as much illegitimacy as native whites." While Frazier's actual argument was that black illegitimacy rates varied based on geography and therefore reflected "social environment" more than culture, Rose hammered away at black culture, even referencing Guy Johnson's study of the "emotionalism of the Negro church" to demonstrate that black culture was pathological. To Rose's mind, charismatic religion only further compounded "the insufficiency and unwholesomeness of Negro recreational activity," "the plethora of [inferior] Negro social organizations," and the tendency of African Americans to support "cultivation of the arts to the neglect of other fields." Oddly oblivious to the value that might be found in any of these categories, Rose jumped to endorse assimilation, arguing that it would be to the "advantage" of blacks in America "to become assimilated into American culture" and to "acquire the traits held in esteem by the dominant white Americans." Although Rose paid lip-service to the basic premise of anthropology that "*all* cultures may be good," he posited that "here, in America," white culture was "highest" and that any minority group "not strong enough to change it" should assimilate into that culture.[41]

Myrdal uncritically endorsed Rose's conclusions, arguing that the chapter represented a "fresh approach" to one of the central premises of the study, namely that white culture was the "highest" form of culture in America and that African Americans needed to "acquire" as many "traits" from the "surrounding white culture" as possible. More important than celebrating black culture, concluded Myrdal, was eliminating white southern violence, ending segregation, and working a gradual shift in white attitudes toward blacks, opening the door to a fully integrated society that also reinforced America's commitment to democracy and equality. Not only did Myrdal discredit the value of black culture; he expressed concern that celebrations of black heritage might actually be used by segregationists to further Jim Crow. Of course, this was precisely what Robert Penn Warren had done by describing racial segregation as a briar patch, a seemingly inhospitable system that actually encouraged black cultural innovation and "art."[42]

Published in 1944, Myrdal's *American Dilemma* enjoyed generally positive reviews, particularly in the North. The New York *Herald Tribune* likened the work to French eighteenth-century author Alexis de Tocqueville's study of American democracy. The *New York Times* declared it an essential guide to understanding racism in the United States, while the *Saturday Review* celebrated *American Dilemma* as "the most penetrating and important book" ever written on "American civilization."[43]

Others, however, dissented. Howard Odum criticized Myrdal's shallow understanding of black folklore, lamenting that there was "little recognition of the compound culture involved in the folk society of the Negro," including a blindness to the manner in which many black cultural practices constituted "as magnificent [a] mastery of environment as can be found in the annals of human culture." Odum's critique fell on deaf ears. In 1947, NAACP attorney Thurgood Marshall cited *An American Dilemma* in a brief filed on behalf of Ada Lois Sipuel, an aspiring law student denied entry to the University of Oklahoma Law School on account of her race. He cited it again in 1950 on behalf of George W. McLaurin, another African American seeking to enter graduate school, and—finally—Marshall took Myrdal to primary and secondary schools in 1952, when he filed a brief on behalf of Oliver Brown and a cadre of black plaintiffs from an array of states, including Kansas, Virginia, South Carolina, and Delaware. Marshall maintained that not only did Jim Crow fail to encourage black development, but it caused tangible, psychological harm to black children, whether school facilities were ostensibly equal or not.[44]

Marshall's southern adversaries balked. In one of the early briefs, T. Justin Moore, the lawyer for Virginia's Prince Edward County, asserted that desegregating the public schools would only "hurt the children in school," both white and black. "Revolution is not desirable and can only breed new and aggravated resentments," argued Moore, positing that under Jim Crow, "evolution" in race relations and racial status had been "occurring." At the heart of the state's reasons for promoting segregation, continued Moore, lay an interest in promoting peace and harmony. "Virginia has established segregation in certain fields," proclaimed Moore, "as a part of her public policy to prevent violence and reduce resentment." One source of resentment was the state's history, which Moore conceded boasted considerable racial violence. Another was racial differences. Moore did not elaborate on what, precisely, these differences were but maintained simply that segregation had "improve[d] the relationship between the different races and between individuals of the different races."[45]

The Supreme Court, of course, disagreed. On May 17, 1954, Chief Justice Earl Warren cited Myrdal's study in a landmark opinion invalidating racial segregation in public schools in the South. The Court listed the report in a critical footnote supporting the claim that racial segregation damaged black youth, even if separate facilities were ostensibly equal. Although southern segregationists would criticize the Court's reliance on Myrdal, its decision to cite the study reflected "the dominant strand of thought within the social science community" at the time, namely "that blacks lacked a distinctive culture." While the Court referenced other social scientists less interested in assimilation than Myrdal, it ultimately discounted the argument that preserving cultural differences was a legitimate defense of Jim Crow.[46] Oblivious to the kind of pluralism that Robert Penn Warren had celebrated over two decades earlier, the Supreme Court set fire to the briar patch.[47]

CHAPTER TWO

The White Mare

"HOW MUCH SATISFACTION CAN I get from a court order for somebody to associate with me who does not wish me near them?" So wrote Zora Neale Hurston from her coastal home in Eau Gallie, Florida, in 1955. Hurston was one of America's most talented writers, a singular voice who had written a groundbreaking novel about black life in Florida called *Their Eyes Were Watching God*, a book on black folklore called *Mules and Men*, and a riveting memoir, *Dust Tracks on a Road.* Outgoing and vivacious, Hurston refused to see herself as a victim of segregation simply because she was black. To her mind, the Supreme Court's *Brown* ruling was based on a false premise, that blacks were damaged by Jim Crow, a lie that masked the Court's true interest, which was to expand federal power. "In the ruling on segregation," noted Hurston, "the unsuspecting nation might have witnessed a trial-balloon," a "relatively safe" move by the Court not to achieve racial justice but to set a "precedent" for government "by fiat," not the "Constitution." It was a conservative critique, that the federal government would use social policy as an excuse to expand its reach, one that resonated in odd ways with Agrarian fears that the federal leviathan was intent on stamping out southern culture.[1]

But Hurston was no Agrarian. Born in Alabama in 1891, she was raised in an all-black town in Florida named Eatonville, a fortuity that would shape her perceptions of race for the rest of her life, convincing her that integration was not a necessary prerequisite for black advancement. Undamaged by segregation, she left Eatonville while still a teenager, traveled, and eventually enrolled at Howard University, where she studied under Alain Locke. Impressed with Hurston's stories about black folklife in Florida, Locke recommended her to Charles S. Johnson, who published two of her stories and a play in *Opportunity.* One of the stories, "Drenched in Light," told of an exuberant young black girl temporarily adopted by a bereft white couple whose "soul[s]" desperately "need[ed]" light. The message Hurston conveyed was clear: African Americans—even in the repressive Jim Crow South—possessed something that whites did not. Not one to view African Americans as a damaged minority, Hurston won two prizes from *Opportunity* for portraying blacks as culturally gifted, prompting her to relocate to New York, where she entered Barnard College and enrolled in classes taught by Franz Boas.[2]

Just as Boas had encouraged Howard Odum to study black folklore, so too did he urge Hurston to do the same, to return to the South and document the black experience. In February 1927, Boas arranged for Hurston to spend six months researching folklore in Florida, Alabama, and Louisiana, a project that she would continue under the supervision of a wealthy white patron named Charlotte Mason. During her travels, Hurston met with average folks and collected a massive amount of fresh, unvarnished material, including folktales, songs, and jokes. Thanks in part to the salty, unrefined nature of many of her discoveries, Hurston rankled more traditional leaders of the Harlem Renaissance like her mentor, Alain Locke, who found Hurston's subjects poor representatives of the race. Locke veered toward presenting black contributions in the guise of "high" culture, lauding the "New Negro Movement" for its "formal" contributions to American "literature and art." Hurston preferred to extol the genius of average, often very poor people—a position that led her to join black poet Langston Hughes in imagining a more granular counterpoint to Charles S. Johnson's *Opportunity.* Together, Hurston and Hughes advanced the claim that high culture was compromised by white influence, and that black culture, by contrast, represented a more authentic representation of the people, or folk, and therefore was more valuable.[3]

Just as Hurston's commitment to black folklore led her to criticize Locke, so too did she become openly critical of Howard Odum and Guy B. Johnson, both of whom she came to view as inexpert. To her mind, they had made substantial "error[s]" in their efforts to capture black music, including a tendency to make "six or seven songs out of one song" or blending different pieces of music together into a single tune, a problem that ran through their highly acclaimed folk music anthology, *Negro Workaday Songs.* Part of their problem, hinted Hurston, was their color. As she put it in her ethnographic work *Mules and Men*, blacks were more likely to be "evasive" in their dealings with whites and less likely to reveal valuable information. "We smile," she noted, "and tell him or her" whatever we think "satisfies" their "white" curiosity, whether it's true or not.[4]

Hurston's experiences collecting black folklore and her role in the Harlem Renaissance help to explain why she feared the negative impact that *Brown* might have on black life. "I regard the U.S. Supreme Court as insulting rather than honoring my race," she complained, balking at the presumption that African Americans wanted to rub shoulders with Caucasians. Blacks wanted opportunity and resources, she argued, not intimacy. "If there are not adequate Negro schools in Florida," she asserted, "and there is some residual, some inherent and unchangeable quality in white schools, impossible to duplicate anywhere else, then I am the first to insist that Negro children of Florida be allowed to share this boon. But if there are adequate Negro schools and prepared instructors and instructions, then there is nothing different except the presence of white people." Hurston termed the Court's presumption that blacks desired to be with whites the "doctrine of the white mare," an allusion to a popular myth that "any mule, if not restrained, will automatically follow a white mare." "Dishonest mule-traders made money out of this knowledge in the old days," she argued, positing that Chief Justice Earl Warren had invoked the tactic in *Brown*, perhaps to lure black supporters back to the Republican Party in the 1956 election, after many had abandoned it during the New Deal.[5]

It was a ruse that reminded her of communists. As she explained it, Reds had long played on the assumption that African Americans wanted to sleep with whites, even to the point of providing black converts with access to white partners. "It is to be recalled that Moscow, being made aware of this folk belief, made it the main plank in their campaign to win the American Negro from the 1920's on," noted Hurston. "It was the come on stuff," she recalled; "join the party and get yourself a white wife or husband." While never official communist policy, Hurston claimed to have witnessed such tactics while living in New York during the 1920s.[6]

Her anticommunism extended to the New Deal, President Franklin D. Roosevelt's campaign to lift the country out of the Great Depression in the 1930s. "That is what your blessed New Deal did for us," Hurston wrote to a liberal friend in 1945. "Crime in Harlem is rampant, and the police are helpless because the New Deal–promoted Negro politicians immediately let out a scream that Negroes are being persecuted the minute a Negro thug is arrested." Rather than look to structural causes of black crime, Hurston blamed New Deal administrators whose "dizzy theories" deemphasized personal responsibility, along with lax politicians eager for the black vote. Among these were Mayor Fiorello La Guardia and his "New Deal gang," who looked the other way when "communists" plotted a race riot in 1935, after a sixteen-year-old named Lino Rivera was beaten for allegedly shoplifting a pocketknife at a five-and-dime shop on 125th Street. "I happened to know that it was promoted by Communists," wrote Hurston, "and nothing was said about it because they had all pledged to vote for Roosevelt in the 1936 election." Although an investigation later found no communist influence, Hurston's antipathy toward the left continued through the 1940s. In 1945, she accused white Georgia writer Lillian Smith of exaggerating instances of racial violence in the South in a polemical novel entitled *Strange Fruit*, a book that flew off the shelves for its provocative portrayal of interracial romance in Georgia. What "zealots" like Smith were "really doing," argued Hurston, was "working for the Communist revolution."[7]

Smith bore no ties to communism, yet Hurston's concerns about Reds were not completely unfounded. In 1929, communist organizers traveled from New York to North Carolina to organize striking textile mill workers in Gastonia and—one year later—the Communist Party divided the South into two districts, numbered 16 and 17, with headquarters in Birmingham and Charlotte. Communist activity percolated through the region, occasionally grabbing headlines as when nine black men were arrested for allegedly raping two white women on a train near Scottsboro, Alabama, in 1931, only to receive legal representation from the Communist Party USA. One year later, a black communist named Angelo Herndon garnered more news after being arrested for soliciting black and white workers into joining an integrated Communist Party in Atlanta in 1932. Just as Hurston suspected, high-ranking communists as far away as the Soviet Union looked to the American South as a likely place for a proletarian uprising, a hope that set many of the region's white elites on edge.[8]

Hurston's politics echoed that of her white peers, as did her thoughts on integration. "Since the days of the never-to-be-sufficiently-deplored Reconstruction," lamented Hurston, "there has been current the belief that there is no greater delight to Negroes than physical association with whites." Not so, she maintained. The very idea was an insult to blacks. "No one seems to touch on what is most important," she argued, namely that the "whole matter revolves around the self-respect of my people." Black self-respect precluded the notion that African Americans wanted anything to do with whites. Those who supported integration, she believed, should look to Native Americans, who fought "valiantly" for their "lands" and did not "seek forcible association with anyone."[9]

As much as the Supreme Court tried to argue that blacks were damaged by Jim Crow, in other words, Hurston argued that African Americans were fine on their own, and it was whites who suffered from shortcomings: not least a perverse penchant for repression. "The idea of human slavery is so deeply ground[ed]" in European history, she suggested in 1942, "that the pink-toes can't get it out of their system." To illustrate, she cited the British colonization of India. "If the English people were to quarter troops in France," argued Hurston, they "would be Occidentally execrated." However, "the British Government does just that in India, to the glory of the democratic way," and "are hailed as not only great Empire builders" but "leaders of civilization." Such pretensions bothered Hurston, who felt that southern whites dressed their cruelty and violence in the garb of cultural superiority. She made this clear in a graphic portrayal of a race riot in Ocoee, Florida, in 1920 during which black efforts to vote prompted whites to "set fire to whole rows of

Negro houses," shooting the inhabitants as they fled. Hurston pulled no punches in describing the savagery of the mob, including the murder of a young black woman "far advanced in pregnancy," the castration of a black carpenter, and the lynching of July Perry, a black man bold enough to stand up to the crowd with a gun.[10]

Just as a penchant for cruelty characterized whites, according to Hurston, so too did a lack of spirituality. "The folk Negro do not crave [white] religion at all," she noted, deriding its "solemn" formalism and stuffy reserve. African Americans "pity" white styles of worship for they "can't do any better," their sermons sounding more like "lectures" than inspired oratory. Hurston also indicated that whites lacked the ability to truly appreciate art, a point she made in a 1928 essay when she described a white companion who accompanied her to a jazz concert but remained unmoved by the compositions. "He has only heard what I felt," observed Hurston. "He is far away and I see him but dimly across the ocean and the continent that have fallen between us. He is so pale with his whiteness then and I am *so* colored." Taking color to coincide with a depth of emotion that whites lacked, Hurston inverted white claims to cultural superiority, positing that African Americans surpassed whites in the cultural domain and were responsible for America's most notable cultural contributions. "Musically speaking," she wrote in 1934, "the Jook is the most important place in America. For in its smelly, shoddy confines has been born the secular music known as the blues, and on blues has been founded jazz." The "jook," as Hurston used the term, referred to black music venues in the Jim Crow South, places where African Americans gathered to listen and perform, free from white interference. Both blues and jazz were born in such venues, argued Hurston, evidence not only that blacks had contributed to American culture but that blacks were actually shaping it in ways that defied easy definition. "What we call civilization," Hurston observed in 1938, was not simply machines or monuments but "an accumulation of recognitions and regulations of the commonplace."[11]

That culture might stem from the grassroots was an increasingly popular notion in the 1920s and 1930s. Critics of mass industry and mass culture, like the Nashville Agrarians, had themselves argued that the highest expressions of the human spirit lay in common things, particularly in the South. For Robert Penn Warren and his Vanderbilt cohort, for example, that was precisely what made the South important and worth preserving: its ties to the land, its resistance to mass culture, and its tradition of creative self-expression. They even agreed with Hurston that African Americans occupied a special place in the region, exemplars of its commitment to creative leisure and "art."[12]

Hurston was not as generous. She showcased her opinion of Confederate-loving "pink-toes" in a 1948 novel entitled *Seraph on the Suwanee*, which focuses entirely on a community of "piney-woods crackers" in Florida. As Hurston told it, white Floridians were no strangers to depravity, having "wore out the knees of [their] britches crawling to the Cross and wore out the seat of [their] pants backsliding." Returning to her view that blacks were more spiritually inclined than whites, Hurston posited that "religious fervor" was "uncommon" among Florida "crackers," a point she underscored by telling the tale of a white girl with "gulf-blue eyes" and "plenty of long light yellow hair" named Arvay, who renounces all worldly pleasures, declaring that "she was through with the world and its sinful and deceitful ways." A personification of white pretensions to moral superiority, Arvay finds herself pursued by a white suitor named James Meserve, a fallen aristocrat whose "ancestors had held plantations upon the Alabama River" but now owned nothing. "The fortunes of the War had wiped Jim's grand-father clean," wrote Hurston. "His own father had had no chance to even inherit." Meserve, whose name invokes selfishness, recalls the penniless pretensions of the aristocratic South, what Hurston likened to a "hamstring" that was "not meat any longer" but still "smelled of what he had once been associated with."[13]

The tale of Jim's and Arvay's relationship projected a white South riddled with intellectual failings, moral blemishes, and physical defects; a comic farce garbed in Confederate rags. In describing Arvay's house, for example, Hurston described a portrait over the mantelpiece of Robert E. Lee sitting on a "fat-rumped" horse "pointing at the blue-clad Union soldiers and looking furious." Hurston mocked Lee's pose, joking that such "battle scenes were in high favor" in white homes, and "though the enemy was always right up under the feet of the general's horse," the generals always "assumed that the men . . . could not see them." Hopelessly dimwitted, white southerners were also savage, a point that Hurston demonstrated by having Meserve court Arvay as a gentleman, only to then rape her beneath a mulberry tree. "Sure you was raped," declares Meserve monstrously, "and that ain't all. You're going to keep on getting raped." Despondent, Arvay leaves her ripped "drawers" hanging from a low branch, "waving in the wind," a white flag connoting her surrender to the lingering violence and sexual depravity of the Old South.[14]

Hurston did not stop there. Just as Meserve confounded pretensions to sexual virtue, personal honor, and moral purity, so too did he defy white claims to genetic superiority, as he and Arvay produce a child with "defects," including fingers that looked like "strings," "practically no forehead nor backhead," and a cranium that "narrowed like an egg on top." The child's deformities lead to disturbing behavioral problems, as Jim and Arvay witness when the boy, named Earl, violently attacks the daughter of a Portuguese immigrant hired to work the Meserves' orchard. While Jim asks that the boy be committed to a mental institution, Arvay protests, identifying him with her line of the family, an extended network of "piney-woods crackers and poor white trash" who, to her mind, deserved to be treated with respect. Shocked that her husband would consider committing their defective son to a "crazy house," Arvay blames the boy's pathological behavior on the immigrant family, who she finds to be nonwhite. "No foreigners were ever quite white to Arvay," notes Hurston, for "real white people talked English and without any funny sounds to it," a clear jab at white southern colloquial speech.[15]

The story proved a darkly satirical allegory, a tale of poor whites (Arvay) brokering a deal with fallen elites (Jim Meserve), only to reproduce the worst traits in both (the violent, bestial Earl). *Seraph* underscored the worst of the white South, its violence, its moral degeneracy, and its absurd pretensions to aristocracy. Meanwhile, blacks played a positive, humanizing role in the novel, both more spiritual and lighthearted than their white peers. For example, Joe, the Meserves' lone black employee, keeps the Meserve property maintained; teaches Meserve's non-defective son, Kenny, to play the guitar; and even shows Jim how to enjoy life, exclaiming that "if you ever was to be a Negro just one Saturday night, you'd never want to be white no more."[16]

Hurston's juxtaposition of positive black traits onto white failings in *Seraph on the Suwanee* prefigured her rejection of *Brown*, especially her contempt for the Myrdalian notion that blacks suffered from cultural bankruptcy because they had not been assimilated into white society, a society that, as she saw it, was itself riddled with violence, pathology, and lies. More important than integration to her was that African Americans be given resources and opportunities sufficient to preserve that which was valuable about their own communities, their own traditions, and their own culture. That observers failed to understand this angered her. She confessed to being "astonished" that her 1955 letter decrying *Brown*, published in the *Orlando Sentinel*, "caused such a sensation," which it did, particularly within civil rights circles. She also showed disdain for the "intense and bitter contention among some Negroes," that is, the NAACP, that blacks wanted integration, or what she framed as "physical contact with Whites," while expressing contempt for white liberals who supported the decision as a means of helping blacks. "I actually do feel insulted," wrote Hurston, "when a certain type of white person hastens to effuse to me how noble they are to grant me their presence."[17]

The letter from Hurston to the *Sentinel* underscored the unsettling fact that liberal social scientists like Gunnar Myrdal actually did harbor a dismissive view of black people. This was clear in *American Dilemma*, which concluded that black culture was pathological and that the solution to America's race problem was to fully assimilate African Americans into mainstream white society. That the Court accepted this view uncritically became apparent in the *Brown* decision, which held that public schools were "a principal instrument in awakening [black children] to cultural values," that is, white values, for which it cited Myrdal.[18]

Hurston, by contrast, blasted southern white society in *Seraph on the Suwannee* while extolling the cultural contributions of embattled minorities by comparing the plight of African Americans in the South to another maligned ethnic group, one that had suffered discrimination for much of European history, Jews. Just as she was penning her critique of *Brown*, for example, Hurston immersed herself in a book project that aimed to rehabilitate the reputation of Herod, ruler of Judea from 40 to 4 B.C.E. Arguably one of the most notorious characters in the Bible for his alleged order to kill male infants for fear that one might usurp him, Herod provided Hurston with an opportunity to drive home themes that she had explicated in her letter to the *Orlando Sentinel* and her white "piney-wood cracker" romance, *Seraph on the Suwanee.* As she put it in a letter on December 3, 1955, her book *Herod the Great* tells the story of "a great and influential character of his time," a king who struggled to free the Jewish people from the clutches of the Pharisees, "a priesthood bent on maintaining their ancient rule over the nation." Hurston told of how Herod backed a less powerful sect known as the Essenes, to whom Jesus of Nazareth and John the Baptist both belonged, and in so doing, "lent his aid to the movement out of which Christianity evolved." Christ's revelations did not come directly from God, argued Hurston, but stemmed from Essene lore. Jesus, to her, was a storyteller, a purveyor of Jewish folklore who brought that lore to gentiles. "It was a movement totally within the Jewish people," argued Hurston of Christianity, "not a sudden and miraculous happening as is told in the New Testament."[19]

Hurston's thesis hewed closely to her own theory of cultural evolution, namely that the most valuable cultural legacies came from the ground up and not from on high, not elites but the folk, not Pharisees but Essenes. Herod warranted praise because he had protected the "genius" of the Jews, a discrete and vilified minority. He also never ordered the execution of infants. "I have consulted every possible source," wrote Hurston in August 1955, "and there is NO historical background for the story in Matthew 2, that Herod butchered those children." According to Hurston, Herod was a "Jew of the Jews," a leader who converted to the religion but, "like many of immigrant stock in the USA," bore a more ardent "patriotism" than those born with Jewish "blood."[20]

No dry historical study, Hurston's book reads like a novel, replete with rousing battles and palace intrigue as Herod repeatedly outsmarts a band of angry Pharisees desperate to quell his rising influence. Hurston even added romance, portraying Herod as a young, strapping hero who found himself the target of recurring female affections, including a young midwife named Cleote, who propositions him in his father's palace; an older woman named Alexandra, who longs to steal him from his wife; and a teenager named Marianne, who fantasizes about him in secret. Part harlequin romance, part cultural theory, *Herod the Great* tells a big story with a subtle theme.[21]

Publishers balked, as did critics, one of whom later deemed the book a "talent in ruins." Accustomed to reading Hurston's stories about black life in Florida, few understood her turn to the Holy Land. Yet *Herod the Great* fell into line with Hurston's theory that minorities often harbored cultural gifts, a notion that combined what today would be called "cultural pluralism" with what Hurston termed ethnic "genius," the idea that an oppressed minority might contribute something valuable and unique to society generally. Set in Galilee, the "melting-pot of Palestine," *Herod* recounts a pluralist world where "Jews were in the minority" and different cultural groups interacted regularly but also preserved their unique cultural identities. Unlike *Seraph on the Suwanee*, her other book about whites, *Herod the Great* sharpened Hurston's theories about the transformative role that particular minorities had played in Western civilization, without reverting to biological racism. Because Herod was not born a Jew, he did not invite an argument that cultural traits were inherited. Rather, he emerged as a custodian of cultural innovation who chose to embrace and preserve the unique "genius" of the Jewish people.[22]

Although African Americans had long identified with Old Testament figures like Moses, Hurston's emphasis on Herod provided a new frame through which to view the black/Jewish analogy—not just an acknowledgment of a shared history of slavery but a declaration of a shared destiny as bearers of culture and enlightenment. This dovetailed with Hurston's critique of *Brown*, which placed assimilation over innovation and ignored the basic fact that if a minority was to effectively fulfill its cultural destiny, then it must be allowed to preserve *itself*.[23]

CHAPTER THREE

Inner Conflict

ROBERT PENN WARREN sat in his cluttered, book-jammed office at Yale University, thinking about home. It was December 1955, several months after Zora Neale Hurston had fired off her letter to the Orlando *Sentinel*, and he too was pondering *Brown v. Board of Education.* It had been twenty-five years since he published "The Briar Patch" defending racial Jim Crow as a cultural incubator, a shield against the alienating, pasteurizing forces of northern industrialism, an industrialism that had, ironically, ensnared him. Yale's glimmer had lured him out of his southern pastoral to New Haven, Connecticut, a drab, once-Puritan city somewhere between Boston and New York.[1]

The aging Fugitive had come a long way but was still on the run. Indeed, something about Warren's northern exile amidst the slate gray turrets of Yale seemed to make him all the more southern, defiantly so, like an ex-patriot who loved his home country precisely because he had left it, and all its problems, behind. He published four novels about the region from 1939 to 1950, including one about a corrupt Louisiana governor that won the Pulitzer Prize in 1947. Entitled *All the King's Men*, the book drew inspiration from Depression-era populist Huey Long but also the rise of fascism in Europe, which Warren witnessed firsthand while visiting Italy in 1939.[2]

Accustomed to infusing his fiction with politics, Warren turned once again to the novel in the aftermath of the Supreme Court's ruling in *Brown*, this time to tell a startling tale about southern slavery. Warren composed a female protagonist, Amantha "Manty" Starr, daughter to a wealthy plantation owner from Kentucky who grows up unaware that her mother, long dead, was a slave, making her a slave as well. She learns the secret of her past upon her father's death, which strikes while she is at college in Oberlin, Ohio, a hotbed of abolitionist thought. Madly in love with a coldhearted antislavery activist named Seth Parton, Manty hears of her father's death and returns to Kentucky, only to be captured by a creditor and sold downriver to a mysterious, handsome slave owner in New Orleans named Hamish Bond. Bond, a burly bear of a man, installs Manty in a luxurious apartment, lavishes her with gifts, and treats her as if she were free, hoping that she might fall in love with him which, of course, she does.

Manty's and Hamish's story advanced two controversial themes. First, that slavery was not simply a white project foisted onto innocent, freedom-loving Africans, but rather an institution that survived in large part due to the willing participation of Africans, including powerful African kingdoms that built fortunes on the procurement and sale of slaves to Europeans. Two, slavery in the American South was softened by intricate, often intimate bonds between slave owners and slaves, bonds that manifested themselves alternately as paternalism—a sense that masters owed a duty of care to their slaves—and/or paternity—the creation of actual familial bonds between masters and slaves. Such bonds, in Warren's telling, humanized slavery in a way that northern abolitionists failed to understand. For example, Warren compared Amantha Starr's indulgent experience as a privileged slave in New Orleans to the harsh, evangelical atmosphere that she endures at Oberlin. Her abolitionist crush demonstrates little empathy for others, even telling her at one point that "we must not be concerned with persons . . . Only with Truth!" Starr counters that while her father may have owned slaves, he treated them well, and so should be judged compassionately, a point that enrages her boyfriend, whose very name, "Seth Parton," evokes the term "parson," pushing him to sermonize that "the good master is the worst enemy of justice," precisely because his "indulgence rivets the shackle" and his "affection corrupts the heart."[3]

Warren had long resented abolitionist zeal, a point he had made clear in his portrait of John Brown in 1929, and now he returned to it following the Supreme Court's ruling on segregated schools. Few readers were likely to miss the political context of the book, not to mention Warren's vindication of the South in its pages. Not only did Warren portray Manty's father/owner as a good man, for example, but the author also cast Manty's subsequent buyer, Hamish Bond, as a benevolent figure. In one of the more improbable passages in the novel, for example, Bond agrees to free Manty by giving her manumission papers and putting her on a riverboat to Cincinnati, only to find Manty running back to him down the gangplank. Terrified at the prospect of returning to the parsimonious North, she abandons her boat at the last minute to remain with Bond, traveling with him to Pointe de Loups, his remote plantation north of New Orleans, where they are welcomed by singing slaves. Only with the arrival of the Civil War do things go awry, as Bond orders Manty, no longer a slave, to leave, pushing her on a course back toward the cold, alienating freedom of the North, a freedom that Warren conveyed by having Manty marry an idealistic Union officer who leaves her upon learning that she is black.[4]

Although set during the Civil War, *Band of Angels* revealed much about Warren's thoughts on race, and racial justice, in the 1950s. Prominent in the book, for example, is the contrast between the impersonal, idealistic, right-thinking North and the intimate, slaveholding, wrong-thinking South, a theme that hearkened back to Warren's biography of John Brown as well as his essay "The Briar Patch." *Band of Angels* reiterated the idea that southern oppression was tempered by human compassion, and that whites and blacks often found themselves entwined in deeply personal relationships, the subjects of legal systems that appeared harsh on the surface but allowed remarkable room for mercy, mutual cooperation, and kindness.[5]

Of course, this was not the experience that most slave women in New Orleans faced. Unlike Manty, young women sold into slavery in the Crescent City were generally treated as commodities who existed to serve the carnal desires of their sellers—and also their buyers. This was particularly true of mixed-race slave women, or "fancy maids," like Manty Starr. Warren made no mention of this in his novel, marking a general tendency on his part to downplay the harsh, violent aspects of southern slavery.[6]

Instead, he focused on the harsh, violent aspects of African societies that the slaves had left behind. For example, Warren included in his novel an astonishing description of a journey that Hamish Bond takes to procure slaves, landing on Africa's western coast and then traveling "seventy miles" into its interior, to "Agbome," a walled city with "mud palaces inside, sixty feet high, with skulls, millions of 'em, set on the wall, and jawbones, and skulls to make pavement for the king to walk on." At Agbome, Bond encounters "Gezo," a black king who drinks rum from a skull and wears a "shirt made out of a red-flowered damask that had been a table-cover in Liverpool before it got promoted to Africa." Gezo commands a brigade of female warriors, or "Amy-Johns," who take Bond on a "war-raid" that is so violent Bond injures his leg and intercedes on behalf of a "black infant" who is about to be clubbed, rescuing it back to America. Bond later christens the infant "Rau-Ru" and personally raises him to become his "K'la," or manager, in charge of his Louisiana plantation.[7]

The tale is startling. Violence, bloodlust, and savagery fill its pages. Yet, Warren hewed close to primary sources in constructing his narrative, carefully cobbling together actual accounts of "Agbome," or "Dahome," in what is now Benin, as told by nineteenth-century British explorers. One such explorer was John Duncan, a Scottish soldier who described a journey inland from the west coast of Africa in October 1845, later published in the *Journal of the Royal Geographical Society of London* in 1846. Like Warren's character, Duncan described a leg wound suffered while exploring the African interior. He also noted that the king of Dahomey, or "Abomey," received him and "commenced a review of about 6000 female troops," just like Warren's "Amy-Johns," all "well armed and accoutred." Warren similarly pulled details from an account penned by British explorer Richard Burton in 1865, describing an inland trip to "Agbome," or Dahomey. Burton recounted great ceremonies or "grand customs" that were "marked almost every day with human blood," bearing a distinct resemblance to Warren's "year customs" in *Band of Angels*, where female warriors danced "by squad, gang and regiment," and the king presided over the "killing" of human "sacrifices." Burton described a grand custom performed in honor of "Gezo," the very same name of the king in Warren's novel, and provided details of the sacrifices made during the customs, noting how some victims were "clubbed" and others "beheaded," their bodies left "hanging head downwards" on massive scaffolds. Warren echoed this account, mentioning that some sacrifices were "bastinadoed," others "throat-cut," and all "hung up by their heels on racks."[8]

It was gruesome. Yet even as Warren seemed to revel in the more violent aspects of Dahomey culture, he failed to mention other reports of the kingdom that were more flattering, including a two-volume study of Dahomey published by Melville J. Herskovits in 1938, detailing its political sophistication and defiance of primitive tribal stereotypes of African culture. Lamenting that "native" African cultures had "too often been written of in a deprecatory tone," Herskovits praised Dahomey's "excellence in technology and art, its complex political and social structure, its profoundly integrated world-view and its mythology rich in elaborate conceptualization," all of which "may prove of help toward a truer and more realistic view of how far removed from the popular idea is the actuality of the cultural heritage of the New World Negro."[9]

Herskovits's argument that Dahomeans were not entirely unlike Europeans did not make it into Warren's novel, nor did the cruelty that Africans faced once they were brought to the New World. For example, Warren made sure to note that during the middle passage, Bond ran a "clean" ship, allowing his slaves the same rations as his white crew, providing them with room to move, and even giving them time "on deck for air and dancing." A romantic rendition of a slave ship, to be sure, but one that helped Warren advance the startling argument that the only person who really suffered in *Band of Angels* was Amantha Starr, who endured a crisis not of violent brutality but identity. Starr's primary problem was her mixed-race heritage, the fact that she had grown up thinking she was white but was in fact black, and therefore suffered from an inner conflict over who, precisely, she was. As Warren explained it in a 1956 interview, "Manty is, of course, a victim too, but in one perspective at least, her view of herself as victim is what stands in the way of her achieving identity."[10]

Read against the Supreme Court's opinion in *Brown*, *Band of Angels* appeared a southern-slanted meditation on racial justice, including a subtle defense of the clear divisions between white and black that had been upheld by Jim Crow. The book made little mention of southern violence, for example, and focused instead on the psychological anxiety caused by interracial liaisons. Amantha's primary challenge, as Warren told it, was to recover who, precisely, she was: an inner conflict, not an outward struggle. "The whole story is about an investigation of the nature of freedom," declared Warren after the novel's publication. "I mean she's never free—you can't set her free from the fact of the relationship to her father. Until she can forgive her father, she's not free." Of course, this downplayed the horrors of slavery, suggesting that the political status of blacks was somehow less important than their psychological self-perception. "You see," Warren explained, "that's the nature of freedom as she experiences it. It's not just a piece of paper in the story, or the Battle of Gettysburg. The story is inside her." If novels about slavery had once encouraged the North to reform the South as *Uncle Tom's Cabin* had before the Civil War, *Band of Angels* suggested the opposite, that legal reform was irrelevant to more personal questions of self.[11]

As Warren added the final touches to his novel, *Life* magazine called, asking him to leave Yale and return South to do a story on race relations in the region. The assignment proved an uncanny chance for Warren to share his views of integration even before his novel came out and to provide his own version of events in the South after *Brown*. Since the Supreme Court's ruling in 1954, grassroots opposition to the decision had exploded, led by an organization based in the Mississippi Delta called the Citizens' Councils. Warren made plans to visit the Delta, both to meet with Citizens' Council leaders and also to catch up with old friends like Hodding Carter, a newspaper editor in Greenville, Mississippi.[12]

As Warren saw it, racism existed everywhere, as did segregation, and northerners had no moral basis to lord it over the South. Instead, they should spend time—as he planned to for *Life*—trying to capture the complexity of southern life. White southerners were not the villains that the NAACP made them out to be, he believed, but rather an embattled minority seeking to preserve their rural, close-knit, pluralist way of life. To drive home this point, he compared them to Jews. "Southerners and Jews," proclaimed one of Warren's characters in the book, "you're exactly alike, you're so damned special." Warren agreed, adding, "we're both persecuted minorities." It was a startling inverse of Zora Neale Hurston's analogy, only involving whites not blacks. It suggested that Warren saw race much like Hurston did, as a matter of cultural heritage, not repression. It also suggested that Warren saw white southerners as the targets of northern aggression, a view that he had first expressed at Oxford. Now, over two decades later, he felt the need to defend his people once again, this time from the NAACP.[13]

Just as *Life* reached out to Warren, news of a racially charged killing made national headlines, as reporters described a kidnapping and murder of a fourteen-year-old African American named Emmett Till by two men in a small town near the Tallahatchie River in Mississippi. The men, Roy Bryant and John William "J.W." Milam, were World War II veterans and half-brothers. Bryant's wife, Carolyn, claimed that Till had approached her at a general store where she worked, sexually assaulted her, and—as she ran for a gun—executed a "wolf-whistle" that was heard down the street, all acts that Roy later avenged by kidnapping Till from his uncle's house and, with the help of Milam, killing him. Till's battered corpse was later recovered in the Tallahatchie River and buried, only to subsequently be exhumed and brought to Chicago by his mother, who put her son's corpse on public display.[14]

Chicago-based black magazine *Jet* ran a piece on Till's murder in its September 15, 1955, issue, including a horrific photograph of Till's mangled corpse, shocking readers. Soon, the national media picked up on the story, sending reporters to the small town of Sumner, Mississippi, to cover the trial of Milam and Bryant. When an all-white jury acquitted the two white men, the verdict drew angry responses in the North—responses that escalated to outrage when the white defendants subsequently confessed to the murder in an interview with reporter William Bradford Huie for nationally distributed *Look* magazine.[15]

The NAACP used the Till scandal to boost national support for civil rights, painting southern whites as racist and violent. On October 12, the organization called for a national boycott of all products made in Mississippi. Three days later, the group asked New York governor Averell Harriman not to return two black fugitives to the South, one wanted for assault and the other for theft, citing a "complete breakdown of law enforcement in the region," based in part on the acquittal of Till's killers. The NAACP also asked President Dwight D. Eisenhower to investigate the killing, along with the murder of two other African Americans in Mississippi, a minister named George Lee and an African American named Lamar Smith. The NAACP subsequently published a disturbing pamphlet entitled *M is for Mississippi and Murder* showcasing the Till killing; the murder of Lee, who was shot while registering to vote; and the killing of Smith on the lawn outside the courthouse in Brookhaven, Mississippi, for the same offense.[16]

By November, the Till killing, the *Look* story, and the NAACP's campaign to paint white southerners as violent and racist had generated enough northern interest to prompt *Life* magazine to run a series on racial sentiment in the region, for which Warren was invited to contribute. Warren agreed, using the *Life* piece as an opportunity to revisit the question of segregation and southern culture. He organized his article around a series of interviews, some formal, some less so, conducted in Mississippi and other places across the South over the winter of 1955–56. He sat down with Citizens' Council organizers and also with black business leaders and educators. He encountered individuals on the street, in hotel lobbies, and at historic sites. He talked with people on planes and visited individuals in their homes. Except for personal musings, however, he kept all identities secret, leaving the reader to assume that he was canvassing a representative segment of the southern population, even if, in fact, he was not. Whether interviewees were quoted fully, or even accurately, was impossible to tell. An abbreviated version of his conclusions appeared in *Life* magazine on July 9, 1956, and an extended book-length edition came out later that year.[17]

Warren opened the book, entitled *Segregation: The Inner Conflict*, with a northerner, a "big, bulging" man with "coal-black grime" under his fingernails who noticed the Yale professor reading an article about civil rights on a plane. The man engaged Warren immediately on the question of race, focusing on Autherine Lucy, a young African American woman who had matriculated into the University of Alabama in February 1956 only to spark immediate protest by white students. After three days of demonstrations, including vandalism, cross burnings, and attacks on black vehicles by white hecklers—all prominently covered in northern newspapers—the university decided to suspend Lucy, citing fears for her safety. The decision, along with the student violence, caused a national uproar, providing concrete evidence that white southerners were unreasonable and uncivilized.[18]

Warren's anonymous northerner, however, took a more nuanced view of the situation. "Somebody ought to tell 'em not to blame no state, not even Alabam' or Mississippi, for what the bad folks do," he explained, in an oddly southern accent, for "folks in Mississippi got good hearts as any place." That not all white southerners were "bad folks" would prove a recurring theme in Warren's *Life* article and subsequent book, as did the notion that instigators on both sides of the equation, whether violent segregationists or radical black activists, were distorting the South's image. "Folks could be more gen'rous and fair-thinking," exclaimed Warren's New Yorker. "You get folks not being affable-like and stirring things up," he argued, "and it won't work out." This applied both to white mobs like those who raged across Alabama's campus and to black activists like Lucy and the NAACP. "Folks on both sides of the question," claimed the New Yorker, were to blame for the crisis.[19]

That Warren chose to feature a northerner sympathetic to the South in the opening lines of his book indicated that he aimed to challenge the NAACP's grim portrayal of the region in *M is for Mississippi and Murder*. Further evidence of this emerged in a subsequent interview in the book, also with an unidentified white man who was "publicly on record against the Citizens Councils and all such organizations," but who argued that *Life* magazine had itself exacerbated the South's negative image by running a story on the Emmett Till murder that deliberately twisted facts, making Till's family out to be more sympathetic than it was. Noting that Till's father had died in the war, the magazine let readers presume that he was killed in combat, even though he had actually been tried, convicted, and executed for rape and murder. "*Life* magazine's editorial on the Till case," argued the unidentified white speaker, "that sure fixed it. If Till's father had died a hero's death fighting for liberty, as *Life* said, that would have been as irrelevant as the actual fact that he was executed by the American army for rape-murder. It sure makes it hard."[20]

Life's story on Till came out on October 3, 1955, describing the Emmett Till murder trial with a series of drawings and photographs, one of a ring that belonged to Till's father who, the caption read, was "killed in France in 1945." While the article did not expressly mention that Till's father died a "hero's death," it also did not mention that he was executed by American forces for murder, which according to a subsequent story in the *New York Times*, he was. Warren's mention of this fact deflated at least some of the NAACP's narrative, casting aspersions onto Till's parents. If, for example, Till had not been the child of a presumably criminal father, then perhaps he would not have been shuttled to his uncle's house for the summer. *Life*'s subsequent effort to rehabilitate Till's family at the expense of the truth lent credence to the interviewee's sense "that the whole thing was a plot by outsiders" to help destroy "the way of life of Southern white people."[21]

Warren worked further to diminish the Till story in a passage that told of a "twenty-one year old" white woman who drove her black cook home only to be heckled by black youths "in the middle of the afternoon." "As she stop[ped] to let the cook out," recounted Warren, "a group of negro boys, upper teen age, had whistled and called at her." This, of course, was one of the acts that Till had allegedly committed against Bryant, though Bryant claimed he went a good deal further. "What did you do?" the white woman's mother asked her. "I ignored it," she responded, to which her mother interjected "That's right . . . you have to ignore it." Rather than hunt down the black youth who whistled at his daughter, the woman's father simply observed, "It's a new kind of Negro we've got around here now."[22]

The passage was curious. The allusion to black youth whistling at white women clearly evoked the Emmett Till story. By including a white family who ignored such a move, however, Warren suggested that not all whites reacted violently to black sexual advances, and that *M is for Mississippi and Murder* was, at best, an exaggeration. *M*, as Warren told it, might have been for moderation. "The cook had come to her for advice," recounted Warren, "about her sons, fifteen and nineteen," both visiting from the North, "showing pictures of their white girl friends," something that Till had allegedly done as well. The white employer whose daughter had been whistled at kept her cook's confidence, explaining, "you just have to live past them. Ignore them."[23]

While the passage on the white daughter who was whistled at did not make it into the final book, Warren did include another incident that minimized the Till case. "I remember the gang rape by four Negroes of a white woman near Memphis last fall," he wrote, "shortly after the Till killing." The crime to which he referred involved a thirty-six-year-old white woman who was allegedly taken "away from her escort" by a group of young black men "on a rural road and raped" in Tennessee, not once but "five times" in revenge for Till's killing. According to Warren, one of the accused rapists exclaimed that "one of our boys was killed down in Mississippi the other day and we're liable to kill you," a threat they made as "they assaulted the man who was with the woman and told him to get going." The incident failed to make major papers like the *New York Times* or *Chicago Tribune* but was mentioned by the *Chicago Defender*, a prominent black newspaper that noted four "juveniles" had been arrested and accused "of kidnapping and raping a 36 year-old white woman" in Memphis in September 1955.[24]

Warren's reference to the Memphis rape suggested that southern whites were not the only violent parties in the South, nor were blacks the only victims of racialized crime. However, the story failed to garner anywhere near the attention that Till's death did, an issue that clearly bothered Warren. As he explained it, northerners were willing to ignore racially motivated killings if they were carried out by blacks but were intent on showcasing killings by whites. Northerners were also more likely, argued Warren, to mask their own complicity in segregation by employing private means, like sending their children to expensive, private schools. "You may eat the bread of the Pharisee and read in the morning paper with only a trace of irony," he commented in a passage that impugned northern liberals, "how . . . some Puerto Rican school boys . . . or Negroes or Italians . . . have stabbed another boy to death, or raped a girl, or trampled an old man into a bloody mire. If you can afford it, you will, according to the local mores, send your child to a private school, where there will be, of course, a couple of Negro children on exhibit. And that delightful little Chinese girl who is so good at dramatics. Or is it fingerpainting?"[25]

Warren balanced his sardonic take on northern liberals with a sympathetic portrait of southern moderates, or what he termed a "fifth column of decency" in the South, who believed that race relations should be guided by civility, mutual cooperation, and respect. To illustrate, Warren included a black interviewee, a "yellow girl, thin but well made," who confessed to Warren that she was contemplating a move North to avoid the racial sleights of ill-mannered whites. "It's how yore feelings git tore up all the time," she confessed, noting that a white store clerk had referred to her husband as a "nigger," prompting her to walk out. "The way folks talk, sometimes." She concluded, "It ain't what they say sometimes, if they'd jes say it kind."[26]

The "yellow" girl's plug for kindness resonated with the New Yorker's argument that if "folks" were simply "more gen'rous and fair-thinking," then race relations generally would be better. This led Warren to contrast southerners who were "affable-like" with southerners who were not, a point that he demonstrated by interviewing a white organizer for the Citizens' Councils "in the tight, tiny living room" of his home near Jackson, Mississippi. The speaker, like all the characters in the book, remained anonymous, presented simply as "a fat but powerful man" who told Warren that he was fighting for what he termed "the old southern way, what we was raised up to," likening the South's struggle to a cooking experiment. "The court caint take no stick and mix folks up like you swivel and swull eggs broke in a bowl," he explained, insinuating that integration would lead to interracial sex. "You got to raise 'em up, the niggers," he claimed, "not bring white folks down to nigger-level." It was an offensive argument, rendered in offensive language. "Segregation is the law of God and Man," declared the organizer, warning that integration would "overwhelm the white race and destroy all progress, religion, invention, art, and return us to the jungle." Warren's speaker provided no data to substantiate his conclusions but spoke freely, using racial epithets and fuzzy logic to explain his opposition to *Brown*. Warren allowed him to rant, letting him impugn himself in the process. Clearly, this was not the best the white South had to offer, a point Warren confirmed by noting that the leader spoke not for educated white southerners but for the "angry," the "disoriented," and the "dispossessed." Warren showed no sign of believing such nonsense but presented the leader's extremist views as a foil for more sensible positions.[27]

Such positions, argued Warren, did not include antiquated theories of racial mixing and civilizational decline so much as concerns that *Brown* represented an assault on "constitutionality" which carried the nation "one more step toward the power state, a cunningly calculated step," and expanded federal power under the guise of advancing a "moral issue" so that all "objector[s]" of such expansion suddenly appeared "enem[ies] of righteousness." This, of course, was one of the central themes in his novel *All the King's Men*, and it was a point that Zora Neale Hurston had raised in her critique of *Brown*. Warren joined her, suggesting that future Supreme Court opinions might not share *Brown*'s "moral façade" but would merely advance "government by sociology, not law." Of course, Warren did not go so far as to call the Court Red, but he nevertheless tolled a decidedly Agrarian bell by linking southern resistance to concerns about a northern "leviathan" that he and his Nashville Fugitive compatriots had long feared.[28]

To skirt charges that his fears of centralized government were simply disguises for racism, Warren confessed that he was open to the idea of integration—so long as it was not forced. Integration would come, he argued, "when enough people, in a particular place, a particular county or state, cannot live with themselves any more. Or realize they don't have to." Certainly more progressive than the Citizens' Council organizer, Warren nevertheless placed the timetable of integration firmly in the hands of southern whites, who at some point would decide that segregation had outlived its usefulness. This, of course, was a case for southern folkways rather than judicial imperatives, an implicit request that the North allow the South to evolve on its own time, gradually. "If by gradualist you mean a person who would create delay for the sake of delay," argued Warren, this was not him. However, "if by gradualist you mean a person who thinks it will take time, not time as such, but time for an educational process, preferably a calculated one, then yes. I mean a process of mutual education for whites and blacks. And part of this education should be in the actual beginning of the process of desegregation."[29]

Here was an arguably progressive impulse, a sense that the most overt, humiliating aspects of Jim Crow—the separate water fountains and bus seats—could be eliminated without also requiring aggressive federal action like integrating schools. Such integration, implied Warren, would come only when the South was ready for it, when its folkways had evolved to a point that no one believed separate education served any further purpose. Until then, the North should lay off, allow the South's fifth column of decency to do its thing, and allow time for a more gradual process of change. Although elements of the South's folkways were violent, to be sure, Warren downplayed this aspect of the southern tradition and stressed conviviality, noting that "the races had made out pretty well in the South," in part due to its fifth column of sympathetic citizens, who conducted their interracial affairs with "some sort of human decency and charity"[30]

To shore up his point that no one in the South really wanted to integrate, Warren included a string of black voices who expressed doubts about *Brown*. For example, Warren interviewed an African American who declared that hopes for immediate integration were "absurd," and it was "foolish thinking for people to believe you can get the South to do in four or five years what the North has been doing for a hundred years. These people are emotional about their tradition," argued the speaker, "and you've got to get an educational program, and this will be a slow process." The black man concluded by noting that "the ultimate goal" of African Americans in the South was not "just to go to white schools and travel with white people on conveyances over the country. No, sir, the Negro, he is a growing people and he will strive for all the equalities belonging to any American citizen. He is a growing people." This was a nod to a latent sense of black nationalism in the South, a sentiment with which Warren sympathized, corroborating his argument that civility and mutual respect were ultimately more important, even to blacks, than the opportunity to go to school with whites. Another black speaker, an "eminent Negro scholar," confirmed this, noting that integration, per se, was not the black South's sole, or even primary, goal. "It's not so much what the Negro wants," explained the scholar, "as what he doesn't. He does not want to be denied human dignity."[31]

Warren seemed particularly interested in black voices that stressed dignity over desegregation. For example, he included an African American woman from Tennessee, a "school inspector for country schools," who was reluctant to integrate. "We don't want to socialize," she confessed. "That's not what we want. But I don't want to be insulted." This hearkened back to Warren's interest in civility and his sense that whites were not the only group in the South averse to forced integration. "We do everything the white folks do already," argued the inspector, "even if we don't spend as much money doing it. And we have more fun." An African American man, also from Tennessee, echoed this sentiment. "My boy is happy in the Negro school where he goes," he declared. "I don't want him to go to the white school and sit by your boy's side. But I'd die fighting for his right to go." A black college student affirmed the man's view, declaring that "the Negro doesn't want social equality. My wife is my color. I'm above wanting to mix things up. That's low class. Low class of both races."[32]

After acknowledging black doubts about integration in the South, Warren included an interview with himself, conceding that segregation as a formal matter of law needed to end but also expressing concern about federal power and the northern press. "Do you think the northern press sometimes distorts southern news?" he asked himself. "Yes," he responded, meanwhile expressing anxiety over the encroaching power of the federal government, or what he termed "the power state," commenting that any process toward integration needed to be gradual, involving "a process of mutual education for whites and blacks." "Gradualism is all you'll get," he observed; "history, like nature, knows no jumps. Except the jump backward, maybe."[33]

Warren's article and book left readers with a distinct impression that *Brown* represented federal overreaching, and that the South was better off sorting out its racial tensions on its own terms, in its own time. Warren foregrounded black speakers who seemed to collectively argue that interracial respect, economic opportunity, and an end to white-on-black violence were paramount, creating the overall impression that integration by itself was not an urgent priority, even among African Americans. Meanwhile, he failed to interview a single black proponent of immediate compliance with *Brown*, a lacuna that was all the more glaring given the simmering civil rights activism in the South at the time, including a sustained bus boycott in Montgomery, Alabama. The boycott began just as Warren started work on *Inner Conflict* in December 1955, sparked by the refusal of an African American woman named Rosa Parks to relinquish her seat on a Montgomery bus. Shortly after her arrest, black leaders organized a general boycott of the city's bus service, encouraging riders to carpool or walk to work. News of the boycott drew national attention as early as December 6, 1955, when the *New York Times* ran a piece on the demonstration, followed by consistent coverage through the spring of 1956, including a series of front-page stories in February, many featuring a twenty-seven-year-old black Montgomery minister named Martin Luther King, Jr. *Life* magazine published a prominent article on the boycott in March, part of a larger string of stories on the South, including Warren's piece.[34]

Warren made no mention of the Montgomery bus boycott in either his *Life* article or subsequent book. While it is certainly possible that Warren felt Montgomery was getting enough attention on its own, prompting him to seek out voices less heard, the absence of an interlocutor sympathetic to King's program of direct action, nonviolence, and immediate compliance with federal law left readers with the profound sense that this was not in fact a popular view among African Americans in the region. By occluding Montgomery, in other words, Warren diminished it. Civil rights, one was left to assume, simply did not coincide with southern folkways.

CHAPTER FOUR

Invisible Man

As Robert Penn Warren's book on segregation hit shelves in New York, golden Italian light filled Ralph Ellison's apartment in Rome, part of the elegant American Academy located at the crest of the Janiculum, a hill named for the two-faced Roman god, Janus. Ellison had been at the academy for over a year, arriving in the fall of 1955 with his wife, Fanny, after an eleven-day sail on the U.S.S. *Constitution*, stopping in Algeciras, Cannes, Genoa, and Florence. The couple occupied a spacious, two-room apartment along with a study in an ancient, one-room cottage overlooking a vegetable garden and attached to one of the city's Aurelian walls, built in 275 C.E.[1]

The writer was there as a fellow, only the fifth chosen for literature since the academy was founded in 1911 and the first African American. He was from Oklahoma originally, but much of his family hailed from North Carolina, where his parents had met. After a stint at Tuskegee for college, Ellison migrated north, eventually settling in New York City. He began writing book reviews, essays, and short stories, many for left-leaning publications, and even flirted with joining the Communist Party. He soured on Marxism, however, during World War II and enlisted instead in the Merchant Marine, after which he began work on a novel that would eventually win the National Book Award in 1953. Styled *Invisible Man*, the book featured an unnamed black protagonist who lived in a basement in New York and struggled, through a series of misadventures, to assert his individual identity against outside pressures from individuals, institutions, and groups, including communists, who tried to pigeonhole him.[2]

Like Zora Neale Hurston, Ellison rankled at the idea that African Americans ought to jettison their traditions, institutions, and cultural heritage for assimilation, or integration, into mainstream, white America. Ellison made this clear in a scathing review of Gunnar Myrdal's *American Dilemma* in 1944, which as he saw it portrayed "the Negro's entire life" as simply a reaction to the "dominant white majority." How, asked Ellison, "can a people live and develop for over three hundred years simply by *reacting*?" Reluctant to view "Negro culture" as pathological, Ellison challenged Myrdal's claim that white culture was somehow better, noting for example that "radio advertising," "Hollywood," and "lynching" were all products of white culture, and that blacks stood to gain little from embracing such phenomena. "Why, if my culture is pathological," asked Ellison, "must I exchange it for these?"[3] Such thinking reemerged in his novel *Invisible Man*, as Ellison's unnamed protagonist declares that his lowly position boasted more positive energy than Times Square. "My hole is warm and full of light," begins Ellison's hero, "I doubt if there is a brighter spot in all New York than this hole of mine, and I do not exclude Broadway [or] the Empire State Building on a photographer's dream night." New York's most iconic locations, argues Ellison's narrator, "are among the darkest of our whole civilization—pardon me, our whole culture."[4]

Precisely because blacks were shut out of white culture—condemned to its basement, as it were—Ellison felt they had gained a critical perspective on its shortcomings, developing instead their own counterculture that boasted "much of great value" and "richness." Such richness needed to be recorded and broadcast, argued Ellison, not erased. Rather than assimilate blacks into white society, in other words, Ellison recommended a change in the "basis of society" that would incorporate black culture into American identity and highlight it. "In Negro culture," he concluded, "there is much of value for America as a whole."[5]

To illustrate, Ellison cited the Negro spiritual. "One ironic witness to the beauty and universality of this art," explained Ellison, "is the fact that the descendants of the very men who enslaved us can now sing the spirituals and find in the singing an exaltation of their own humanity." This was a tribute to songs that slaves in the American South had composed, of course, but also a prescient foretelling of what was about to happen in the South in the 1950s and 1960s, as black ministers and their congregations began to mount a grassroots movement for civil rights that would awaken the nation to its highest democratic ideals. The leader of this movement, or at least the individual who would come to be most recognized as its leader, was a young minister from Atlanta named Martin Luther King, Jr., who would take the cultural traditions of the black Baptist church and use them to elevate and inspire white listeners across the country, for at least the next decade.[6]

Certainly, King would not have agreed with the Swedish sociologist's indictment of the very institution that he represented, a point that Ellison caught. To Ellison, Myrdal not only failed in his analysis of black culture but failed in his analysis of America. The "dilemma" that faced the nation was not that African Americans had been excluded from mainstream, white society, he argued, but that mainstream America was itself violent, racist, and spiritually bankrupt. That blacks had been excluded from this culture, mused Ellison, was not necessarily bad, for they now stood in a position—an illuminated basement as it were—from which to rehabilitate it, by extolling—not erasing—black traditions, institutions, and art, a black chorus to a white tragedy.[7]

This was a celebration of the black experience that pointed not to black separatism, a position Ellison rejected, but rather black syncretism, a reorienting of American life along new lines, drawn in part by black people. The black ministerial tradition that King represented factored prominently here, as did black folklore. Ellison echoed Zora Neale Hurston's enthusiasm for folklore, explaining that the time had come not to junk black history but to meditate on "what in our background is worth preserving," the first "clue" to which lay in black folklore, "which offers the first drawings of any group's character." As Ellison saw it, folklore "preserves mainly those situations which have repeated themselves again and again in the history of any given group." In so doing, "it embodies those values by which the group lives and dies. These drawings may be crude but they are nonetheless profound in that they represent the group's attempt to humanize the world. It's no accident," he concluded, "that great literature, the products of individual artists, is erected upon this humble base."[8]

Ellison compared black folklore in the South to European folklore, arguing that European artists frequently drew inspiration from traditional art forms, even if they then manipulated those forms in order to create something new. Pablo Picasso, he argued, had "never abandoned the old symbolic forms of Spanish art," including "the guitar, the bull, daggers, women, shawls, veils, [and] mirrors," thereby providing his audience with "an orientation, both emotional and associate, which goes so deep that a total culture may resound in a simple rhythm, an image." Of course, such a notion of culture implied a certain degree of homogeneity and continuity through time, enough to create a generally recognizable set of artifacts and practices that could, in turn, be associated with a particular people. Black poet Vilma Howard and white novelist Alfred Chester, both writing for the *Paris Review*, questioned Ellison's analogy, doubting its applicability to the United States precisely because the nation was so deeply divided by race. "But these are examples from homogenous cultures," they countered during an interview with the writer. "How representative of the American nation would you say Negro folklore is?" Ellison balked. To his mind, black culture lay at the heart of the American experience, one of its truest expressions of a collective, lived experience. "The history of the American Negro," argued Ellison, "is a most intimate part of American history," not only because it reflected a "courageous expression" of the will to defy oppression, itself a core American ideal, but also because it boasted a transformative quality, a capacity to change the very lives of those responsible for that oppression. Ellison made a case both for recognition of the African American experience as an otherwise marginal chapter in the American drama and a repositioning of that experience at the center of that drama.[9]

Like Hurston, Ellison understood that black folklore provided a point of orientation not just for African Americans seeking to celebrate themselves but for Americans generally, particularly those interested in better understanding their national identity, a point that Ellison raised in *Invisible Man*, which suggested that the search for identity was "the American theme," a quest complicated by the fact that aspects of American society "prevented" Americans from "knowing who we are." No racial essentialist, Ellison argued not for some idealized European or African past but rather an engaged, deliberate reconstruction of the present. Ellison reiterated this theme in his acceptance speech for the National Book Award, during which he described *Invisible Man* as a departure from "hard-boiled" protest literature and a move instead "to express that American experience which has carried on back and forth and up and down the land and across, and across again the great river, from freight train to Pullman car, from contact with slavery to contact with a world of advanced scholarship, art and science." Rather than hope to speak simply for the African American experience, in other words, Ellison sought to place the African American experience at the center of the American experience, and to use the black perspective as a lens through which to view the United States, perhaps even remake it. Citing Mark Twain as an inspiration, Ellison observed that "the Negro was the gauge of the human condition as it waxed and waned in our democracy," for "the Negro symbolized both the man lowest down and the mysterious, underground aspect of human personality," a theme that he underscored via the metaphor of the illuminated basement.[10]

Rather than limit the significance of the black experience to African Americans, in other words, Ellison argued that it was also significant to whites, who were "invisible" in their own ways, struggling to assert their identities in the face of overwhelming pressures from outside—forces not of racism, necessarily, but industrialism, modernism, regionalism, and so on. This was true for the rich as well as for the poor, both confined by preconceived expectations of who, or what, they should be. Ellison remained careful to leave open the possibility that his protagonist was in fact the ultimate American, a "tinker" cobbling together his identity from the confines of "a border area," or frontier, that also happened to be an urban basement, a place that should be dark but that the protagonist had ingeniously illuminated with electric filament light. In Ellison's telling, the basement was not just a refuge but a place of regeneration, a fertile frontier like the one that historian Frederick Jackson Turner famously argued was central to the American experience: an uncertain, at times hostile environment where Americans forged their nation's culture.[11]

Ellison celebrated the United States as a nation filled with "rich diversity" and an almost "magical fluidity and freedom," a place that warranted more than simply a protest novel about what he called the "narrow naturalism" of black suffering. Racial oppression, argued Ellison, was real but needed to be balanced with "images of hope, human fraternity and individual self-realization." America's "truth," Ellison claimed, "lies in its diversity and swiftness of change," a change ushered in less by government than art, including black art. Artists struck Ellison as uniquely suited for effecting change by influencing the manner in which average Americans saw themselves and their country. "What has been missing from so much experimental writing has been the passionate will to dominate reality," observed Ellison, "as well as the laws of art." That writers might "dominate" reality was a bold aspiration, to be sure, perhaps an overestimation of the role that art could actually play in the course of events. Yet the idea that he might impact events through his writing revealed a sense on Ellison's part that just because he lacked interest in "protest" literature did not mean that he was disinterested in effecting reform.[12]

Some did not see it that way. Prominent literary critic Irving Howe derided Ellison for adopting an overly optimistic tone in *Invisible Man,* conveying the "ideological delusion" that his narrator might actually access "infinite possibilities" of self-definition in the United States. To Howe, who was white, African Americans remained bounded by racial prejudice, constricted in what they could achieve and who they might become. Howe found Ellison's take on the transformative potential of the black experience to be overly optimistic, perhaps even naive. He argued that American racism was more pernicious than Ellison let on, and *Invisible Man* was simply not angry enough.[13]

Ellison roared. To his mind, he had adequately captured the pernicious nature of racism in the United States, as evidenced by his unrelenting portrait of white prejudice and white people in his novel. Out of the ten or so white characters that peppered the story, none was sympathetic. Some, like the aged northern benefactor of an all-black college in the South, were condescending and paternalist, while others were violent and perverse. None were more violent than the southerners, who Ellison referenced in a passage about slave owners bidding on “a beautiful girl the color of ivory,” and later depicted in a scene about a “Battle Royal” that involved whites from Mississippi orchestrating boxing matches among African American teenagers. The scene opens with a cadre of black teenagers arriving at a bizarre soiree where they are invited to view a naked white woman and then encouraged to fight one another for loose change. Acknowledging that this was a dramatization, Ellison argued that similar, if less striking rituals of “initiation” and “preservation” happened all the time in the South, forming one of the cultural “patterns” of southern white society. Ellison situated his protagonist against this backdrop, showing how he struggled against white preconceptions of blackness to forge his own identity, a point Ellison underscored by putting his protagonist through a series of trials, including expulsion from a southern black college, time in a white paint factory, time with a white communist cell, and an encounter with a black separatist movement led by a figure reminiscent of Marcus Garvey named “Ras.” “Before he could have some voice in his own destiny,” explained Ellison to the *Paris Review*, “he had to discard these old identities and illusions.”[14]

Even as he presented an unflinching portrait of the “South’s stony injustice,” Ellison conceded that aspects of black life in the South remained more cohesive than in the North. Black culture had suffered during the Great Migration, he argued, a disruptive event that “sent the Negro people hurtling, without clearly defined trajectory, from slavery to emancipation, from log cabin to city tenement, from the white folks’ fields and kitchens to factory assembly lines; and which, between two wars, have shattered the wholeness of its folk consciousness into a thousand writhing pieces.” Ellison seemed to agree with Hurston that the South had fostered a coherent black “folk consciousness,” even if it had also promoted violence and terror. By carving out black spaces, the institution of segregation had, despite its brutality, allowed for a “microscopic degree of cultural freedom,” a space—albeit small—for black self-expression.[15]

That expression, Ellison believed, was worth preserving, for black voices said something about the nation that was important and singular. As he put it in 1953, "there is in progress between black and white Americans a struggle over the nature of reality," a struggle to discern who, precisely, was destined to write the American narrative. "Despite the impact of the American idea upon the world," argued Ellison, "the 'American' himself had not . . . been finally defined. So that far from being socially undesirable this struggle between Americans as to what the American is to be is part of that democratic process through which the nation works to achieve itself. Out of this conflict the ideal American character—a type truly great enough to possess the greatness of the land, a delicately posed unity of divergencies—is slowly being born." Here lay one of Ellison's core interests, a commitment not simply to assimilating African Americans into the white mainstream but rather to redefining that mainstream, and using the black experience to do it. This ambition helped explain his anger at Gunnar Myrdal, whose prescription that blacks should simply be absorbed into white society presumed that their history was worthless, a point with which Ellison emphatically disagreed.[16]

Ellison's theory of the relationship between the black experience and American culture boasted far-reaching implications, including an effort to redefine the nation—to rewrite its narrative, as it were—using literature as a tool. This was ambitious, to be sure, but not necessarily naive. After all, the Court's decision in *Brown* had accomplished little in the South save spark a furious backlash. To truly gain compliance would require federal legislation—a point that would finally become clear in 1964 with the first Civil Rights Act—and that meant winning the hearts and minds of voters in the North and West. That a novelist might accomplish such a task was not without precedent. Harriet Beecher Stowe had faced a similar predicament prior to the Civil War, and her novel *Uncle Tom's Cabin* had done much to win northern sympathy for abolition. Ellison hoped to do the same for Jim Crow.

He was not alone. Hurston too had struggled to upend stereotypes in her fiction, repositioning the African American experience at the center of cultural life in the South. But Ellison was more explicitly national in his agenda. He saw in fiction both the potential for preserving and elevating a cultural tradition and the power of remaking the country itself, redefining it in a way that would press average Americans into reevaluating themselves, their nation, and the links between the two.

Ellison would explore these themes in Rome, a city that impressed him with its beauty, if not its influence. "I've given up any faint notions I might have had that the salvation of the world lay in Europe," he wrote from Rome in 1955, "just as I've learned that a lot of the crimes against taste which the Americans are charged with are just so much hoeky." "Hell yes, Hollywood is lousy," he continued, "but it just isn't powerful enough to be responsible for all the degeneration of Italian taste." Ellison lamented Italian television and Italian cuisine, even as he balked at the idea that European culture might somehow be superior. New York, with its "art shows, music, opera, etc. and Louis Armstrong," had replaced Rome, Paris, and London as "the center of the world's cultural activities."[17]

After enduring Rome for a year, Ellison received an invitation from Eugene Walter, an Alabama native who had helped found the *Paris Review*, to join him in an interview with a new fellow at the academy, a novelist and poet from Kentucky, Robert Penn Warren. Warren had been in Italy that summer, writing in an old fortress on the coast, and trained to Rome in the fall of 1956 just as his book *Segregation: The Inner Conflict* was coming out. Ellison met him there, with Walter, in Warren's new apartment. Warren served Pernod on ice as Ellison and Walter asked questions.[18]

Ellison began by noting that much of Warren's work seemed interested in "moral judgments," particularly judgments about race in the South. "It never crossed my mind," responded Warren, "that I could write about anything except life in the South," a point that led Ellison to question whether "as a Southerner" Warren might have been particularly aware of "the complexity of American social reality," particularly matters of race. Warren said yes, recalling the impact that World War I had on the region. "After 1918," he explained, "the modern industrial world, with its good and bad, hit the South and all sorts of ferments began." Among those ferments was a rethinking of the racial order. "More than mere general cultural or personal shocks," he explained, "there was a moral shock in the South, a tension that grew out of the race situation. That moral tension had always been there," he continued, "but it took new and more exacerbated forms after 1920. For one thing, through the growing self-consciousness of the Negroes was involved the possibility of expanding economic and cultural horizons." Black self-consciousness had spiked post–World War I because African Americans had enlisted in the armed services and fought overseas, leading them to return with a renewed sense of America's democratic promise. African Americans had also expanded their economic horizons, moving North and gaining new, better paying jobs while creating new spaces from which to critically evaluate their experiences in the South, a turn of events that manifested itself most publicly in New York as the Harlem Renaissance. That Warren recalled the impact of such shifts on him at the time was noteworthy, not least because his work during the period seemed unaware. After all, his "Briar Patch" essay from 1929 oozed blissful ignorance of black frustrations with Jim Crow, even casting segregation as a mutually beneficial arrangement. However, Warren seemed to suggest to Ellison that he knew more than he had let on, writing the piece not simply as an explanation of the South's system to the North but also perhaps as a deliberate attempt to counter more critical black assessments of the South, and maybe even to keep blacks in the region, by promising more in the way of procedural justice and economic opportunity. This might explain Warren's discussion in "The Briar Patch" of the need for a black working class sufficient in size to support a black creative class, lest that class leave. The essay may not simply have been a defense of a repressive system, which it was, but also an aspirational blueprint for what Jim Crow could, in an ideal world, become.[19]

Ellison pressed the point, noting that there was "an exciting spiral" from Warren's "Briar Patch" essay to *Segregation: The Inner Conflict* and his novel *Band of Angels.* "It would seem," argued Ellison, "that these works mark stages of combat with the past. In the first, the point of view seems orthodox and unreconstructed," but "in recent years your work has become more intense and has taken on an element of personal confession." Warren perked up. Ellison could have taken him to task on *Angels* for portraying slavery in a sympathetic light, but he refrained. Instead, Ellison focused on the inner turmoil that Amantha Starr felt over her identity, a theme that coincided with his own explorations of identity in *Invisible Man.* This hinted at a shared interest. Although Ellison's protagonist and Starr were different, both struggled with stereotypes, with definitions of who they should be based on the perceptions of others. Ellison seemed to appreciate Warren's effort to write a black character in this way, not as a one-dimensional stereotype but as an individual struggling with her core identity, "a young girl trained as a white gentlewoman," Ellison explained, "who suddenly finds herself on the slave block."[20]

Others had been less forgiving. "One reviewer, a professional critic," complained Warren to Ellison, "said that *Band of Angels* is an apology for the plantation system," a point Warren tried to deny. "The story of *Band* wasn't an apology or an attack," he argued. "It was simply trying to say something about something. But God Almighty, you have to spell it out for some people, especially a certain breed of professional defender-of-the-good, who makes a career of holding the right thoughts and admiring his own moral navel." Warren's anger was palpable, perhaps because he knew that *Band of Angels* was an apology for slavery, regardless of its other themes.[21]

Ellison gave Warren a pass, finding instead a refreshing avoidance of stock ideas in Warren's work, including assumptions about black aspirations such as their desire to integrate with whites. Warren made his aversion to this liberal impulse clear, for example, by suggesting that the push to integrate the South belied an oddly liberal form of authoritarianism. "You know the kind of person who puts on a certain expression and then talks about 'solving' the race problem," declared Warren, "well, it's the same kind of person and the same kind of expression you meet when you hear the phrase 'solve the sex problem.' This may be a poor parallel, but it's some kind of a parallel. Basically the issue isn't to 'solve' the 'race problem' or the 'sex problem.' You don't solve it, you just experience it. Appreciate it." That one might appreciate race was an odd formulation, particularly in light of the Supreme Court's assertion that African Americans were damaged and their institutions worthless—better forgotten and absorbed into the white mainstream. Warren, long an advocate for a plural South, thought differently. To his mind, preserving racial difference seemed an important goal, perhaps because he retained a sense that race and culture were linked, and that the destruction of black identity would bring with it the destruction of black art. He also seemed to find something authoritarian lurking behind the

Court's mandate in *Brown*, an effort not simply to achieve legal equality but to make everyone the same—as if stamped on a conveyor belt. "What I'm trying to say is this," he continued, "a few years ago I sat in a room with some right-thinking friends, the kind of people who think you look in the back of the book for every answer—attitude A for situation A, attitude B for situation B, and so on for the whole damned alphabet. It developed that they wanted a world where everything is exactly alike and everybody is exactly alike. They wanted a production belt of human faces and human attitudes." Ellison concurred. "Hell, who would want such a world?"[22]

That Ellison shared Warren's concern that "right-thinking" liberals might threaten diversity was significant. He harbored no love for segregation, or white southerners, a point he had made clear in a letter that he wrote to fellow black writer Albert Murray while in Rome. "We're trying hard as hell to free ourselves," Ellison explained to Murray, "so that when we got the crackers off our back we can discover what we (Moses) really are and what we really wish to preserve out of the experience that made us." "Moses" was Ellison's euphemism for African Americans, a group that he believed possessed valuable information and important traditions, forged in the violent crucible of Jim Crow. "Crackers," by contrast, were whites, whose culture left much to be desired. To jettison black traditions for "crackerdom," as Ellison called white society, was undesirable, leading him to side with Warren, cracker though he was, on the issue of diversity or what Warren termed "pluralism." "I want variety and pluralism," explained Warren to Ellison, and "appreciation" of the differences and divisions in America, the divergent traditions and cultures that enriched the national tapestry. "Man is interesting in his differences," declared Warren, a point that did not preclude reform, to be sure, but placed restrictions on it, particularly on grand schemes like integration, which sought cultural assimilation. Warren acknowledged to Ellison that "some sort of justice and decency" should be achieved, maybe even with government help, but not at the cost of diversity. Government campaigns to achieve justice by eliminating diversity struck Warren as fundamentally wrong, bids to legislate "undifference." "I feel pretty strongly about attempts to legislate *undifference*," explained Warren to Ellison. "That is just as much tyranny as trying to legislate difference."[23]

The conversation was fascinating, in part because the two writers seemed to arrive at a consensus that rejected the basic principle of *Brown*, avoided almost any mention of civil rights, and focused nearly entirely on the relationship between diversity and state control. Both seemed to find an authoritarian streak in the Supreme Court's call for integration, and both prized pluralism. Warren's vision of a separate, valuable black "art," a vision he had first articulated in his 1929 essay "The Briar Patch," seemed to find a corollary in Ellison's celebration of the black experience in the South, even if Ellison's indictment of "crackerdom" paid no compliments to whites, like Warren, who had supported Jim Crow.

The bond forged between Ellison and Warren spoke not simply of a mutual affection but of a shared vision. Both writers prized difference, praised diversity, and viewed America as an oddly divided nation, a position that led them to question the logic behind *Brown*. Both also harbored doubts about the feasibility, nay desirability, of big-government solutions to social problems. This was Warren's point in Rome, which Ellison agreed with, and it was a point that both writers had confronted in their work: Warren in *All the King's Men* and Ellison in *Invisible Man*, where his narrator clashes with communists who promise revolution but practice exploitation. Warren portrayed a similar phenomenon via Willie Stark, the governor in *All the King's Men* who rises to power on promises of ending poverty while focusing on the centralization of power around himself. Both authors seemed to recognize that talk of universal equality and revolutionary reform were not only naive but opened the door to even more frightening, totalitarian tendencies.

CHAPTER FIVE

The Color Curtain

As Ralph Ellison and Robert Penn Warren sipped Pernod in Rome in the fall of 1956, Richard Wright left his home in the French town of Ailly for Stockholm. Born on a plantation in Mississippi in 1908, Wright had taken a long road to Europe. Much of his childhood was spent in the Deep South, not in the protective embrace of an all-black township like Eatonville but banging up against white racism and violence. Early memories included white children attacking him with broken bottles in Arkansas, sadistic employers in Mississippi, and a maze of prohibitions and restrictions so Byzantine that Wright had trouble doing things as simple and mundane as borrowing books from the Memphis local library. By the time he turned nineteen, Chicago beckoned.[1]

Wright spent ten years in the Windy City, working odd jobs, joining the Communist Party, and writing. In 1937, he moved to New York, joined the editorial staff of the *Daily Worker*, and published his first collection of short stories under the title *Uncle Tom's Children* to widespread acclaim. While working on *Children*, Wright befriended Ralph Ellison—then a twenty-four-year-old aspirant—helping him publish some of his first pieces in left-leaning journals like *New Challenge* and *New Masses*, and securing him a job with the New York Writer's Project, a subsidiary of the Works Progress Administration. Ellison looked up to Wright, drew inspiration from his political views, and even served as best man at his wedding in 1939, to a ballet dancer named Dhima Rose Meadman.[2]

However, the two disagreed on Gunnar Myrdal's *American Dilemma.* Ellison found the study dismissive of black culture and uncritical in its endorsement of mainstream white ideals, a point he had made in a scathing review. Wright, on the other hand, hailed the project. As he saw it, Myrdal had captured the harsh nature of white racism in the South, showing how it created perverse incentives that in turn forced African Americans to debase themselves simply to survive. He told this story himself in 1945, a year after *American Dilemma* came out, in a memoir called *Black Boy*, which presented a battery of grim vignettes about Jim Crow, all drawn from Wright's own experiences. In one, a black elevator operator let a white patron kick him for a quarter. In another, Wright himself agreed to fight a black acquaintance before a crowd of leering whites in the hopes of earning five dollars. Anyone who refused to grovel before whites suffered recriminations, usually violent, and anyone who aspired to any kind of professional achievement, education, or self-fulfillment met white opposition. "This was the culture from which I sprang," he concluded before recounting his exodus to Chicago; "this was the terror from which I fled."[3]

Wright's indictment of southern culture was not new. In 1938, he panned Zora Neale Hurston's novel *Their Eyes Were Watching God* for adopting a "minstrel technique that makes the 'white folks' laugh" at the cost of ignoring deeper questions of social injustice in the South. The book tells the story of an African American woman named Janie who endures two failed marriages before meeting an attractive drifter named Tea Cake and establishing a fulfilling relationship, only to confront tragedy when Tea Cake suffers a rabid dog bite, forcing Janie to shoot him. Although later celebrated for its nuanced depiction of black life and its reliance on black vernacular speech, *Their Eyes Were Watching God* struck Wright as a caricature, its prose "cloaked in that facile sensuality that has dogged Negro expression since the days of Phyllis Wheatley," an African American poet who lived in the eighteenth century and extolled American ideals, even though she was a slave.[4]

Hurston returned fire, critiquing Wright's work for being overly violent and deliberately dismissive of black achievement. Others joined, including Alain Locke, who expressed private reservations about *Black Boy*, and Ben Burns, who derided Wright's memoir in the prominent black newspaper the *Chicago Defender*, criticizing it for exaggerating "the hopelessness of the Negro's lot."[5]

Wright dismissed such complaints. For him, African Americans occupied an important place in American society not simply as exponents of a special culture—à la Hurston—but also as critics and reformers. This was particularly true, he believed, of African American writers, a point he made in 1937—a year before panning Hurston's novel—about the relationship between black culture and social change. According to Wright, "two separate cultures" had emerged in black America, "one for the Negro masses, unwritten and unrecognized," and one for the "rising Negro bourgeoisie, parasitic and mannered." Wright respected authors like Hurston who focused on the culture of "the masses" by exploring folklore, an aspect of black culture that was important precisely because it contained "the collective sense of Negro life in America," and also because it held "memories and hopes" of the African American "struggle for freedom." However, Wright felt that writers active in the Harlem Renaissance, also like Hurston, had focused too heavily on catering to white patrons and not enough on elevating "the consciousness of the Negro people," which was one of the black writer's primary functions. This explained Wright's critique of their *Eyes Were Watching God*, a novel that struck him as more of a "minstrel" show than a bid to raise black awareness. Of course, Hurston disagreed, seeing her work as not simply a form of plantation entertainment but rather a tribute to the creative genius of the black folk, a literary and artistic contribution that elevated the profile of African America, for black and white alike.[6]

To the extent that Wright believed black writers should write for white audiences, he leaned toward rubbing their noses in their own racism, not celebrating black folklore. He took this role seriously, excoriating the South for its mistreatment of African Americans and indicting the North as well, a point he made vividly in 1940 by publishing a novel about a black protagonist named Bigger Thomas who worked for a wealthy white family in Chicago, "the Daltons," only to find himself committing two brutal murders. Thomas's first victim, Mary, is the Daltons' daughter; a budding communist who invited Thomas out with some friends only to become severely drunk, leaving Bigger to help her home and into bed. Once in her room, however, Thomas fears being discovered by Mary's mother, prompting him to silence her with a pillow, accidentally killing her. To evade detection, Thomas burns Mary's body in the family furnace, kills his girlfriend Bessie after she suspects he was responsible, and ends up on death row.[7]

Although Wright prepared himself for white backlash, critics hailed it. The *Atlantic Monthly* declared the novel a "performance of great talent," while the *New York Times* found it "enormously stirring," an "American tragedy" evocative of Theodore Dreiser. Most understood *Native Son* to be a tale not of innate criminality but the perverse incentives engendered by northern racism. For example, Mr. Dalton, a real estate broker, only rents apartments to African Americans in overcrowded, segregated ghettos. Thomas lives in one such apartment and finds himself with few opportunities to support his family other than menial jobs or crime, an ironic dilemma given that he chooses a menial job but then feels it necessary to commit violence after Mary Dalton's mother—who is blind—walks in on him and her daughter. As Wright saw it, Bigger's actions were completely rational given the racist norms of the day. He did not kill Mary Dalton because he was innately violent but because he was responding to irrational American taboos against interracial sex. Similarly, Bigger killed his black girlfriend not out of primal rage but from a desperate bid to escape the electric chair by preventing her from serving as a witness against him.[8]

Even as *Native Son* became a bestseller, Wright found himself hounded by many of the same problems that had stalked Bigger Thomas, including discrimination in housing. He first encountered this while trying to purchase a house in New York's quaint Greenwich Village neighborhood in 1945, only to meet a snarl of restrictions against black buyers that forced him to hide his identity. When white neighbors finally learned his race, they moved to outbid him, a desperate gambit that failed but outraged the black author. Wright and his wife subsequently moved to purchase a country house in Vermont, only to make a deposit and then suffer rejection once again when the seller learned that he was black. Wright later identified this final humiliation as a pivotal moment in his Sisyphean struggle against American racism, an event that convinced him to leave the United States for good.[9]

Wright relocated his family to France in 1947, a move that inspired him to take his critique of the United States and apply it to the West generally. From Europe, Wright saw that many of the same evils he had witnessed in America were also inherent in European colonialism. By colonizing Africa and Asia, observed Wright, European nations like Britain, the Netherlands, and France had spread racism around the globe, threatening a violent backlash by colonial peoples. To avoid such a cataclysm, Wright came to believe that Western powers needed to aid in the creation of postcolonial states, but not along lines that replicated imperialism. Instead, the West should aid in the creation of independent nations where Asians and Africans could exercise independence free from white prejudice and control, somewhat like Zora Neale Hurston's Eatonville.[10]

While Wright derided Hurston's depictions of black life in Florida, he shared her view that vibrant black communities were normatively more attractive than integrated communities, particularly if those communities were dominated by racists. He did not oppose desegregation, to be sure, and even admired Gunnar Myrdal, but remained convinced that white racism was so pervasive in America that it actually made sense to leave. France struck him as an improvement, but the continent that most drew his attention was Africa.

Wright visited Africa in 1953, sailing by ship from Liverpool, England, to Sierra Leone and then the Gold Coast, a sub-Saharan British colony that was in the midst of a rousing movement for independence, led by a former educator named Kwame Nkrumah. Nkrumah had studied in the United States and England, met W. E. B. Du Bois, and come to the conclusion that Africa needed to gain independence from white rule in order to advance, meanwhile developing a new culture along African lines, free from economic exploitation, respectful of African traditions, and devoid of condescending white rulers. By the time Wright arrived, Nkrumah had risen to the position of prime minister and seemed on the verge of breaking from Britain.

Wright puzzled at many aspects of African society, such as its "disorder," "polygamy," and "strange burial customs," but grew to respect Nkrumah for overcoming "tribal differences" and building "a bridge between tribalism and twentieth-century forms of political mass organization." Nkrumah seemed to Wright an inspirational figure who had restored African confidence after the British "smashed" it with an obnoxious insistence on Anglo-Saxon cultural supremacy. "All that the African personality seemed to have gotten from the West," observed Wright, "was a numbed defensiveness, a chronic lack of self-confidence." Nkrumah's vision of an independent state defied this, holding out hope for a new, decidedly African future.[11]

However, Wright also saw a looming danger in the prospect of independence, a possibility that Africans might simply adopt a version of the same racism that their white overlords had embraced, mixing it with superstition and religion, two forces that threatened progress. Wright crystallized these ideas in April 1955, two years after his Africa trip, when he traveled to the former Dutch colony of Indonesia to report on a conference held by postcolonial nations at Bandung. No whites were allowed, and Wright proved one of the few Americans, along with New York congressman Adam Clayton Powell, Jr., to attend. He was struck by two things: First, he recoiled at the heavy-handed legacy of Dutch colonial rule, its absolute insistence on treating people of color as servants and inferiors, much like the British had done in the Gold Coast. Second, Wright became intrigued by the surging racial and religious fervor exhibited by many of the participants at the conference, all from former European colonies.

Wright conveyed his views of the Bandung conference in a book about the meeting entitled *The Color Curtain*, published in 1956. "It was strange," he recalled, "how the moment I left the dry, impersonal, abstract world of the West, I encountered at once: religion . . . And it was a passionate, unyielding religion, feeding on itself, sufficient unto itself." Wright had suffered negative experiences with religion as a child in the South, mainly from his Seventh-day Adventist grandparents, and found the developing world's religiosity frightening, "irrationalism meeting irrationalism" as he put it. To Wright, the developing world's adherence to religion made it "static," a condition that needed to be addressed before poverty, illiteracy, and other problems could be ameliorated. While some blamed Western imperialism for this, Wright found indigenous causes as well, in particular a tendency by Africans and Asians to view society not from the standpoint of individuals but rather through "collectivist visions" that lent themselves "toward hierarchy" and "social collectivities of an organic nature."[12]

Collectivist thinking struck Wright as rooted, again, in religion, a sense that social organization stemmed from a communalist, almost sacred view of the world. "It was no accident," he observed, "that most of the delegates were deeply religious men representing governments and vast populations steeped in mystical visions of life." Third-world mysticism struck Wright as fertile ground for racism, particularly antiwhite racism stoked by centuries of colonial rule. "Racial feeling manifested itself at Bandung in a thousand subtle forms," he believed, commenting that one of the few things uniting the diverse participants was their hatred of Europeans. "The feeling of inferiority that the white man has instilled in these people corrodes their very souls," he noted, opening the door to hostile, anti-Western alliances.[13]

Although critical of colonial attitudes toward indigenous people, Wright also understood that certain aspects of the "dry, impersonal, abstract world of the West" were positive. He praised the West's "secular, rational base of thought and feeling" and explained that it was in many ways superior to the "traditional and customary" worldviews that had "stagnated" developing countries "for centuries." This included the West's adherence to science, which had debunked racial stereotypes, and also America's commitment to rights, which Wright found rooted in a larger concept of the individual as the primary unit of society. Rights had no place, he surmised, in a truly communal world. Nor did rights have any place in a truly religious state.[14]

However, the West's commitment to rights and science were undermined by its irrational commitment to white supremacy, a problem that had actually stirred anticolonial sentiment across the globe, threatening a violent, reactionary backlash. As Wright saw it, Europe's racist actions engendered equal and opposite reactions—much like American racism engendered Bigger Thomas—jeopardizing that which was most positive about European and American civilization. "It is not difficult to imagine Moslems, Hindus, Buddhists, and Shintoists," warned Wright, "launching vast crusades, armed with modern weapons, to make the world safe for their mystical notions."

The entire conference at Bandung seemed to simmer with resentment and thoughts of revenge against Europeans, threatening new global alliances hostile to Western interests. Because these alliances were forged on religious and racial grounds, Wright believed, military solutions were futile: "To wage war against racial and religious emotion is ultimately meaningless and impossible; atom and hydrogen bombs would only inflame racial and religious passions."[15]

Like Max Weber, Wright saw the world through the lens of culture, with efficient, scientific, secular nations rising above what he perceived to be inefficient, superstitious, "pagan" nations. Even some European nations struck Wright as pagan, including Spain, a country "as sacred and irrational as the sacred state of Akan in the African jungle." Wright's thoughts on Spain, which he toured in 1954, led him to believe that certain isolated segments of the West were themselves rooted in superstition and irrational thought—like the American South. "I grew up in the Methodist and Seventh Day Adventist churches," noted Wright, "and I saw and observed religion in my childhood; and these people are religious."[16]

The South's religiosity, to Wright's mind, was not unconnected to its unflinching adherence to racism. Both were rigid ideologies that stifled individuality and trampled creative self-expression. They were similar, he believed, to communism, also a rigid ideology that demanded conformity and discouraged diversity, whether artistic or political. Although originally enthusiastic about communism, Wright became increasingly disenchanted with its authoritarian leanings, both in the Soviet Union and the United States, ultimately abandoning the party in 1944. While listening to the Chinese delegates at Bandung, for example, Wright came to fear that communists might exploit third-world religiosity and racial solidarity for their own ends, merging the communalism of traditional societies with the communalism endorsed by Marxist theory. China was an obvious candidate for such an operation, since it had itself melded Marxist thought onto thousands of years of Chinese culture, a process that it could conceivably replicate throughout the developing world, essentially "rip[ping]" postcolonial countries "out of the traditional and customary soil in which they have stagnated for centuries."[17]

Communism, however, exacted an even steeper price than American racism. Joseph Stalin's policies of collectivization and political consolidation in Russia and Ukraine alone had led to millions of deaths, both through political persecution and famine, leading Wright to warn of communism's appetite for "limitless murder and terror, its wholesale sacrifices of human freedom and human life." This was arguably even worse than Jim Crow, which for all its violence in the name of white supremacy had never even come close to the number that Stalin killed in the name of egalitarian, proletarian ideals. Yet, if the West did not reach out to the developing world, precisely such promises of equality might drive that world into communist hands. "I think that the very intensity of their racial and religious conditioning would," he argued, "lead these masses to accept such a desperate path," for their traditional communalist cultures had "prepared them to re-enact on a global scale ceremonies of collective crucifixion and rituals of mass rebirth." Faced with this imminent threat of "horror and blood," Wright concluded by wondering whether there was "no stand-in for these sacrifices, no substitute for these sufferings?"[18]

The answer, he concluded, was Western intervention. Not imperial intervention aimed at extracting resources from undeveloped nations, to be sure, but an active effort aimed at helping postcolonial states develop into independent, secular powers, in part by educating "static" peoples in secular, Western values, and in part by aiding in the construction of functioning economies that did not hinge on sending raw materials to Europe only to then demand that colonials buy them back once they had been made into finished goods. It would be "far preferable," Wright reasoned, for the West to assist African economic development, even if it meant a "radical adjustment of the West's own systems of society and economics, than to face militant hordes buoyed and sustained by racial and religious passions."[19]

Wright elaborated on these ideas back in Europe, first at his country house in Ailly, France, then on a speaking tour of Scandinavia. Swedish publishing house Bonniers invited him to Stockholm in November 1956, culminating in a series of lectures in a string of cities that built on some of the same ideas that Wright had developed in the Gold Coast and Bandung, all of which he published in a 1957 book entitled *White Man Listen!* Standing before auditoriums full of blue-eyed Nordics, Wright talked of the Gold Coast, describing how black revolutionaries like Kwame Nkrumah had drawn from European ideas and merged them with indigenous traditions to forge a new national identity, calling for universal male suffrage and a representative—rather than imperial—government, meanwhile bringing back the "ancient national dress of the Gold Coast, togas draped about the body in Roman style." The result was not an emulation of Europe so much as a reinvention of Africa with the help of specific Western ideas, a sudden jump "into the twentieth century, with its present tribal structure and all." For Wright, the role of Europeans as overlords was over, and the way forward was for Europeans to check their privilege and engage Africa "in the spirit of civil servants rather than civil masters." Meanwhile, there was also an important role for Europeans to play in Europe, building on the critique of Western imperialism that leaders like Nkrumah had pioneered in Africa. "In my opinion," declared Wright, "the greatest aid that any white Westerner can give Africa is by becoming a missionary right in the heart of the Western world, explaining to his own people what they have done to Africa." It was a role that Wright himself had played, and was playing again, this time in Scandinavia.[20]

That Ellison was also in Europe underscored the rift that had opened between the two writers. Once Wright's protégé, Ellison did not follow his mentor's exodus. His séjour in Rome was temporary, and his interest in America far exceeded any interest that he may have had in Africa. However, both writers shared a critical view of whites. Ellison saw them as blind to their nation's past; Wright saw them as sadistic. Both believed strongly that even if whites may have had positive qualities, their racism corrupted them and they needed help—from blacks. This was not the view that the Supreme Court had taken in *Brown*, which declared that segregation had instilled a sense of inferiority in African Americans—quite the opposite. Both Ellison and Wright viewed whites critically, not as natural overlords but flawed beings, blinded by their violent obsession with status. Ellison believed they could be reformed by reading black literature, while Wright saw them as useful servants to African elites. Both agreed with Zora Neale Hurston: white pretensions to superiority were just that—pretensions.

CHAPTER SIX

Intruder in the Dust

As RICHARD WRIGHT toured Scandinavia demanding that white men listen, William Faulkner checked into the Algonquin Hotel in New York. It was October 1956, and President Dwight D. Eisenhower had tapped the Mississippi writer to lead a new program aimed at easing Cold War tensions by bringing "People to People" together, literally. The appointment bore some irony; Faulkner was not known to have been particularly personable. According to Allen Tate, a member of the Nashville Fugitives, Faulkner was "arrogant and ill-mannered," a curmudgeon who "usually failed to reply when spoken to" and refused to socialize with other southern writers, preferring instead to hold himself out as a simple, down-to-earth "farmer." Tate found this "pretentious," partly because Faulkner's reputation hinged on his literary genius, not farming, but also because Faulkner refused to associate with "serious" writers like Tate, preferring to surround himself with "sycophants."[1]

It was a harsh assessment, colored perhaps by envy as much as truth. Faulkner was known for being aloof—a loner compared to the cliquish Fugitives—but he was also a major figure, popular not simply among writers but New York socialites, Virginia fox hunters, French intellectuals, even Hollywood. To cast Faulkner's fans as sycophants oozed of sour grapes. Certainly, nonliterary types liked him, but he also mingled with America's literary elite, including figures better known than Tate. After checking into the Algonquin, for example, Faulkner cabbed up to East 64th Street to have drinks with John Steinbeck and Saul Bellow, both acclaimed novelists, and William Carlos Williams, a respected poet. Armed with a "gigantic Old Fashioned glass" full of bourbon, Faulkner engaged his peers on how they might best serve People to People, prompting Williams to suggest that the group strive to free Ezra Pound, an American poet who had been confined to a mental institution in Virginia after supporting fascism during World War II. Bellow balked, citing Pound's anti-Semitic views, while Steinbeck wondered whether the group might support airlifting Hungarians from the clutches of the Soviets, who had recently seized Budapest. Faulkner listened skeptically, sipped bourbon, and waited quietly to hear from another writer who he had contacted about People to People, a Fugitive and old friend of Allen Tate's, Robert Penn Warren.[2]

Warren had long held Faulkner in high regard. In 1941, he publicly defended the Mississippi author against charges that one of his novels, *The Hamlet*, miscast the South as a heap of "gothic ruins" populated by grotesque characters preternaturally obsessed with "the horrible and disgusting." The attack came from a reviewer who had focused on a scene in *The Hamlet* depicting a sexual relationship between a man and a cow. Warren recognized the grotesquery of the liaison but read it symbolically, concluding that the character embodied a southern archetype of Faulkner's invention, a "Snopes," someone who traded tradition, morality, and "humanism" for self-interest, immorality, and "animalism." The counterpoint to such venality was another Faulkner invention, the "Sartoris," a member of a fictional clan that embodied the moral sensibility and honor of the Old South, not just its plantation elite but also its independent yeoman-farmer class.[3]

Faulkner conjured the struggle between "the Sartoris world" and "the Snopes world" repeatedly in his fiction, locating their battles in an imaginary landscape, Yoknapatawpha County, based on his home in Mississippi, a place where the honorable Sartoris clan was joined by equally honorable families like "the de Spains" and "the Compsons," who boasted noble pasts but struggled, usually in vain, against modernity, industrialism, and the Snopes. The Snopes rejected paternalism and possessed a "bitter hatred and fear and economic rivalry of the Negroes," siding with vicious populists like

Theodore Bilbo, a two-term governor of Mississippi who exploited racial fears of miscegenation to garner votes in the 1920s. The Snopes also joined the Ku Klux Klan—not its first Reconstruction-era iteration, which Faulkner found to have been "honest and serious" in its struggle against Yankee occupation, but the second Klan, a group who emerged in the 1920s endorsing Prohibition, opposing immigration, and targeting Catholics and Jews as well as blacks.[4]

It was a complicated mythology. Faulkner's views of southern declension seemed to suggest a romantic—if deluded—portrait of the Old South, a sense that the region had been governed by codes of honor and noble principles, not violence and exploitation. This was certainly how the Fugitives—also blind to the harsh realities of slavery—read him. Allen Tate declared that arrogance aside, Faulkner's greatest achievement was his ability to convey the manner in which "the destruction of the Old South released native forces of disorder and corruption," namely free blacks and violent, Snopish whites, "accelerated by the brutal exploitation of the Carpetbaggers and an army of occupation," essentially Reconstruction, a tragic episode not because it failed to uphold the rights of former slaves but because it replaced the antebellum South's "old order of dignity and principle" with "upstarts and cynical materialists" like the Snopes. Cleanth Brooks, an old Fugitive friend of Tate and Warren, found a similar thread in Faulkner's work, noting that Faulkner tended to focus on "the breakup of the traditional society of antebellum times and the abandonment of its code," a slow ruin that left "children bereft of proper fathers or mothers, reared as orphans, thrown too much upon their own resources, or deprived of the healthy resources of a big family."[5]

However, Faulkner's portrait of the Old South was not all moonlight and magnolias. In a 1936 novel entitled *Absalom Absalom!* Faulkner told the story of a poor white character named Thomas Sutpen who emerges from obscurity to build a vast plantation, Sutpen's Hundred, in northwestern Yoknapatawpha County. The story echoed the lives of many plantation owners in early Mississippi, a frontier state that joined the Union relatively late and lacked the settled rhythms of older dominions like Virginia. Faulkner underscored the Mississippi/Virginia dichotomy by having Sutpen visit an established plantation in Virginia as a teenager only to be denied entrance through the front door by a black slave because he lacks the appropriate social standing. Outraged, Sutpen travels to Haiti where he becomes an overseer, then to Mississippi, where he claims one hundred square miles of Indian land and creates his massive plantation, replete with an ostentatious mansion. Once ascendant, Sutpen appears to have attained the planter ideal, only to then lose most of his property during the Civil War, finally suffering death at the hands of a poor white farmer, the very class of southerner that he had tried to escape.

At first blush, *Absalom Absalom!* was an allegory of the Old South—a rise-and-fall drama that mapped onto Faulkner's own mythology of an ascendant plantation elite wiped out by war and poverty. However, Faulkner's story plumbs darker depths, casting Sutpen's tale not simply as a romance about the Old South but a discordant set of memories recovered by Quentin Compson, a crumbling Sartorian who pieces together Sutpen's tale while a student at Harvard in 1909, almost half a century after the Civil War. Like a generation of southerners born after 1865, Quentin struggles with Sutpen's legacy, in part because the plantation owner had fought valiantly for the Confederacy and lost, in part because he lacked "honor" and defied many of the norms later associated with the planter elite, including many of the ideals that Faulkner and the Fugitives themselves admired. For example, Sutpen is rough, unrefined, and ruthless in his business dealings. He also competes with his slaves, a hallmark of Snopesism, demanding that they physically wrestle with him in his off-time. Such odd behavior leads Sutpen to suffer rejection at the hands of his plantation-owning peers, suggesting that he is not an archetypical hero after all, not a Sartoris but a Snopes.[6]

For those who read *Absalom* as an allegory of the Old South, Sutpen's rise proved a paradox. If Sutpen was more like a Snopes than a Sartoris, then what sense did it make for Faulkner to argue that the Snopes's had not risen to ascendance until after the Civil War? What was there, if anything, to the idea that the Old South had adhered to a code of honor and principles? According to Cleanth Brooks, the answer to the riddle was that Sutpen was an outlier, and his story not necessarily an allegory of the Old South at all. "Sutpen resembles the modern American," noted Brooks, not the southern planter. He was "a 'planner' who works by blueprint and on a schedule," someone who is "rationalistic and scientific, not traditional," and who ultimately resembles a "Yankee, not a southerner at all."[7]

Sutpen's outsider status, suggested Brooks, was linked to his downfall. Unlike the mythic gentleman planter, he pursues modern ideals: individual achievement, naked ambition, and immediate self-gratification. He flouts conventional norms and suffers for it. Perhaps the most important norm that he tramples, the "dark secret" that prompts the "Sutpen tragedy," as Brooks put it, is his violation of the South's longstanding prohibition against interracial sex. Careless in his pursuit of sexual partners, Sutpen fathers two interracial children, first in Haiti by accident, then intentionally in Mississippi with a former slave, yielding a daughter who burns down his mansion.[8]

Although many critics read *Absalom, Absalom!* as a story about "the curse of slavery," this was, in Cleanth Brooks's view, "an oversimplification." "Slavery was an evil," he conceded, "but other slaveholders avoided Sutpen's kind of defeat and were exempt from his special kind of moral blindness." That blindness proves central to the novel, not a critique of slavery per se but rather a problem with slavery that had long bothered white southerners: interracial progeny. While an embarrassment to polite society, interracial children proved a recurring byproduct of the South's peculiar institution, particularly in Mississippi, a frontier region that was also a "sexual playground" for rapacious slave-owners. While the children born in this playground were initially identified as black and rendered slaves, subsequent generations of interracial children blurred the "invisible line" of race, not only fooling hapless owners like Thomas Sutpen but undermining the moral basis of slavery itself.[9]

This was a dilemma. If slavery hinged on a clear delineation between white and black but also incentivized liaisons between white and black, how could the South's racial order survive? According to Thomas Jefferson, who was himself involved in an interracial relationship with a slave, the answer was "manners and morals." Sutpen had neither. He fails to vet his partners appropriately, exhibiting an "innocence" about racial pedigree that would lead him to carelessly father an interracial child in Haiti, Charles Bon, who would follow him to Mississippi and ultimately destroy the lives of

Sutpen's legitimate progeny, first by courting his white daughter, Judith, and then by suffering death at the hands of his white son, Henry—all because he is black. "So it's the miscegenation, not the incest, which you can't bear," exclaims Bon towards the end of the novel, referring to his love for his half-sister—just before his half-brother kills him.[10]

The juxtaposition is stark. As Faulkner told it, Henry had been alerted to the fact that Charles is his half-brother prior to the Civil War, agonized over it, but finally concluded that Charles should marry Judith regardless, even though she is kin. However, once Henry learns that Charles is black, Henry moves to stop the marriage, leading Charles to raise the specter of "miscegenation" as an offense even worse than incest. This underscores the centrality of interracial sex to Sutpen's demise, even as it provides a clue into Faulkner's own attitudes about race at the time he wrote the novel in the 1930s. Interracial sex had been a persistent problem in the antebellum South. "Miscegenation," however, was a postbellum word. Slave owners used the term "amalgamation" to describe interracial liaisons, not "miscegenation." The term only became popular in the region after the Civil War, first coined by two New York "politicos" in 1864 and then publicized by southern proponents of Jim Crow, a system that, unlike slavery, made prohibitions against interracial sex the very "foundation of post–Civil War white supremacy," a sharp turn away from slavery's tacit encouragement of interracial progeny and a move toward a new society that encouraged separate racial "development." This was the world that Faulkner grew up in, and the world that Quentin Compson grew up in as well. By having Compson narrate the story of Charles Bon and Thomas Sutpen, Faulkner quietly invited readers to reconsider the antebellum South through the lens of Jim Crow, a story where Sutpen's crime is not exploitation but integration: integration in the fields, integration in the wrestling arena, integration in the bedroom.[11]

That Faulkner would locate miscegenation at the center of slavery's "curse," transforming Sutpen's grand plantation into what Faulkner called a "burning house," foreshadowed Robert Penn Warren's gothic romance *Band of Angels*, which also focuses on the dilemma of interracial progeny, with Amantha Starr as a female counterpoint to Charles Bon. Both writers seemed intrigued by characters who could cross the color line, suffering "tragic alienation" as a result. More normal and well-adjusted were black figures who remained firmly in their racial sphere—whether or not they possessed interracial heritage—a point that Warren made in his book *Segregation: The Inner Conflict*, and that Faulkner made in two novels, *The Sound and the Fury* and *Intruder in the Dust*. In the first, Faulkner told the story of the Compson family's harrowing decline from antebellum grandeur to postbellum squalor, a saga in which the only unbroken character is the family's black maid, Dilsey, who labors selflessly for the Compson family while drawing strength and hope from the black church. By contrast, the once-dignified Compsons emerge as a ship of fools suffering various forms of moral degeneration and mental illness. They include Benjy, Quentin's mentally impaired brother; Quentin himself, who suffers a nervous breakdown and commits suicide at Harvard; and finally Jason, Quentin's amoral brother who ends up stealing money from his sister, Caddy, after blackmailing her. Compared to such human wreckage, Dilsey appears heroic and composed—itself a type of stereotype—though one that was more positive than negative. Faulkner's heroic, if one-dimensional portrait of Dilsey hinted that, in his mind, segregation served as a shield protecting blacks from white pathology, a point Dilsey herself makes when she warns her daughter Frony to "tend to yo business en let de white folks tend to deir'n," a policy she violates only once, when she brings Benjy to her segregated black church, a display of black compassion directed at the South's white ruins.[12]

Perhaps Faulkner's most powerful black character is Lucas Beauchamp, an "intractable and composed" figure who boasts mixed heritage but stands up defiantly to whites, refusing their handouts, resisting their advances, and waiting patiently in jail while he is gradually exonerated from a false murder charge—the main theme of Faulkner's 1948 novel *Intruder in the Dust*. Even more than Dilsey, Beauchamp emerges as an exemplar, not just of the black South but of the South itself, one of the few descendants of southern aristocracy in Faulkner's fiction who had not succumbed to moral decline. That Beauchamp happens to be black was important, for it underscored Faulkner's larger sense that racial discrimination in the South had forged black character—tempering it like steel—itself a stereotype rationalizing segregation as a type of social defense mechanism, or what Warren termed a briar patch. Beauchamp's white attorney Gavin Stevens hints at this, reasoning that southerners were a "homogenous people," and black southerners possessed even "better homogeneity" than whites, for they had exhibited "patience even when [they] didn't have hope" and possessed not "just the will but the desire to endure." Black endurance was exemplified by Beauchamp, a character who remains resolute despite the looming threat of his own death for a crime that he did not commit. He also exemplifies southern "homogeneity," an intriguing allusion to the idea that African Americans comprised a "coherent social group" embodying the best of the South: a committed resistance to the vagaries of modern life and a stoic integrity unshaken even by the threat of imminent death. Stevens indicates as much, arguing that African Americans were the most southern of southerners for they appreciated "the old few simple things," including "music," religion, and "a little earth for his own sweat to fall on among his own green shoots and plants."[13]

Stevens's point is oddly reminiscent of the argument that Donald Davidson had made in the Agrarian manifesto *I'll Take My Stand*, essentially that African Americans exemplified southern traits, a commitment to community, a tie to the land, and a will to endure, even against insurmountable odds. Like Warren, Faulkner recognized injustice in Jim Crow but also saw something inspirational about the black struggle. "We," argues Gavin Stevens, "should confederate: swap him [African Americans] the rest of the economic and political and cultural privileges which are his right, for the reversion of his capacity to wait, and endure and survive." The idea of a racial "swap" seemed to merge the Agrarians' vision of extolling black virtues with Ralph Ellison's and Richard Wright's interest in black moral superiority, a type of gentlemanly arrangement that recognized black virtues and avoided the destruction of black culture called for by Gunnar Myrdal. For Stevens, and possibly Faulkner as well, this was the way out of the burning house. Blacks should gain white privileges, and whites should acquire black virtues. "Then we would prevail," declares Stevens, "together we would dominate the United States; we would present a front not only impregnable but not even to be threatened by a mass of people who no longer have anything in common save a frantic greed for money and a basic fear of a failure of national character which they hide from one another behind a loud lipservice to a flag."[14]

Speaking through Gavin Stevens, Faulkner provided a redemptive vision of America with the black South as a beacon, extolling perseverance, endurance, and a resistance to the cowardice, self-interest, and superficiality of the modern era. This was a resounding rejection of Myrdal's *American Dilemma*, a call not to subsume black culture into the white mainstream but to extol it.

Whether Faulkner had been angered by Myrdal was not clear, though he did engage one of Myrdal's supporters as he mulled over the plot for *Intruder in the Dust:* black author and Mississippi native Richard Wright. Wright had drawn inspiration from Myrdal's study in the composition of his own autobiography, *Black Boy*, which was published in 1945. Faulkner read the memoir and felt moved enough to contact Wright directly, commending his work. "I have just read *Black Boy*," exclaimed Faulkner in a personal letter to Wright. "It needed to be said, and you said it well." What was said, of course, was that the American South harbored virulent racism, far more than the injustices portrayed in Faulkner's own fiction. "I hope you will keep on saying it," encouraged Faulkner, a comment suggesting that he at least partially understood Wright's perspective, a trait that separated him from many other prominent white Mississippians at the time, including Mississippi congressmen Theodore Bilbo and John Rankin, who issued a joint statement declaring *Black Boy* "the dirtiest, filthiest, lousiest, most obscene piece of writing" that they had ever seen.[15]

Faulkner adopted a more positive view but expressed doubts about Wright's larger project. "I am afraid," he lamented, that *Black Boy* "will accomplish little of what it should accomplish, since only they will be moved and grieved by it who already know and grieve over this situation." The sentence was telling. Faulkner seemed to suggest that he understood Wright's critique of the South, and maybe even sympathized with it. He also seemed to indicate, however, that those who most needed correction, the Bilbos and Rankins of the world, would reject the book—which, of course, they did. Instead, Faulkner counseled Wright to return to the novel and abandon the memoir. "I hope you will keep on saying it," encouraged Faulkner, "but I hope you will say it as an artist, as in *Native Son.* I think you will agree that the good lasting stuff comes out of one individual's imagination and sensitivity to and comprehension of the suffering of Everyman, Anyman, not out of the memory of his own grief."[16]

Why Faulkner found *Native Son* more compelling than *Black Boy* was not completely clear. He seemed to indicate that it was a matter of genre, not content, and that the novel lent itself to more creativity, perhaps more general appeal. Then again, perhaps *Faulkner* liked *Native Son* because it was set in Chicago, not his own backyard. Only a year earlier, a Georgia writer named Lillian Smith had published a controversial novel about an interracial romance rent apart by violence and racism. The protagonists included a young man—white—who is ultimately murdered by his paramour's brother—black—and an innocent African American lynched for his death. The book, entitled *Strange Fruit*, caused a stir in cities like Boston and Detroit, where it was banned, and drove home the theme that Jim Crow distorted human relationships, incited violence, and incentivized pathological behavior. Wright's memoir followed soon after, a double punch that may have left Faulkner, the South's preeminent man of letters, feeling some pressure to respond. Smith's book proved a major literary event, as did the publication of *Black Boy*, the latter soaring to the top of the bestseller list in April 1945 and remaining there through the summer. Prominent critics like Lionel Trilling and Sinclair Lewis embraced Wright's book, Wright himself embarked on a high-profile speaking tour, and *Life* magazine sent a crew to Mississippi to report on the places where Wright grew up. Many read the memoir as a complement to the "Double V" campaign, an effort by African Americans to link America's fight for democracy abroad during World War II with a similar fight for racial justice at home, spearheaded by the federal government.[17]

Talk of federal intervention in the South spiked in December 1947, when a committee assembled by President Harry Truman issued a report calling for federal laws against lynching, police brutality, poll taxes, school segregation, racial covenants, and discrimination in employment. Faulkner sat down in the wake of the report and composed *Intruder in the Dust,* relying on Gavin Stevens to speak out against federal meddling in southern affairs. "That's why we must resist the North," declares Stevens in the book, for the North had already tried to reform the South, "and have been admitting for seventy-five years now that they failed." Abraham Lincoln had humiliated the region, argued Faulkner, a problem that still haunted Dixie. "Lucas Beauchamp's freedom was made an article in our constitutions," argues Stevens, referring to the 13th, 14th, and 15th Amendments, "and Lucas Beauchamp's master was not merely beaten to his knees but trampled for ten years on his face in the dust to make him swallow it, yet only three short generations later they are faced once more with the necessity of passing legislation to set Lucas Beauchamp free." It seemed a direct allusion to the president's civil rights report, which called for a battery of new laws, all enforced by an expanded Department of Justice with regional offices in every southern state.[18]

Faulkner found such measures counterproductive, more likely to stoke southern hatred than calm it. Instead, he envisioned a more organic process by which southerners would themselves come to accept blacks gradually. "What we are really defending," declares Stevens in *Intruder in the Dust,* is "the privilege of setting [African Americans] free ourselves: which we will have to do for the reason that nobody else can." Not the North but the South had to address racial injustice, argued Faulkner, because prejudice was ultimately a matter of personal distaste, not something to be legislated away. Of course, this omitted the elaborate network of rules that comprised Jim Crow, even as it presupposed that white southerners would spontaneously stand up to fight discrimination, not something that seemed particularly likely at the time. Faulkner, though, seemed to hold out hope that if white southerners could only be led to appreciate that which was most valuable about the black South, its ability to "endure" for example, then some kind of alliance between the races could be forged, just as Gavin Stevens predicts.[19]

Faulkner extolled black virtues in a series of public appearances in the 1950s, beginning with an august address before the Nobel Prize Committee in Stockholm on December 10, 1950. Standing before a room full of Gunnar Myrdal's countrymen, Faulkner took the opportunity to strum an Agrarian chord, explaining that modernity had pushed humankind to the brink of nuclear destruction. "There are no longer problems of the spirit," lamented Faulkner in Stockholm, "there is only the question: When will we be blown up?" Sounding like a Fugitive, Faulkner invoked southern virtues to counter impending global apocalypse, the very same virtues that his African American characters had long exemplified. "I believe that man will not merely endure," he announced, relying on the same wording that he frequently invoked when speaking about blacks, but "he will prevail," an optimistic prediction that Faulkner attributed to "soul, a spirit capable of compassion and sacrifice and endurance," all qualities that he had associated with the African American experience in *The Sound and the Fury* and *Intruder in the Dust.* Although he did not mention race explicitly, Faulkner's words conjured images not of Quentin Compson or Thomas Sutpen—both flawed white men—but his most powerful black characters, Lucas Beauchamp and Dilsey, the maid who brings her poor, suffering, mentally impaired charge Benjy to church.[20]

From 1950 to 1954, Faulkner wove together black virtues and Agrarian themes in a string of public addresses that would ultimately foreshadow his reaction to the Supreme Court's decision in *Brown v. Board of Education.* On May 28, 1951, for example, he told a class of graduating high school students in Oxford, Mississippi, that the "danger" facing America was not racial discrimination or even nuclear annihilation but big government, a problem threatening "individuality" by reducing individuals to an "unthinking mass," whether by "giving" them "free food" or "valueless money" which they had not worked for. In another talk a year later, Faulkner sounded a similar note, lamenting the increased reliance of Americans on government programs, "relief roll[s]," and "gravy trough[s]," compromising the virtue of "responsibility," a trait exemplified by Daniel Boone, Thomas Jefferson, and Booker T. Washington, the same black leader who had endorsed segregation in Atlanta in 1895, and that Robert Penn Warren had praised in his "Briar Patch" essay. Faulkner's nod to Washington coincided with his larger campaign to write positive black characters into narratives that whites themselves would find sympathetic while extolling black independence and isolation from white corruption.[21]

Then came *Brown.* On May 17, 1954, the Supreme Court cited

Gunnar Myrdal directly to support the argument that southern states needed to desegregate their public schools, a decision that sparked a prompt backlash. Mere weeks after the ruling, a prominent state judge in Mississippi named Thomas Pickens Brady delivered a charged address in Greenwood—only eighty miles from Faulkner's home—warning that school integration would lead to miscegenation, the very same problem that Faulkner had broached in *Absalom, Absalom!* An alarmed audience member became so incensed by Brady's words that he summoned a group of community leaders in Indianola to form the first Citizens' Council, the same group that Warren had targeted in his book *Segregation: The Inner Conflict*.[22]

The backlash was roughly what Gavin Stevens predicts in *Intruder in the Dust*. Rather than boost support for integration, *Brown* antagonized white people. Faulkner found himself picking up the pieces at the Peabody Hotel in Memphis, where he delivered an address before a roomful of historians on November 10, 1955. The Nobel Prize winner began by noting that Cold War pressures demanded America do more to live up to its ideal of racial equality. "We have no other weapon to fight communism with but this," he declared, confessing that "to live anywhere in the world of A.D. 1955 and be against equality because of race or color, is like living in Alaska and being against snow." Echoing Richard Wright, Faulkner noted that a frightening trend was emerging in the developing world, a place where "in only ten years, we have watched the non-white peoples expel, by bloody violence when necessary, the white man from all of the middle east and Asia which he once dominated." The answer, which echoed Wright again, was for the United States to right its racial wrongs and then "teach all other peoples" in the world about American values, including freedom and equality.[23]

However, Faulkner did not make an emphatic plea for integration. "I am not convinced that the Negro wants integration in the sense that some of us claim to fear that he does," he declared, alluding to Brady's fears that integration would lead to interracial sex. Instead, Faulkner echoed Warren, suggesting that blacks may have been happy with some level of separation provided they were guaranteed equality, not "equality *per se*" as he put it but equality of opportunity, or at least the possibility to exercise one's talents and reap some reward, "to make the best one can of one's life within one's capacity and capability, without fear of injustice or oppression or threat of violence." If the South had only lived up to its promise of providing equal accommodations to blacks, he hinted, "there would have been no Supreme Court decision about how we run our schools."[24]

Not long after his Memphis address, Faulkner received an invitation from *Life* magazine to submit a piece in the same series that featured Robert Penn Warren's travelogue. Faulkner agreed but took a slightly different tack from Warren, not touring the South with a notepad but writing instead a "Letter to the North." The missive came out in March 1956 and criticized the NAACP, which had taken events like the killing of Emmett Till to stereotype white southerners as violent racists, "a people decadent and even obsolete through inbreeding and illiteracy." Although Faulkner had written his share of books about white decadence, he felt that black activists were obscuring the existence of moderates like himself who respected black achievements and were open to the idea of doing away with "compulsory segregation," meaning Jim Crow laws. However, Faulkner also maintained that no one in the South—white or black—longed to spend more time with members of the opposite race. He even mentioned a letter he had received from a black woman who, he asserted, was "writing for and in the name of the pastor and the entire congregation of her church," worried that he was taking a stand too favorable to civil rights. "Please, Mr. Faulkner," began the woman's letter, "stop talking and be quiet . . . you are not helping us. You are doing us harm. You are playing in to the hands of the NAACP so that they are going to use you to make trouble for our race that we don't want." The woman then impugned Emmett Till, complaining that "the Till boy got exactly what he asked for, coming down there with his Chicago ideas, and that all his mother wanted was to make money out of the role of her bereavement." Whether Faulkner actually received such a letter was not clear, but his reveal coincided with his longstanding view that African Americans themselves harbored doubts about integration. Not surprisingly, he opposed the idea that the government should move aggressively toward achieving "compulsory integration," a goal that Faulkner found unrealistic. "I must go on record as opposing the forces outside the South which would use legal or police compulsion to eradicate that evil overnight," declared Faulkner in his *Life* piece, noting that "I don't believe compulsion will work." Faulkner cautioned the NAACP to "go slow," admitting outright that he sided neither with them nor the Citizens' Councils, but stood in "the middle," opposed to the "immorality of discrimination by race" but also more prone to work "to help the Negro improve his condition" than to endorse "immediate and unconditional integration," a bid for the same type of gradualism that Gavin Stevens endorses while mulling over the fate of Lucas Beauchamp in *Intruder in the Dust.*[25]

CHAPTER SEVEN

Fire Next Time

As William Faulkner sipped bourbon with John Steinbeck and Saul Bellow in New York in the fall of 1956, James Baldwin picked up a copy of *Life* magazine in France, the same edition that featured Faulkner's "Letter to the North." Baldwin had left the United States for Paris in 1948, when he was only twenty-four, to escape racism and prove that he could be more than just a "Negro writer." He was slight, with big eyes, and hailed from New York City. His parents, however, were from the South, a topic he broached in his first semiautobiographical novel, *Go Tell It on the Mountain*, which he completed in Paris. As Baldwin saw it, the South was the "old country," a place where African Americans in New York had immigrated from, like Italy for Italian Americans. Save for one thing, the South was violent, "stifling," and oppressive.[1]

When Baldwin read Faulkner's letter, he boiled. Faulkner's arguments struck him as thoroughly "dishonest," mere subterfuges masking a deeper commitment to segregation. He belittled the Nobel Prize winner as the "squire of Oxford," a Confederate fogey who expected blacks to thank him for not lynching them, while rebuking Faulkner's passive "middle of the road" approach to reform. "Faulkner," complained Baldwin, "is so plaintive concerning this 'middle of the road' from which 'extremist' elements of both races are driving him that it does not seem unfair to ask just what he has been doing there until now. Where is the evidence of the struggle he has been carrying on there on behalf of the Negro?" Baldwin was skeptical of Faulkner's claim that southern moderates wanted to help blacks, perhaps realizing that extremists actually did more to stoke national interest in civil rights. This, after all, was why the NAACP had focused on racist killings in *M is for Mississippi and Murder*, a document that angered Faulkner for casting whites as violent and "decadent." That the squire of Oxford counseled the NAACP to "go slow" struck Baldwin as an effort not to quell violence but to subvert civil rights.[2]

Of course, Baldwin's diatribe against Faulkner threatened to expose a gap in his own credibility: as much as he disagreed with southern whites, he had never himself been below the Mason-Dixon line. Thirty-two years old and an emerging voice in American letters, Baldwin had yet to visit "the old country." His parents both hailed from southern states, to be sure, but Baldwin had yet to go, in part because his mother had regaled him with horror stories of the South as a youth, including a tale about his brother, who "had his front teeth kicked out by a white officer" in Atlanta." Baldwin also possessed aspirations that went beyond simply being a "Negro writer." He had just published a novel called *Giovanni's Room* about an American ex-patriot who found himself embroiled in a romantic affair with another man, an Italian bartender named Giovanni. The book raised eyebrows for its open discussion of homosexuality but featured no black characters. It was a bold move given that black writers were often expected to write about black things. It was also a serious character study, not a parade of stereotypes like Zora Neale Hurston's vicious, "piney-wood cracker" romance, *Seraph on the Suwanee*.[3]

Yet events in Dixie beckoned. Baldwin understood that white writers like Faulkner were, in many ways, his logical antagonists, literary peers whose voices promised to influence the very same intellectual and literary circles in the North that he hoped to influence, and therefore warranted a more sophisticated response than white morons in the Citizens' Councils. Much like Robert Penn Warren had left Yale to return home following *Brown*, so too did Baldwin fly from Paris to New York and then proceed by plane to Charlotte, North Carolina, where he confessed to feeling like "the son of the Italian emigrant who finds himself in Italy, near the village where his father first saw the light of day."[4]

It was September 1957 and an odd homecoming, a return to a place he had never been, though the landscape, the speech patterns, and "the ways of the people" were all familiar. Charlotte struck Baldwin as "pretty" but otherwise painfully middle class, "bourgeois," "Presbyterian," and "hermetic," almost completely isolated from the outside world. The town seemed proof-positive that white moderates had done little to help the cause of civil rights. Four years had passed since *Brown* had been handed down, and the city had engaged in "legal stratagems designed to get the least possible integration over the longest possible period," a process endorsed by North Carolina's widely respected, moderate governor, Luther Hodges, who supported plans that assigned students to schools by racial proxies, decentralized admissions decisions, and encouraged African Americans to segregate themselves so as to better preserve their own "culture." Hodges was, in many ways, the political corollary to William Faulkner and Robert Penn Warren, someone who viewed Jim Crow as a mutually agreeable arrangement that allowed for whites and blacks to exist side by side while pursuing their own unique, cultural destinies, whatever those might be. "Unless we can, through good will and pride in the integrity of our respective racial cultures separate schools voluntarily," explained Hodges during a televised address on August 8, 1955, then the state's progressive reputation, its ability to attract northern investment, and its overall prospects would suffer.[5]

Georgia proved equally recalcitrant, as Baldwin realized when he traveled to Atlanta, a city that struck him as a place "manipulated by the Mayor and a fairly strong Negro middle class" nonplussed about integration. Atlanta's black middle class resided in a "wealthy Negro section" of town that was "very pretty" despite unpaved streets, a stark contrast to the neighborhood where he stayed, "composed of frame houses in various stages of disrepair and neglect, in which two and three families live, often sharing a single toilet." The town was a dual society, a place where "a high proportion of Negroes own their own homes and exist, visibly anyway, independently of the white world."[6]

This was not exactly what Baldwin had expected. The black

leaders that he met in Atlanta mocked him for being from the North, a place where—as they saw it—African Americans tended to be less educated—and less sophisticated—than in the South, a point they drove home by forcing Baldwin to admit that he did not own a car nor had he attended college. This was an ironic byproduct of Jim Crow: most black college students in America from 1895 through 1965 graduated from southern schools, a trend that would not change until northern schools abandoned their discriminatory policies in the 1970s. Until then, black students in the North faced discrimination in admissions, substandard housing on campus, and social ostracism, prompting many, like Ralph Ellison, to go south for college, precisely to enjoy the educational opportunities and social inclusivity of historically black education.[7]

Baldwin met graduates of these schools in Atlanta, observing the manner in which they contrasted the South's cohesive black communities to the North's alienating, disorganized ghettos. Despite the horrors of lynching and the KKK, they argued, African Americans in the South had retained a sense of community, even autonomy, thanks to the region's dual society. They owned their own cars, ran their own businesses, and attended their own churches, all while avoiding close contact with whites. Of course, this did not mean that African Americans raised in such an environment liked Jim Crow; they did not. But Atlanta's elite remained pragmatic, more likely to negotiate concessions from whites than oppose them openly in the streets.[8]

Except for one. The eldest son of one of Atlanta's most prominent black families, the Kings, had become publicly involved in the Montgomery bus boycott. An ordained minister with a Ph.D. in theology from Boston University, Martin Luther King, Jr., boasted an academic pedigree far beyond what most southern whites possessed, including Georgia governor Marvin Griffin, who possessed no advance degrees and cultivated a folksy style that made him appear even less educated than he was, someone who likened desegregation to "Armageddon" and fought viciously to keep Georgia football segregated, even though it threatened certain death for the sport in the state. King left Griffin, and Atlanta, for Montgomery in 1954 to serve as minister of the Dexter Avenue Baptist Church, a historic congregation that would quickly become the headquarters of the boycott. Over the course of the protest, which began in December 1955, King became head of the association charged with leading it and delivered a series of startling speeches on behalf of the bus riders, not least an address delivered shortly after his house was firebombed by white terrorists. Rather than call for revenge, King declared, "We are not advocating violence." Rather, "we want to love our enemies," a bid for magnanimity that deftly elevated the moral stature of Montgomery's black community above that of its white overlords. "Be good to them," beseeched King, "love them and let them know you love them": a moral imperative that echoed the teachings of Jesus himself, recasting blacks as the saviors of Alabama's violent, morally compromised white population.[9]

Baldwin was fascinated. He knew well the deep seated resentment that southern blacks felt toward their white counterparts—a resentment that had driven his parents from the region—but he had not seen the rhetoric of love used to assert black moral supremacy in the way that King did. King described whites, the self-proclaimed masters of southern society, as violent, unruly children, precisely the role that they had long reserved for blacks, who now emerged as their moral superiors.

Baldwin sought out the young minister in Atlanta and then followed him to Montgomery, "the cradle of the Confederacy," to hear him preach. "When King rose to speak," recalled Baldwin, "I began to understand how the atmosphere of this church differed from that of all other churches," a factor that stemmed from King's ability to take the black religious tradition, a tradition that had always been a "sanctuary" for African Americans, and mobilize it in a way that communicated to his congregants their special role as agents of change in a campaign of spiritual renewal that went far beyond the NAACP's bid for simple, legal equality. To King, the struggle for legal reform was inextricably linked to a larger struggle for moral reform, led by blacks, aimed at helping whites reach a deeper understanding of themselves. "Along with the Negro's changing image of himself," argued King, "has come an awakening moral consciousness on the part of millions of white Americans," a consciousness that promised to address the nation's "schizophrenic" approach to race, its faith in democracy coupled with its mistreatment of blacks.[10]

King's claim that America suffered from schizophrenia intrigued

Baldwin, who also began to cast racism in terms of psychological deficiency, a point he made while describing whites in Montgomery as confused and distressed. Baldwin boarded an integrated bus in Montgomery and noted the silence that greeted him from white passengers, a "silence" like that "which follows a really serious lovers' quarrel," leaving the black writer with a sense that local whites felt "betrayed" by the black community who refused "to be controlled by the town's image of them." This betrayal, in turn, had left whites in the midst of an identity crisis, "abruptly and totally lost," since "the very foundations of their private and public worlds were being destroyed."[11]

That the black struggle for freedom might dismantle white personality intrigued Baldwin, as did the idea that African Americans might seize the moral high ground from their white peers. The end result, he realized, could yield a rewriting of the American narrative with blacks at the center, not a downtrodden fringe but spiritual redeemers, architects of a more spiritual, more humane nation. Inspired by what he saw in Montgomery, Baldwin jettisoned the complex approach to white characters that he had displayed in *Giovanni's Room*, adopting instead King's tendency to portray whites in one-dimensional terms, as violent and immature. Baldwin expanded this indictment to include whites in the North, for as he saw it, the "venom and villainy" of the South could not alone be blamed for racial inequality in the United States, since it had also been aided by the "tacit consent of the North," a consent that now barred the North from "any claim to moral superiority."[12]

By denying northern whites the moral high ground, Baldwin opened the door for blacks to become arbiters of white behavior, a move that echoed King's approach, even as it confirmed Ralph Ellison's interest in preserving that which was important, nationally, about the black experience. Neither expressed any interest in sacrificing the black perspective for the chance at full assimilation into mainstream white society, even though this had been mandated by the Supreme Court. Instead, all three attacked that mainstream. Baldwin elaborated on this after he returned from his southern trip during a symposium at San Francisco State where he noted that "I thought that the white world was very different from the world I was moving in," a place that was "cleaner," "safer," "more polite," only to realize that there wasn't "anyone in that world who didn't suffer from the very same affliction that all the people I had fled from suffered from and that was that they didn't know who they were." Like Ellison, Baldwin seemed to suggest that Americans struggled with their identity, a concept that drew strength from recent developments in psychology, not least the invention of a condition called "identity crisis" by the psychologist Erik Erikson in 1950. Erikson coined the term to explain how ostracism, exclusion, and alienation at a young age could permanently impact one's psychological development, even into adulthood. Baldwin tied this notion to the question of race by arguing that whites did not know who they were because their identities hinged on baseless presumptions about white superiority, a condition that was true of whites in the North as well as the South, for even if white northerners did not identify with segregationists, they did identify with being white, itself a construct rooted in the nation's history of oppression. Before America, argued Baldwin, most Europeans considered themselves to be ethnically and even racially distinct from one another—"minorities," as Baldwin put it—grouped according to their nationality, language, or regional culture. Once in the United States, however, such minorities quickly melted into a single group—whites—who defined their position or "status" vis-à-vis blacks. "The Negro tells us where the bottom is," noted Baldwin, in a larger social "ladder" that demanded "rung-by-rung ascension to some hideously desirable state."[13]

Baldwin's notion that race was linked to status enabled him to explain why, precisely, whites endorsed racism. Even if they did not harbor any personal animus toward blacks, for example, their desire for status meant that they had to remain superior to blacks or their self-worth would be compromised. Baldwin characterized America's obsession with status as a type of "social paranoia," a condition that created a sense of "bottomless confusion" at the heart of "the American republic." To cope with this confusion, whites clung to racial stereotypes as a type of "fixed star," a reference point from which they could make sense of each other and themselves. This was true not just of the South, Baldwin maintained, but the nation as a whole, where race "persists as a problem" precisely because "it fulfills something in the American personality. It is here because the Americans in some peculiar way believe or think they need it."[14]

Baldwin took heart in the idea that the civil rights movement was not just reforming the South but pressing the nation to reconceptualize itself. To his mind, the debunking of racial stereotypes opened the door to new ways of thinking about America, ways that were not only less racist but also less materialist. "Cadillacs, refrigerators," and "all the paraphernalia of American life," he argued, only contributed to the shallow manner in which Americans assessed themselves, a perception that the civil rights movement—in Baldwin's view—sought to upend. Not simply a struggle for more Cadillacs and newer refrigerators, the movement was ultimately an effort to raise awareness about the profound ways in which American society was itself unfree. "It seems to me," Baldwin observed in San Francisco, "that the myth, the illusion, that this is a free country . . . is disastrous," in part because so many Americans were bound by their restrictive obsession with status.[15]

Baldwin's views on the black project of national redefinition congealed over the winter of 1961–62, leading him to write a public letter to his nephew describing the relationship between race, racism, and America. He submitted the epistle for publication in *The Progressive*, a move that raised obvious questions about its intended audience. If Baldwin had simply wanted to contact his nephew, for example, he could have written him privately. But he did not, indicating that he really wanted to stir white readers by describing racial inequality in stark, simple terms, as one might speak to a child. Baldwin even described whites as childlike and "innocent," a point that became central to his piece, which began with a lament that so many blacks had "left the land," that is, the South, to settle in "cities of destruction," northern ghettoes beset by poverty, exclusion, and hopelessness. As Baldwin saw it, such slums did little more than cage African Americans, restricting their physical movement and social mobility in a way that amounted to a national "crime." "This is the crime of which I accuse my country and my countrymen," he wrote, "that they have destroyed and are destroying hundreds of thousands of lives and do not know it and do not want to know it." Baldwin's indictment of unknowing whites coincided with his claim that whites were driven by a desire for status, not irrational hatred, a point that resonated with what would later be called structural racism, a system that perpetuated inequality minus invidious intent. This included the macro-consequences of micro-decisions like leaving low performing school districts for better ones, moving out of urban cores for better accommodations in suburbs, and rejecting state expenditures on social programs to lower individual tax burdens, all of which contributed to persistent, systemic inequality.[16]

For blacks to assimilate into this mainstream, argued Baldwin, would be simply to extend America's "crisis of identity," a problem that the Supreme Court had missed. "There is no reason for you to try to become like white people," he declared to his nephew, "and there is no basis whatever for their impertinent assumption that they must accept you." Echoing King, Baldwin suggested that Gunnar Myrdal had the equation backward and that blacks needed to accept whites, not vice versa. "You must accept them and you must accept them with love," he declared, "for these innocent people have no other hope. They are, in effect, still trapped in a history which they do not understand." Here again was the notion that whites did not know themselves, and did not recognize how their obsession for status contributed to black suffering. Only when blacks led whites into a deeper understanding of themselves "as they are" could there be change.[17]

Baldwin's sense that whites suffered in dungeons of their own delusion resonated with King's notion that whites needed moral reform and Ellison's notion that whites suffered a type of moral narcolepsy and needed to be shaken awake. All agreed that whites, not blacks, needed to change, and that African Americans certainly did not need to abandon their institutions and traditions to advance. Although Baldwin had personally left the black church behind, he adopted King's tactical use of Christian forgiveness to upend Myrdal and place blacks in a position of moral authority over whites, explaining to his nephew that "if the word integration means anything, this is what it means: that we, with love, shall force our brothers to see themselves as they are, to cease fleeing from reality and begin to change it."[18]

Baldwin reiterated his interest in national transformation one year later in another epistolary essay, a "Letter from a Region in My

Mind," published in the *New Yorker* in November 1962. The piece was not addressed to his nephew but to whites directly. Baldwin opened with a quote from Rudyard Kipling, the British poet who championed the once-dominant view that white Anglo-Saxons needed to uplift blacks, assume their racial "burden," and bring enlightenment to the less-advanced races of the world. Baldwin mocked this pretension, arguing that "the Negro's experience of the white world cannot possibly create in him any respect for the standards by which the white world claims to live." White standards, argued Baldwin, were pretexts, ruses, phony slogans that whites invoked to mask the fact that their privilege rested on violence, that they had "robbed black people of their liberty," "profited by this theft," and then relied on "judges, the juries, the shotguns, the law—in a word, power" to maintain their supremacy. It was a dystopian portrait even more grim than the one he had painted for his nephew. If America was blindly innocent in some respects, it was downright malicious in others, a toxic combination that led Baldwin to repeat his doubts about the logic of integration. "Do I really want to be integrated," he posited, "into a burning house?"[19]

Baldwin's characterization of America as a burning house was startling. It conjured the image of Sutpen's Hundred in Faulkner's novel *Absalom, Absalom!* a mansion built on greed and exploitation, without even a sideways glance to community or civility. Although Baldwin had himself criticized Faulkner's moderate stance on civil rights, he seemed to share aspects of Faulkner's contempt for modern American society, a society ruled by Sutpens and Snopes, a society on fire. By contrast, both writers seemed to find something redemptive in the black struggle. For Faulkner, it was Lucas Beauchamp and Dilsey. For Baldwin, it was black culture generally. The only way that the white man could be "released," argued Baldwin, was "to consent, in effect, to becoming black himself, to become a part of that suffering and dancing country that he now watches wistfully from his heights of lonely power."[20]

Baldwin's vision rivaled anything that Wright, Ellison or Hurston had suggested about white America, though all three had indulged in their share of gripes—Wright in his portrayal of the ignorant Daltons in *Native Son*, Ellison in his depiction of the condescending founder in *Invisible Man*, and Hurston in her caricature of "piney-wood crackers" in *Seraph on the Suwanee*. Baldwin joined his peers in trampling whiteness. "There is certainly little enough in the white man's public or private life that one should desire to imitate," he argued, for not only did whites suffer moral deficiency but they lacked emotion, feeling, even humanity. "They are terrified of sensuality," argued Baldwin; they suffer from an emotional "deep freeze," sing with "sexless" voices, and "supposed 'Europe' and 'civilization' to be synonyms—which they are not." Baldwin's portrait of whites had become so negative by 1962 that it raised the question whether he had come to believe in a form of racial essentialism, a sense that white Americans were congenitally different from blacks —a view that was itself racist—or whether he still thought that whites had been conditioned to behave the way that they did and could therefore be saved. He seemed to indicate the latter, noting that white Americans could be transformed were they only to "re-examine themselves and release themselves from many things that are now taken to be sacred, and to discard nearly all the assumptions that have been used to justify their lives and their anguish and their crimes so long." Among those assumptions, of course, was the lie that whites were somehow superior, a delusion that led to a "labyrinth" of other misconceptions from which whites could only be free if they came to understand the black perspective and the black past. "This past," wrote Baldwin, "this endless struggle to achieve and reveal and confirm a human identity, human authority, yet contains, for all its horror, something very beautiful."[21]

Much like Hurston, Ellison, and Wright had found something profound in the black struggle, so too did Baldwin find something uniquely American, and uniquely valuable, in the black experience. But whereas Hurston remained satisfied with preserving that experience apart from whites, and Wright imagined a new reality in Africa, Baldwin joined Ellison in wanting to transform whites in America. Both joined King in a bid to reform their oppressors but went farther than King in arguing for a type of pluralism not of blood, to be sure, but of experience: a recognition that the black perspective was important, perhaps even critical, and that Gunnar Myrdal and the Supreme Court had been wrong to decry African American traditions and institutions as pathological. African Americans, argued Baldwin, enjoyed "the great advantage of having never believed that collection of myths to which white Americans cling: that their ancestors were all freedom-loving heroes, that they were born in the greatest country the world has ever seen, or that Americans are invincible in battle and wise in peace . . . Negroes know far more about white Americans than that; it can almost be said, in fact, that they know about white Americans what parents—or, anyway, mothers—know about their children, and that they very often regard white Americans that way." Here again was a sense that African Americans stood above whites, like parents to children, not racially superior necessarily but superior in their understanding of the realities of American life, a superiority that carried over into their views of their white peers. "The tendency has really been," Baldwin argued, "to dismiss white people as the slightly mad victims of their own brainwashing."[22]

Once Baldwin identified whites as "mad" and the United States as a country in crisis, he began to chart out a path somewhere between the Supreme Court's call for full assimilation into white society and the call by early black nationalists like Marcus Garvey for separatism. Such hopes, argued Baldwin, were a delusion, for "the value placed on the color of the skin is always and everywhere and forever a delusion." Here, his view of identity, or the loss of identity in America's perpetual struggle for status, allowed Baldwin to move the conversation in a direction that resonated with Ellison, in part by suggesting that the African American experience had molded black identity and engendered a unique, important black voice. In 1962, Baldwin concluded that such black wisdom could one day benefit the United States, and that African Americans had no other choice but to contribute to the United States, for they had "no choice but to do all in [their] power to change that fate."[23]

Like Ellison, and to some extent Hurston as well, Baldwin would seek to carve out a pluralist vision of the United States, a vision that included a heavy emphasis on the black experience as a source of truth about the nation's history, an awareness that whites lacked. Part of this involved a critique of consumerist, middle-class status-seeking and materialism—a position that he shared, ironically, with Warren and the Agrarians and also Faulkner, whom he loathed. Still, Baldwin joined his white peers, indirectly, in lamenting an anti-intellectual, antihistorical bent in the United States. Both blacks and whites, argued Baldwin, had become caught up in the middle-class "dream." "No other country in the world has been so fat and so sleek, and so safe, and so happy, and so irresponsible, and so dead for twenty years," he wrote, in part because America had been built not so much on a dream of equality and freedom but a "dream of a Plymouth and a wife and a house with a fence and the children growing up safely to go to college and to become executives." Much like Warren and Faulkner, Baldwin found mainstream America "joyless," materialist, consumerist, more interested in "the selling of Coca-Cola" than democracy—a land of Snopes. The nation's "only hope," according to Baldwin, was to "undermine the standards by which the middle-class American lives." This was an intriguing twist: not only did blacks hold out the hope of racial enlightenment, for example, but Baldwin saw them playing a redemptive role in the struggle against bourgeois materialism as well, their very poverty a virtue. Baldwin criticized middle-class status-seeking again in 1961, confessing that he was not "terribly worried about color TV and split-level houses," for the middle class was a "pretty sorry lot," suffering "in their tawdry splendor." Like Faulkner and Warren, Baldwin questioned the materialist ethos, including the emphasis placed on rising into the middle class. "As for the rise of the Negro into the middle class," he noted, "I am not certain that what is happening in this country can be summed up quite so neatly. It doesn't look much like a rise to me; it looks more like an insane rout, with white people fleeing to the suburbs of cities, hotly pursued by Negroes. In any case, by the time anything we can comfortably speak of as a 'rise' has occurred, this country will be, for better or worse, unrecognizable."[24]

Warren would probably have agreed; it was a point the Fugitives had long made, as had William Faulkner, who had imagined the pursuit of status culminating in a burning house.

CHAPTER EIGHT

Everything That Rises Must Converge

FLANNERY O'CONNOR FUMED. "THE kind I don't like is the philosophizing prophesying pontificating kind," she wrote, the "James Baldwin kind" of "Negroes" who were excoriating southern whites like herself in prominent literary magazines like the *New Yorker*. The journal had published "Letter from a Region in My Mind" to rave reviews, prompting Baldwin to reissue it, along with the "letter" to his nephew, in a small book entitled *The Fire Next Time* in 1963. The title hailed from a Negro spiritual and alluded to the second coming of Christ, something that O'Connor, a devout Catholic, did not take lightly. She was thirty-nine, only a year younger than Baldwin, and a successful writer in her own right, having published two novels, *Wise Blood* and *The Violent Bear It Away*, along with a series of acclaimed short stories, many with Christian themes. Born in Savannah, Georgia, she lived on her family's farm, Andalusia, outside Milledgeville, and suffered from a debilitating case of lupus, a tragic disease that caused her immune system to turn on itself. To her, Baldwin was a self-righteous outsider who knew little about the South, her South, a region characterized by charity, manners, and Christian values, values that O'Connor embraced in her work.[1]

She also embraced segregation. A friend had inquired about the possibility of Baldwin visiting O'Connor during his trip through the South in 1959, but she declined, arguing that "the traditions" of her society precluded it. "I can't see James Baldwin in Georgia," she wrote to her friend. "It would cause the greatest trouble and disturbance and disunion. In New York it would be nice to meet him; here it would not." That was before Baldwin published *The Fire Next Time*, which rankled O'Connor for its insinuation that white southerners were morally undeveloped, "trapped in a history which they do not understand," and unable to grasp the magnitude of evil in the world, including the evil that they themselves had wrought on blacks. "Baldwin can tell us what it feels like to be a Negro in Harlem," she spat, "but he tries to tell us everything else too." Her observation was brusque, as was her language. She peppered her comments about race with the n-word, made fun of her black help, and mocked the civil rights movement, as became obvious in June 1961 when one of her employees, a farmhand named Shot, injured himself on her estate near Milledgeville and threatened to sue. Although he had already collected insurance, O'Connor joked to friends that he might call the NAACP, a jab at black attempts to enlist the courts in their pursuit of equality. O'Connor also mocked black activists, writing to a friend in 1962 about a failed sit-in protest in Milledgeville, orchestrated by four flamboyantly dressed African Americans from Atlanta who hoped to integrate a local drugstore, only to retreat when they found the establishment crowded with rednecks pretending to read the newspaper. O'Connor found the scene amusing, mocking both the black activists from Atlanta and their white redneck adversaries, hinting at a larger contempt for white extremists and the civil rights movement alike, a contempt that led her to refer to the black freedom struggle as "the race business," an endeavor that promised little for southern art. When an acquaintance asked her whether the "race crisis was going to bring about a renascence" in southern literature, she replied, no, for "that was to romanticize the race business to a ridiculous degree."[2]

Yet, behind O'Connor's bigoted bluster nestled a variety of ideas about race that resonated, oddly, with Baldwin's own claims in *The Fire Next Time*. For example, O'Connor published a story in the *Sewanee Review* just before she excoriated Baldwin that portrayed African Americans as inhabiting a higher moral plane than whites—a

notion that Baldwin himself had advanced in "My Dungeon Shook," the title he gave to his nephew's letter. The story is set in a doctor's office in the Deep South and features four main characters: a white matronly woman named Ruby Turpin; her "florid and bald" husband Claude; a "well-dressed gray-haired lady"; and her "fat," college-age daughter who happens to be home for the summer from Wellesley College in Massachusetts. Also present in the waiting room is a "white-trashy" family who Turpin deems "worse than niggers." Turpin fancies herself to be "neat," "clean," and "respectable," anguishing over the annoying ubiquity of poor whites, at one point even conceding that she would rather be a respectable "Negro woman" than "white-trash." Turpin views the South's social order as a type of ladder, with poor "colored people" and "white-trash" together on the bottom; then "home-owners," white and black, above them; "home-and-land-owners" beyond them; and, finally, at the apex of southern society, "people with a lot of money and much bigger houses and much more land." Turpin considers herself a "home-and-land owner," though she suffers nightmares that she may one day slip into the lower rungs like some whites who, despite their "good blood," had "lost their money and had to rent." By underscoring Turpin's obsession with social rank, O'Connor made the material quest for status a centerpiece of her story, much like Baldwin had focused on the pervasive quest for status in *The Fire Next Time.* O'Connor joined Baldwin in linking the pursuit of status to the question of race, suggesting that racial prejudice was itself somehow a reflection of status anxiety. For example, Turpin complains at one point that she can't find employees to work her farm because "you can't get the white folks to pick [cotton] and now you can't get the niggers—because they got to be right up there with the white folks," a problem that manifests itself not just in refusal to work but also in a desire to integrate—sexually. "What they all want to do," argues Turpin, is "go to New York and marry white folks and improve their color." The notion of improving one's "color" was a recurring paranoia within certain racist circles in the South, a fear that African Americans wanted to ascend the social order by marrying whites and bearing light-skinned children, a concern sufficiently serious that the Supreme Court refused to hear a case challenging bans on interracial marriage in 1955 for fear of sparking a backlash.

Baldwin scoffed at such arguments, as did O'Connor, whose portrayal of Turpin's fear bordered on the ridiculous. However, her humor conveyed her larger point that status anxiety presented itself both in materialist concerns over property and houses and in racialist concerns of black ascension and white decline—a point that Baldwin had also made.[3]

Turpin's anxiety about status peaks when the "fat" Wellesley student grows so tired of her condescending remarks that she pounces from her chair and throttles her, prompting a moment of confused silence during which Turpin asks the student what, precisely, provoked the attack, waiting "as for a revelation" for the response. The revelation, it turns out, is that Turpin struck the student as a beastly person, a "warthog from hell," which Turpin takes to be a sign from God that "she had been singled out" even "though there was trash in the room to whom it might justly have been applied." The scene is striking. O'Connor used Turpin's attack to underscore the notion that she was beset by an anxiety regarding her position in society, and therefore her identity. Her confusion as to why the Wellesley student attacked Turpin echoed Baldwin's theme that whites were blind to their own repugnance, "innocent" as he put it, of the manner in which their obsession with status translated into racial prejudice, condemning them to a lower moral plane than blacks. For example, Turpin recovers from her assault only to suffer a horrifying vision of "a vast swinging bridge extending upward from the Earth" to heaven, upon which trudge a procession of "souls" reminiscent of Matthew 20:16, where Jesus of Nazareth declares that the last on Earth would be the first to enter paradise. To her horror, Turpin notices that she is not first in line but somewhere in the back, behind "bands of black niggers" who magically outrank her, despite—or perhaps because of—her social prestige. The scene provided a startling glimpse of Jim Crow through a biblical lens, essentially inverting the theory of white supremacy by suggesting that those who enjoyed white privilege were morally compromised and damned to hell, while those who occupied the lowest social positions on Earth, blacks, were closest to God.[4]

Although some invoked biblical arguments to justify white supremacy, O'Connor seemed to take a different view, suggesting that whites, particularly privileged whites, existed in a spiritually precar-

ious position. While this echoed Baldwin's notion that white insistence on maintaining racial primacy compromised white integrity, O'Connor did not follow Baldwin in suggesting that Turpin's "revelation" should therefore prompt some kind of social change. Instead, she found social change itself to be shallow, a worldly effort to advance blacks' social and political positions while moving them farther back on the great "swinging bridge" of salvation. Grace, suggested O'Connor, was reserved for the downtrodden and the oppressed, not those dedicated to elevating them.

This was, to some extent, a conundrum. If O'Connor's status put her farther from God than blacks, why did she not endorse the relinquishment of white privilege to improve her spiritual position? At a deeper level, why adopt a theology that put herself in a hopelessly compromised position in the first place, above blacks politically but below them spiritually? Most white southerners did not share O'Connor's view, believing instead that it was possible to live a Christian life from within the confines of Jim Crow, viewing material wealth, or privilege, as evidence of God's blessings, not his rejection. Of course, such whites could also not come up with a compelling biblical explanation for why civil rights should not be granted to African Americans, a problem that confronted many white Christians who opposed *Brown.*[5]

O'Connor could. She rejected the notion that God expressed his blessings through prosperity and wealth, and she also rejected Protestant millennialism, the idea that society was progressing toward an ideal state of peace and justice, a vision that included a place for social reform as part of a larger Christian campaign of vanquishing evil and transforming Earth—all leading up to the second coming of Christ. This, of course, was the language that Baldwin had invoked in *The Fire Next Time*, the "fire" being a direct allusion to Christ's return, which, for some millennialists, would involve a cataclysmic day of judgment.[6]

O'Connor's aversion to millennialism, by contrast, stemmed in part from her Catholic upbringing, which did not place the same emphasis on the second coming as Pentecostals and Baptists. However, even the Catholic church endorsed the notion that Christians owed a duty to the poor and disfranchised, a concept first enunciated by Pope Pius XI in 1931 under the rubric of "social justice."[7]

O'Connor made no mention of social justice in her work, nor did she endorse the theology of black preachers like Martin Luther King, Jr., who worked diligently to link the idea of Christian duty to the struggle for civil rights. King called expressly on white Christians to address "social issues" and to resist the temptation to commit themselves to "other-worldly religion[s]" unconcerned with racial oppression, a point he made in a widely celebrated letter from Birmingham, Alabama's city jail in 1963. "I have been so greatly disappointed with the white church," lamented King in his epistle, "some have been outright opponents, refusing to understand the freedom movement and misrepresenting its leaders; all too many others have been more cautious than courageous and have remained silent behind the anesthetizing security of stained-glass windows." O'Connor rankled at such sanctimony, finding King's theology little more than a self-serving distortion of Christ's teachings aimed not at salvation but at moving African Americans ahead materially. This explains her reverence for the black poor on the great swinging bridge in "Revelation," and her contempt for the Atlanta activists who attempted to integrate a soda fountain in Milledgeville. It also helps contextualize her story about Ruby Turpin. Written in the wake of King's "Letter from Birmingham Jail," O'Connor's story suggests that King himself was due for a "revelation" about the nature of God's grace. It did not come from winning the right to buy lunch at Woolworth's, she implied, but from going without.[8]

While the value of suffering was central to most mainstream Christian traditions, O'Connor's aversion to reform was not. Her faith in segregation coincided with an odd awareness that African Americans suffered repression yet did not deserve reform. This tolerance for evil, an evil that arguably put her farther from grace as well, was an aspect of O'Connor's thinking that did not stem from Catholic or Protestant thinking so much as a strand of intellectual thought dating back to the post–Civil War South. According to southern theologian Ralph C. Wood, the South's "humiliating defeat" in the Civil War instilled in the region "an ineradicable sense of the tragic"—an awareness that "many things broken cannot be mended, and that much evil must be patiently endured." The idea of reform for southerners like O'Connor rankled precisely because it defied southern experience, feeding into a "millennial sense of destiny" that was endemic to the North, not the South. Even if Jim Crow was done away with, for example, O'Connor believed that there would still be evil in the world, maybe even more evil, as blacks abandoned their historically Christ-like tolerance of suffering and vied with whites for status, power, and material wealth.[9]

Although younger than the Nashville Agrarians, O'Connor had gained some of her ideas from their work, having studied under Agrarian poet Andrew Lytle as an undergraduate. "The Fugitives at Vanderbilt in the '20s felt that the South they knew was passing away," she recounted to *Atlanta Magazine* in 1963, "and they wanted to get it down before it went, but they had a larger vision than just the South. They were against what they saw coming, against the social planner, fellow traveler spirit that came along in the next ten years." "Social planners," of course, referred to scientists like Gunnar Myrdal, who espoused sweeping social reforms to eradicate systemic social problems. O'Connor shared the Fugitives' doubts about such figures and traveled to Nashville in 1959 to rejoin the group for a symposium at Vanderbilt University, where she found herself on a panel with Robert Penn Warren. The two writers took turns criticizing modernity, industrialization, and suburbanization, painting all three as threats to individual identity and diversity. "I think as it gets to be more and more city and less country," lamented O'Connor, individuals will be reduced to "the same flat level," there would be less diversity in human relationships, and "we'll be writing about men in gray flannel suits." Warren agreed, noting that suburban America was even more devoid of diversity than urban America. "The city has sort of a new romance after the supermarket civilization of the suburbs," argued Warren, a point that O'Connor conceded. "I shouldn't say 'city' in that sense," she quipped, "I mean just the proliferation of supermarkets." "Cellophane," responded Warren; "plastics," retorted O'Connor, as both agreed that "everybody wants the privilege of being as abstract as the next man." The two writers hinted that consumerism and progress were rendering America less interesting, more homogenous, a problem that was even afflicting the South. "I think in the South we're losing that regional sense," lamented O'Connor, whose celebration of the poor in "Revelation" coincided with her critique—and Warren's—of the status-conscious, striving middle class.[10]

Of course, integration also threatened to make the South more homogenous, a problem that Warren had raised with Ralph Ellison in Rome, and that O'Connor explored in a story written shortly after her Vanderbilt visit. Published in 1961, the tale begins with a white woman boarding a recently integrated bus joined by her son, a college graduate and aspiring writer named Julian, en route to a weight-loss, or "reducing," class. Before departing, the woman dons a "hideous" hat with "a purple velvet flap" that "came down on one side of it and stood up on the other; the rest of it was green and looked like a cushion with the stuffing out." If garish, the hat cost $7.50, a large sum for the woman, who lives in an apartment in a rundown section of town, "struggled fiercely to feed and clothe" her family, and even subsidizes her son, who has failed to achieve his literary dreams. She justifies purchasing the hat by announcing that it makes her distinct, a clear indication that the accoutrement is a status symbol, something that prevents her from "meet[ing]" herself "coming and going." Although poor, the woman flaunts her antebellum heritage, explaining to her son that his great-grandfather had been a "former governor" who owned "a plantation and two hundred slaves," the slaves too being clear markers of prestige. "I've always had a great respect for colored folks," blathers the woman, reminiscing on how her childhood "nurse" had been "an old darky" named Caroline. The woman's son recoils at such blatant efforts by his mother to boost her profile by condescending to blacks, prompting him to sit down next to a "large Negro" on the bus, even as his mother "turned an angry red." Tensions boil over when a black woman boards the bus wearing the same exact hat as Julian's mother, joined by her four-year-old son, Carver. While Julian's "face was suddenly lit with joy" at the thought of his mother's hat losing its prestige, she proves undaunted and condescendingly hands Carver a penny, prompting Carver's mother to bash her with a handbag, at which point she suffers some kind of psychotic break, wandering down the street mumbling, and collapses. Julian does not notice his mother's episode until it is too late, after he has already harangued her by declaring that the woman was her "black double" whose attack symbolized "the whole colored race" and its refusal to "take your condescending pennies." Julian's words revealed the extent to which O'Connor herself understood how racial condescension and the quest for status were linked, and how African Americans might resent this. The scene also demonstrated the manner in which white notions of identity hinged on black inferiority, including the false presumption that African Americans might actually want patronizing gifts. Julian's mother loses her mind precisely when Carver's mother strikes her, an event that seems to shatter her personality.[11]

Hardly a tribute to civil rights, "Everything That Rises Must Converge" undermined the image of the humble, nonviolent bus rider epitomized by Rosa Parks, replacing it with a violent, status-conscious, black matron. The story also portrayed pro–civil rights whites as self-righteous prigs, epitomized by Julian, whose effort to humiliate and punish his mother for her racial chauvinism backfires, filling him with regret as she expires on the street, casting him into "the world of guilt and sorrow." Julian's awakening comes not from his fight for black rights, which O'Connor mocked, but from the realization that his impudent, self-righteous behavior seriously harmed the woman closest to him. By the end of the story, Julian's sanctimonious nod to racial justice proves just as condescending as his mother's sanctimonious nod to black inferiority, both evidence of their impious pride.[12]

Rather than lead to some type of social utopia, the integration of public buses only exacerbated the problem of status, a point that O'Connor underscored by concluding her tale with a black woman exacting violent revenge on her white doppelganger. Just as the title suggested, the "rise" of blacks led them, inevitably, to "converge" with whites, that is, to wear the same garish hats and display the same obnoxious, status-conscious, even violent behavior. Even if Carver's mother was legitimately affronted by the offer of a condescending penny, for example, her savage response is disproportionate to the offense, hardly an expression of the type of brotherly love and forgiveness that had been celebrated by Martin Luther King.

Published a year after student-led sit-in demonstrations rocked the South, O'Connor's story about hats highlighted her doubts about Baldwin and King, both of whom struck her as self-righteous and spiritually confused. For example, her story paid little attention to the struggle that blacks had gone through to desegregate public accommodations, a victory that she seemed to find pyrrhic. "White people and colored people are used to milling around together in the South," she noted nonchalantly in 1963, "and this integration only means that they are going to be milling around together in a few more places. No basic attitudes are being changed." Rather than a transformative achievement, in other words, integration promised little save a reordering of public space, perhaps even opening the door to more open conflict and violence. The only thing that might prevent such violence, believed O'Connor, was "manners," a code of conduct that had evolved in the South over decades of interracial interaction. "It requires considerable grace for two races to live together," she explained in 1963, "particularly when the population is divided about fifty-fifty between them and when they have our particular history. It can't be done without a code of manners based on mutual charity." Charity and manners were, to O'Connor, cornerstones of southern society, values that warranted preservation with or without Jim Crow. In fact, she believed that the dismantling of Jim Crow prompted a renewed emphasis on such codes, a position O'Connor expressed in a rare concession to civil rights. "The Negro will in the matter of a few years have his constitutional rights," she declared to *Atlanta Magazine* in 1963, "and we will all then see that the business of getting along with each other is much the same as it has always been, even though new manners are called for."[13]

Like the Fugitives, O'Connor saw race relations in the region as largely harmonious, precisely because the races adhered to strict codes of conduct, softened by charity. This, incidentally, was not the case in the urban North, where whites and blacks had failed to develop a gracious *modus vivendi*, prompting even worse tensions than in the South. O'Connor explored this theme in a story about a Georgia farmer who moves to New York to be with his daughter, only to suffer at the hands of an angry black neighbor. Entitled "Judgement Day," the tale focuses on "Tanner," an elderly white man from Corinth, Georgia, who is taken to New York City by his daughter once she discovers that he has fallen on hard times and is living in squalid conditions with a poor black man named Coleman on property owned, ironically, by a wealthy black doctor. Tanner resents his New York captivity and fantasizes about returning to Georgia to reconnect with Coleman, who sends him a postcard from Corinth inquiring about his health. Unfortunately for Tanner, however, his daughter cannot countenance her father "settl[ing] in with niggers," prompting her to keep him in Manhattan. Desperate for the fellowship that he left behind in Georgia, Tanner attempts to befriend African Americans in his daughter's apartment building, to horrific end. He leaves his daughter's apartment on one occasion and tries to engage an African American actor living in the same building but condescendingly refers to him as "preacher," a title that Coleman considers complimentary but that the actor finds pejorative. Outraged, the actor declares that "there ain't no Jesus" and proceeds to slam Tanner against the wall, ultimately shoving him into his apartment. Convinced that New York is "no kind of place," Tanner tries to escape but falls down the stairs and is found again by the actor, who shoves his head through the stair rail and kills him after Tanner insists once again on calling him "preacher."[14]

The story presented O'Connor's views of race, grace, and the South in stark terms. The black actor echoed the black matron in "Everything That Rises Must Converge," who demonstrated her newfound equality by abandoning manners for violence. The actor also projected faint emanations of James Baldwin, who rejected religion in *The Fire Next Time* and threatened whites with violence, or "fire," as he put it. Like Julian's mother in "Everything Rises," Tanner's death startles precisely because it does not seem commensurate with his offense, underscoring O'Connor's insinuation that integration would only bring about more violence under the guise of equality. Tanner does not believe in equality, of course, and prides himself on the fact that Coleman is his "servant," but the two essentially occupy the same social rank and enjoy a close personal bond. Tanner's daughter, by contrast, emerges as a villain for refusing to allow her father to live with Coleman on black-owned land, imprisoning him in an urban, northern hell where he is brutally killed.

"Judgement Day" proved O'Connor's final story. She died as it went to press on August 3, 1964, from lupus. The disease had ravaged her for over a decade, sapping her strength, compromising her organs, and dissolving her bones. Although she claimed that the suffering wrought by her condition did not affect her writing, this is hard to believe. Her personal experience with lupus—which essentially amounted to a protracted, painful death sentence—coincided closely with her emphasis on suffering and salvation, on the idea that those who suffer do not endure for nothing but draw closer to

God. It also explained her dismissive attitude toward white privilege. While Baldwin carped about the harms caused by white racism, his depictions of whites as a categorically privileged class who did not know suffering clearly fell flat with O'Connor, partly because she was southern, to be sure, but also because she was dying. If she knew anything, it was pain, a constant discomfort that she would probably have traded for a lower rank in society, a slot closer to heaven on God's great swinging bridge.

CHAPTER NINE

Who Speaks for the Negro?

As Flannery O'Connor suffered her final, agonizing months in Milledgeville, Robert Penn Warren sat down with James Baldwin and a tape recorder. It was April 1964—Baldwin had just finished a play inspired by the murder of Emmett Till named *Blues for Mister Charlie*, and Warren was in the midst of a new project, a book about black leadership and civil rights. There was much to cover. Since 1955, African Americans had launched a push for constitutional rights unprecedented in American history. Early signs of the campaign had exploded in Montgomery—which, of course, Warren had failed to mention in *Segregation: The Inner Conflict*—but then caught fire in Greensboro, Richmond, Nashville, and other cities in 1960 as black college students entered white lunch counters and refused to leave, often provoking bitter, racist attacks. Such assaults embarrassed Warren even as they sparked renewed interest nationally in civil rights, an interest that continued to generate smoke and flame in 1961 as a series of widely publicized integrated bus trips, or "Freedom Rides," rolled through the Deep South, crisscrossing the region and provoking outrageous displays of white violence in forgettable places like Anniston, Alabama, where a bus was torched, and Montgomery, where mobs attacked riders. The inspiration and planning for these protests came from different organizations and different leaders but were invariably portrayed in the northern press as part of a larger, organized "movement," a term that first began to gain national currency in 1962. Warren became interested in writing something about the "movement" in 1963, in part due to the kaleidoscope of black organizations that had been formed to lead it, groups like the United Defense League, formed in Baton Rouge in 1953; the Montgomery Improvement Association, formed in Montgomery in 1955; the Alabama Christian Movement for Human Rights, formed in Birmingham in 1956; and the Inter-Civic Council, formed in Tallahassee in 1956. In 1957, longtime civil rights activist Bayard Rustin, himself a member of an organization called the Fellowship of Reconciliation (FOR), lobbied Martin Luther King, Jr., and other prominent black ministers to form a group charged with coordinating the bus boycotts across the South, a project that inspired the creation of the Southern Christian Leadership Conference (SCLC). The SCLC emerged as a prominent force in southern racial politics for the next decade, in part due to the charisma and eloquence of King, but still failed to unite the various protest strands in the region. For example, students tired of answering to senior leadership in the SCLC formed their own organization, the Student Non-Violent Coordinating Committee (SNCC) in 1960. Soon thereafter, yet another civil rights group took center stage, the Congress of Racial Equality (CORE), orchestrating the Freedom Rides in 1961. By the close of 1962, proponents of unity in Mississippi called for an umbrella group to bring CORE, SNCC, SCLC, and the older, more established NAACP together, this time leading to the formation of the Council of Federated Organizations, an entity that enjoyed some success but ultimately failed to dampen the institutional pluralism then rampant in southern black protest circles.[1]

The simmering alphabet soup of black organizations behind the "movement" intrigued Warren, not least because it pointed to a political landscape that was at once decentralized, diverse, and populated with precisely the kind of "individual variety" that he had heralded as a bulwark against "standardization and anonymity" in the plural South. Warren named his new project *Who Speaks for the Negro?* The title oozed ambivalence, almost as if composed to underscore black divisions—divisions that were not necessarily known to whites in the North, who tended to associate black leadership with one man, Martin Luther King, Jr. King had worked diligently to project a united black front in his speeches and writings, including a memoir of demonstrations in Birmingham published in June 1964 entitled *Why We Can't Wait.* In his memoir, King told the Birmingham story with authorial surety—and singularity—casting the movement in the South as an expression of a cohesive black will that had manifested itself in a determination to face police dogs, fire hoses, and terrorist attacks. Although King had been only one of many actors in the Birmingham campaign, he retold events in a unified, almost Homeric style, referring to African Americans in the singular by noting repeatedly that "the Negro" had grown tired of waiting for *Brown*'s promise, become frustrated with federal dawdling, and was now awakening from "a stupor of inaction" to sound "a declaration of freedom with his marching feet across the pages of newspapers, the television screens, and the magazines."[2]

Warren was dubious. His title questioned King's presumption of singularity, suggesting instead that there were many African American perspectives and many African American leaders, some of whom disagreed with King on who precisely "the Negro" was and what precisely "he" wanted. In fact, Warren's title evoked an earlier anthology of fourteen essays edited by Howard University historian Rayford Logan in 1944 entitled *What the Negro Wants,* another singular reference to black America that Warren seemed eager to engage. Logan's volume enlisted a diverse panel of speakers, including Roy Wilkins, W. E. B. Du Bois, and Langston Hughes, all of whom joined in a unanimous call to end racial segregation in the American South, a show of solidarity that shocked whites at the time, even liberals who did not anticipate the kind of overwhelming hostility to Jim Crow that the collection's contributors expressed.[3]

Warren's interlocutors told a different, more fractured tale. Some lobbied for immediate integration, others for gradual change. Some argued for separatism, others for pluralism, and yet others for vague, unrealizable objectives that Warren took not to be genuine bids for reform so much as opportunities to rant angrily against the South and the United States. Rather than identify a common thread running through black politics, Warren explored dissensions, underscored disputes, and highlighted differences of opinion regarding tactics and goals hiding behind unifying slogans like the "civil rights movement." The end result was a 454-page Tower of Babel that suggested no one "spoke" for African Americans nor did African Americans necessarily agree on what they wanted or believed. The heroes of the study, to the extent there were any, proved to be blacks supportive of gradual reform, black self-help, and pluralism, themes Warren had long endorsed himself. Meanwhile, the least sympathetic characters were those with the most defiant ideas and the fewest realizable solutions.[4]

James Baldwin emerged as one of Warren's most eloquent, and complicated, interlocutors. On the one hand, Baldwin seemed to argue for integration, or a world in which race "would count for nothing." On the other, he made a strong case for the importance of preserving a distinctly black perspective on America, its history, and its shortcomings, values that Baldwin found tangled up with "centuries of cruelty and bad faith and genocide and fear." African Americans, argued Baldwin, should not go quietly into the white mainstream, but rather their history and their voices should be celebrated, for they had developed a critical perspective on America that was valuable and worth preserving.[5]

Baldwin even hinted that blacks possessed superior traits, beyond simply a more critical lens on the American experience, traits like "sensuality" that whites lacked, as well as a capacity "to respect and rejoice in the force of life, or life itself, and to be *present* in all that one does, from the effort of loving to the breaking of bread." Warren found some aspects of this view compelling, others ridiculous. "On the matter of sex," observed Warren, "some of Baldwin's pronouncements are difficult to reconcile with one another. All his comments on the defect of white sexuality, etc., clearly carry the implication of some happy norm of Negro success in this department," a norm that Warren called into question. "What all the studies show," argued Warren, "is that Negroes, given the same psychic strains react exactly as white people do."[6]

More interesting to Warren were Baldwin's thoughts on diversity, on the desire to maintain a distinct black perspective, independent of white mainstream values. "In the last few years," stated Warren, "there is a movement toward an acceptance of and a pride in negro identity," a movement that Warren related to earlier efforts, first mounted by W. E. B. Du Bois at the turn of the century, by blacks to "identify" with "American Negro culture as opposed to

American white culture," or what Warren rephrased as "the Western European American white tradition." Of course, Warren had been interested in this point—and in Du Bois—since his 1929 essay "The Briar Patch," which declared Jim Crow instrumental in developing an independent black "art." Baldwin reviled Jim Crow, to be sure, but conceded that "it was very hard" for him to "accept Western European values" because "they didn't accept me." "No matter how many showers you take," he continued, "no matter what you do, these Western values simply—absolutely resist and reject you. So that inevitably at some point you turn away from them or you re-examine them." Although Baldwin's turn from white culture seemed to stem from white rejection—a point that distinguished him from Zora Neale Hurston and Ralph Ellison, who argued for an appreciation of black traditions independent of white acceptance or rejection—his sense that blacks were engaged in a constant reassessment of America was a notion all three shared. They agreed that African Americans possessed a more honest, clear-eyed view of mainstream American society than did whites. "The slaves who, you know, who adopted the bloody cross," explained Baldwin to Warren, "did know one thing, they knew the masters could not—those masters could not be Christians because Christians couldn't have treated them that way. You know what I mean—this rejection has been at the very heart of the American Negro psyche from the beginning." This, of course, was an indictment of southerners like Flannery O'Connor, who placed Christianity at the center of their worldview, including their view of Jim Crow, which relegated blacks to second-class status. O'Connor reconciled this system with her Catholic faith, but Baldwin suggested that such reconciliations—to be truly legitimate—had to pass African American muster, which O'Connor's did not.[7]

Having established the importance of the black perspective, Warren queried Baldwin on black leadership, beginning with Martin Luther King, Jr., whose efforts to build a movement in the North had not succeeded as well as in the South. Rather than address differences in the legal landscape of the North, Baldwin focused on the tight-knit nature of black communities in the South. "Negroes in the South still go to church," argued Baldwin, "and Negroes in the South—which is much more important—still have something resembling a family around which you can build a great deal. But the Northern Negro family has been fragmented for the last thirty years, if not longer, and once you haven't got a family then you have another kind of despair, another kind of demoralization, and Martin King can't reach those people." It was an intriguing argument, and controversial. Since at least the 1930s, anthropologists and sociologists had debated the relationship between black family life and the existence of a separate black culture in the American South. Most northern-based scholars concluded that disorganization in black family life, including single-parent homes and illegitimacy, were environmental rather than biological in origin, and therefore did not have a direct biological tie to race. Black sociologist E. Franklin Frazier made this point in 1939 in a book entitled *The Negro Family in the United States*, which rejected arguments that black family disorganization was a cultural trait unique to African Americans. Yet, Frazier did concede that black family patterns had evolved along particular lines in the American South—largely due to slavery and emancipation—yielding a black "folk culture" that was "recorded and transmitted orally and which was isolated from the influences of modern urban society." This culture was precisely the same culture that Zora Neale Hurston extolled in her writings, though she focused on music, storytelling, and folklore, not marriage rates. For Frazier, however, black folk culture was also marked by single-parent homes, "'matriarchal' family organization," and "illegitimacy." However, even Frazier concluded that these were not particularly damaging or pathological because they formed part of a larger, extended kin conception of family. Other scholars, like black sociologist and Harlem Renaissance contributor Charles S. Johnson, concurred, arguing that southern rural blacks had carved out their own "culture" marked by "'matriarchal' pattern[s]" and "freer sexual mores." Anthropologist Hortense Powdermaker confirmed this notion, also finding matriarchal family patterns prominent in black communities in the South and concluding that they were not particularly negative or damaging. White sociologist John Dollard joined her, arguing that extended black families in the South provided children with a nurturing environment, even if their parents were not always married.[8]

Baldwin may have been aware of this work and may have relied on it to argue that black communities in the South were, despite the lynchings and violence of Jim Crow, more cohesive than in the North. Of course, this was something Warren wanted to hear, not least because it resonated with his longstanding argument that black communities had fared better in the segregated South than in the integrated North. Baldwin's point also resonated with Warren's interest in the development of a separate black culture in the South, a product of separate black communities.

Warren concluded his interview by asking Baldwin about the state of black leadership, a query that led Baldwin to claim that civil rights organizations were "on their way out" since established leaders like King had failed to connect with black youth. "It has created a tremendous struggle for power," explained Baldwin, "but that's not yet such a menace as a split in the leadership—as a real split which is, you know, an open secret." Baldwin's concern over the split in black leadership dovetailed with Warren's own interest in exposing dissension within black America's civil rights elite, a recurring theme of his book. While willing to acknowledge that African Americans possessed legitimate gripes with whites in the South, Warren was also invested in underscoring the complexity of views within black protest circles, a move that opened the door to nuanced discussions about the implications of reform for black culture, black perspectives, and black identity—topics that King did not broach. Baldwin's interest in preserving black identity therefore coincided with Warren's interest in "variety and pluralism," a phrase he had invoked with Ralph Ellison in Rome several years before. And, Baldwin's indictment of mainstream, middle-class values, or what he had once termed "a burning house," appealed to Warren in part because Warren had himself raised questions about mainstream America culture intermittently since the 1920s. Even if Baldwin was not southern-born, in other words, aspects of his thinking made him a fugitive from the modernizing, homogenizing thrust of American middle-class culture. This, perhaps, was the most resonant chord in Warren's book, a chord that he strummed not just with Baldwin but with a series of black interlocutors, from a variety of occupations and walks of life.[9]

For example, Warren followed his interview with Baldwin by talking to James Farmer, a civil rights leader based in New York who happened to be the head of CORE, the same group that sponsored the Freedom Rides. Warren met Farmer in his "big, bare shabby" office at 38 Park Row in New York City, across from City Hall, in a Dickensian building replete with "sodden cigarette butts and old gum wrappers on the floor," a "creaky elevator," and a "waiting room with bulging and broken cartons stacked in a corner," the walls covered in a "grime-stained plaster." Warren's description of the building shaded the portrait that he painted of Farmer, "comfortable but solid in his ample coffee-colored flesh, not notable for humor, but ready to smile out of his round face."[10]

Warren mentioned Farmer's early activism, which began in the 1940s working for FOR, the same "pacifist organization" that Bayard Rustin belonged to. Farmer then cofounded the Committee for Racial Equality, later renamed the Congress for Racial Equality, in 1942, with the goal of fighting segregation by adopting Gandhian principles of nonviolence. In 1961, Farmer played a critical role in organizing the Freedom Rides, themselves modeled after earlier integrated bus trips sponsored by FOR in the 1940s.[11]

Warren questioned Farmer about his commitment to integration, wondering "whether the Negro wants real integration, with the shocks and the sharpened competitiveness entailed by that, or a token, a superficial integration, with the insult of formal segregation removed but a self-imposed segregation maintained, blurred around the edges of public contact but hard at center." Farmer conceded that a "crucial debate" on precisely this point was going on "in the Negro community," and that "most Negroes—'the ordinary John Does whose skins are black'—are not concerned with the issue of segregation or of separation versus integration. 'The real issue for them,'" argued Farmer, "is getting the heel of oppression off their neck." Personally, Farmer favored integration, but only of a certain kind. Warren asked him, for example, whether integration would "mean the absorption of the Negro into white culture, perhaps even the blood stream," or "would it mean that the Negro, with 'pride in culture and history' and with a sense of 'identity,' could enter as a 'proud and equal partner who has something to give, something to share, and something to receive'?" Farmer favored the latter, arguing for what he called "unity through diversity," meaning a pluralist society in which groups retained their cultural identities but were not discriminated against because of them. This appealed to Warren, partly because it resonated with his own view that blacks themselves did not particularly want to integrate with whites but rather preferred a voluntary "self-separation characteristic of much minority life in America after 'success' and 'acceptance.'" However, Farmer also cautioned against rigid segregation on account of a "special danger," namely the encouragement of "nationalistic sentiment and anti-white feelings among Negro children." Warren seemed to agree with this. At no point did he indicate support for maintaining the laws of segregation outright, preferring to leave open the possibility that individuals and communities might work out their own arrangements. This, of course, led him to confront the single most influential proponent of integration in the South at the time, Martin Luther King, Jr.[12]

Warren interviewed King on March 18, 1964, in Atlanta at the SCLC headquarters on Auburn Avenue in the heart of the city's black business district. King struck Warren as a "tidily made, compact man" with "lips rather full but drawn back at the corners under a narrow close-trimmed mustache to emphasize this impression of compactness." Warren was clearly impressed with King's resume, noting his role in the Montgomery bus boycott, his leadership of the SCLC, and his recent Nobel Peace Prize, marking the culmination of a decade of high-profile work, not just in Montgomery but also Albany, Birmingham, and other places, including Washington, D.C., where he had delivered an electrifying speech at the Lincoln Memorial, the main theme of which was a "dream" that King had of racial harmony, integration, and equality in the United States.[13]

Warren began by asking King about his father, a prominent minister in Atlanta who had long worked within the confines of Jim Crow to advance black interests. King explained that his father had waged a struggle for reform long before he had, and that he was simply carrying the torch. Warren found this intriguing and dropped a footnote in his book about how rare it was for black ministers to be interested in politics. "The Negro churches," explained Warren, "have not traditionally been concerned with the rights of the Negro," in part because, as an institution, "the Church is a victim of its own heritage—segregation. Its strength came from segregation, and its leaders hardly shared any desire to shift the foundations."

This was an old argument in the South, the same one that whites like Henry Grady had made at the turn of the century. Warren conjured it in passing, fusing legends of the black church with problems King himself had confessed to about rallying the black community. For example, Warren cited in his note a passage in *Why We Can't Wait* where King expressed frustration at "the reluctance of many of the Negro clergy of Birmingham to support the demonstration[s] there in 1963," as well as the uncomfortable fact that "no church was made available for a mass rally" in Montgomery in 1963, "not even the Dexter Avenue Baptist Church, where Dr. King had begun his ministry." Before King even had a chance to tell his remarkable story, in other words, Warren dropped a subtle grenade fracturing the idea of a unified "movement" in the South by exposing the latent pluralism within the one southern institution most sacred to King, the black church.[14]

Warren moved on to the ideal of integration, asking King what the next stage of the movement would be after Jim Crow was dismantled. King sounded an assimilationist note, suggesting that individuals strive for "genuine inter-group, inter-personal living." Skeptical, Warren pressed the minister on whether integration was actually feasible, particularly in places like Washington, D.C., where "some eighty-five per cent of the children in public school" were black. King responded by referencing the need to fix the problem of segregated housing and white flight, perhaps through busing. Warren parried, asking the minister about situations where bus rides for children would simply be too long to be feasible. King conceded, noting that in some cases integration would simply not work. "I agree," he confessed, "that the problem will not be solved if we have these situations."[15]

Once Warren got King to admit that integration might not work in all cases, he then pressed King to reconsider the ramifications of integration generally for black identity. He asked the minister about the "pull, on the one hand, toward Negro tradition, or culture, or blood, and the pull on the other hand toward the white cultural heritage with, perhaps, an eventual absorption of the Negro blood?" This was not one of King's regular themes, to be sure, but the leader conceded Warren's point, acknowledging that it was "a real issue," particularly among the "Negro middle class." Yet, King maintained that cultural pluralism and civil rights could coincide. "One can live in American society with a certain cultural heritage," explained King, "African or what have you—and still absorb a great deal of this [mainstream] culture." Blacks who rejected their culture, argued King, suffered for it. "Often," black individuals who "reject psychologically anything that reminds [them] of [their] heritage" find themselves "with no cultural roots."[16]

Warren beamed. This was a point that he had been trying to make for decades, namely a positive aspect of the South's separate racial traditions. Now he appeared to have an ally in King, of all people, whose public writings and speeches seemed to stress assimilation, a dreamscape where "the sons of former slaves and the sons of former slave owners" would attend the same schools, play at the same theme parks, and sit "down together at the table of brotherhood." Warren's careful questions teased out a different dream, namely a society in which black and white might sit down together, perhaps at school or work, but then go their separate ways at night. Of course, this was not what Gunnar Myrdal had imagined, since he found black culture to be pathological. But Warren sensed—correctly—that this aspect of Myrdal's thought was not something even King ascribed to.[17]

After finding a remarkable commonality with King, Warren turned to a black leader who, initially, seemed more aligned with his thinking: Malcolm X. Born Malcolm Little in Omaha, Nebraska, in 1925, Malcolm had converted to a black religious sect called the Nation of Islam (NOI) while serving a prison term for burglary, ultimately rising to become one of the Nation's highest profile officials, which at the time was led by an enigmatic character from Cordele, Georgia, named Elijah Muhammad. Muhammad inspired Malcolm X, convincing him of the church's central precepts that whites were devils, blacks superior, and integration heresy. Muhammad also sold Malcolm on the Koran, a commitment that culminated in a rift between the two when Malcolm discovered that his leader had fathered several children out of wedlock, a violation of Islamic law so egregious that it prompted him to leave the church. Warren found all this mildly amusing, leading him to introduce his conversation with Malcolm X at the Theresa Hotel in Harlem on

June 2, 1964, by portraying the NOI as "doomed" and Malcolm as a quixotic leader "without a real organization," lodged in a hotel conference room alone, by "himself," with few prospects.[18]

Warren's ensuing conversation took some unexpected turns. As a believer in pluralism, one might have assumed that the Fugitive poet would have found the Nation of Islam to be a kindred faction. However, Malcolm X's lack of interest in the black experience in the South irked Warren, defying his sense that African Americans had forged something significant under Jim Crow. For example, Warren pressed Malcolm on why, precisely, African Americans joined the Nation of Islam, a point Malcolm responded to by saying that an identity crisis lurked at the core of the African American experience, a sense that "the main problem that Afro-Americans have is a lack of cultural identity," making it "necessary to teach him that he had some type of identity, culture, civilization before he was brought here." This was an odd take on black culture, essentially ignoring the black experience in America and focusing exclusively on seventeenth- and eighteenth-century civilizations in Africa. Warren, of course, knew something about those civilizations, or at least believed he did, having included extended sections of his novel *Band of Angels* on the kingdom of Dahomey. However, he seemed to think the black experience in the United States more important than distant memories of Africa, which he found little more than a "dream—sad, angry," and "vainglorious."[19]

Warren also took issue with Malcolm X's blanket indictments of whites as "devils," a core NOI position. "Let's take an extreme case," posited Warren, "a white child of three or four—an age below decision or responsibility—is facing death before an oncoming truck . . . Is he guiltless?" He wasn't, responded Malcolm, a view that Warren found unreasonably absolutist, even totalitarian. "Does he mean to imply that moral value equates, simply, with consequence? Many people have believed that. Machiavelli, for one . . . Stalin, for another." Ultimately, Malcolm X emerged, in Warren's view, as a menacing, angry demagogue gripped with a searing "illogic," more polemical than persuasive.[20]

More sympathetic was Warren's old acquaintance Ralph Ellison, who Warren interviewed "high above the Hudson River" on Manhattan's Upper West Side, picking up on some of the themes that they had discussed in Rome eight years before. For example, Warren asked Ellison about the "split in the Negro psyche" between a desire to assimilate with whites and a desire to remain apart, to which Ellison responded by invoking the "implicit cultural pluralism of the country," noting that "the real goal of the pressure now being asserted by Negroes is to achieve on the sociopolitical level something of the same pluralism which exists on the level of culture." "My problem is not whether I will accept or reject American values," explained Ellison; "it is rather, how can I get into a position where I can have the maximum influence upon those values." Ellison's interest in values suggested that his vision of pluralism was not about exiting America, or even living in a separatist NOI-type enclave, but rather enriching America by recognizing black achievement. "I want to help shape events and our general culture," confessed Ellison, "not merely as a semi-outsider but as one who is in a position to have a responsible impact upon the American value system." Warren interpreted Ellison's comment to mean that there was something that the black writer appreciated about being black, a sense of "enrichment" that went beyond anger and frustration. "Then it's not merely suffering and deprivation," queried Warren, "it's challenge and enrichment?" Ellison concurred, noting that even though some black leaders insisted that segregation constituted "total agony," the danger in this "lies in overemphasizing the extent to which Negroes are alienated, and in overstressing the extent to which the racial predicament imposes an agony upon the individual." This was an important statement, one that went directly to Warren's longstanding sense that Jim Crow had been a livable system. Ellison sharpened his point, however, arguing that much of the movement's "discipline" came from the black experience with violence in the South, "out of long years of learning how to live under pressure, of learning to deal with provocation and violence." Warren pivoted, asking Ellison whether he feared losing "Negro identity" under fully integrated conditions. "I don't fear Negro blood being absorbed," explained Ellison, "but I am afraid that the Negro American cultural expression might be absorbed and obliterated through lack of appreciation and through commercialization and banalization." Warren warmed. This was a point he had long made, that mass culture threatened identity and that the South was a holdout against northern influence. Ellison, much like Zora Neale Hurston, found in the South something "present in our lives to sustain us," a certain "power of character" and "self-control" evident in black cultural expression, including "folklore."[21]

Ellison's view of pluralism paralleled many of Warren's own views about the South, a sense that the region possessed two cultures, and two peoples, with their own positive traditions. To Ellison's mind, this was something of value and worth saving. "I watch other people enjoying themselves," declared Ellison. "I watch their customs, and I think it one of my greatest privileges as an American, as a human being living in this particular time in the world's history, to be able to project myself into various backgrounds, into various cultural patterns, not because I want to cease being a Negro or because I think that these are automatically better ways of realizing oneself, but because it is one of the great glories of being an American." "In fact," continued Ellison, "one of the advantages of being a Negro is that we have always had the freedom to choose or to select and to affirm those traits, those values, those cultural forms, which we have taken from any and everybody . . . We probably have more freedom than anyone; we only need to become more conscious of it and use it to protect ourselves from some of the more tawdry American values. Besides, it's always a good thing to remember why it was that Br'er Rabbit loved his brier patch, and it wasn't simply for protection." Warren rejoiced. He, of course, had used the briar patch to describe segregation three decades earlier. Now he pressed Ellison to explain how racial separation might promote pluralism and growth. "I know some people, Ralph," stated Warren, "white people and Negroes, who would say that what you are saying is an apology for a segregated society. I know it's not. How would you answer such a charge?" "I've never pretended for one minute that the injustices and limitations of Negro life do not exist," Ellison responded. "On the other hand I think it important to recognize that Negroes have achieved a very rich humanity despite these restrictive conditions. I wish to be free not to be less Negro American but so that I can make the term mean something even richer."[22]

Ellison's affirmation of pride in his black past, and of the South as a pluralistic region, impressed Warren. "Ellison is more concerned," he proclaimed, "with the way man confronts his individual doom than with the derivation of that doom; not pathos, but power, in its deepest sense." Warren then mentioned an essay that Ellison had written challenging Gunnar Myrdal, who, to Ellison's mind, created "a sensation that [the African American] does not exist in the real world at all—only in the nightmarish fantasy of the white American mind." This appealed to Warren. "What Ellison would reject," he argued, is the violation of the density of life by an easy abstract formulation. Even militancy, if taken merely as a formula, can violate the density of life." Instead, Ellison embraced the complexity, and tragedy, of American life: "Not only the basic unity, but the rich variety, of life is what concerns him; and this fact is connected with his personal vision of the opportunity in being an American: The diversity of American life is often painful, frequently burdensome and always a source of conflict, but in it lies our fate and our hope." Here was a position that Warren could embrace, an endorsement of pluralism that took into account the nation's difficult past without categorically condemning it.[23]

Warren could have concluded his study with Ellison, for the black writer had confirmed his own beliefs, but Warren went on to add one section dedicated to "the young," the college-age black students who had been central to much of the grassroots protest in the South. His interviewees included Izell Blair, one of the four black students who had integrated lunch counters in Greensboro, along with three other student activists: Lucy Thornton, Jean Wheeler, and Stokely Carmichael, all of whom he met in a "disheveled," "none-too-clean basement apartment" at Howard University. The walls were a "calsomined a bilious green," noted Warren, the air "hot and sticky" from steam pipes in the ceiling. As they sipped "whiskey and water" from "paper cups" and "jelly glasses," Warren asked Blair about the Greensboro sit-ins four years earlier.[24]

Blair claimed the idea came from his "roommate," Joseph McNeil, also a freshman at Greensboro Agricultural and Technical College, or simply A&T. McNeil came up with the idea of a "boycott" that involved sitting at the counter at Woolworth's until they were served. They contacted a "local merchant" who happened to also be a member of the NAACP, as well as the local NAACP chapter president, George Simpkins, to alert them about the students' plans. The merchant provided the students with money to purchase items in the store and agreed to notify the press and police. However, Simpkins proved reluctant to involve the NAACP directly, opting instead to call CORE.[25]

Warren pressed Blair on the originality of the protest, wondering whether they had not modeled their action off earlier events, including student protests in the 1940s. Blair confessed that the 1940s had not been an inspiration but that there had been an earlier student demonstration in Wilmington, North Carolina, "in 1959" that they were aware of. Intrigued by the notion that hidden channels of protest existed between black communities in the South, including channels relaying information and ideas about possible avenues of resistance to whites, Warren invoked his old metaphor for Jim Crow, the briar patch. As he saw it, the nonviolence adopted by the students was less "a way of life" than a tactic, an adaptation of the same strategies of resistance that the "defenseless Br'er Rabbit" had used to "outwit all the powers, thrones, and dominions arrayed against him." As such, nonviolence joined the "thousand subtle and disguised ways" that African Americans in the South "express[ed] [their] natural resentment," including "the slovenly broom stroke, the crooked nail, the idiotic 'yassuh,' the misplaced tool, [and] the Uncle Remus story." It was an intriguing comment, evidence that Warren was aware of strategies of black resistance that anthropologists would eventually come to call "hidden transcripts" and "weapons of the weak." However, his inclusion of nonviolence into this category suggested that black activists were also employing the guise of spirituality to accomplish secular objectives. For many in the movement, he argued, nonviolence provided "a means of evoking and swaying the moral sense of the uncommitted and the moderate in local situations and, through the national press, that of the general public." Nonviolence, in other words, embodied a particularly savvy form of black resistance, a way to advance black interests by reversing stereotypes, making southern whites look savage and unsympathetic, a point that seemed to resonate with his interlocutors at Howard. "Most segregationists seem to think that Negroes are really nothing but cannibalistic savages," noted one black student, "and if we start fighting this would give them more reason to believe this." "Morally it looks better," argued another, "having a nonviolent protest than it does to be waiting in the woods, with a gun and bombs and things to destroy human life."[26]

Reticent through much of the conversation, black activist Stokely Carmichael expressed ambivalence about nonviolence as an ethical ideal, preferring to see in it an expression of black "inner power," a point that he would refine and rearticulate two years later as "Black Power." "I never took the approach we've got to teach them to love us," confessed Carmichael. "I thought that was nonsense from the start. But I was impressed by the way they [demonstrators] conducted themselves, the way they sat there and took the punishment." Warren warmed to Carmichael, questioning him on whether nonviolence may have been an active assertion of black identity, even superiority, over southern whites. "You mean not just by their fortitude," queried Warren, "but by self-discipline and personal power, inner power?" "Right," agreed Carmichael, suddenly conceding that nonviolence might simply have been an early iteration of the very spirit of black power that he would later invoke in 1966. No abrupt turn from past practice, in other words, Carmichael's rejection of nonviolence might simply have been a continuation of his longstanding admiration for black resolve and self-reliance.[27]

Carmichael's revelation that nonviolence was simply an incipient iteration of Black Power proved a coup for Warren, enabling him to demonstrate that pluralism reigned even among young black activists, who demonstrated little interest in joining white society or culture. To establish this point, Warren concluded with a "small, delicately formed young woman" named Ruth Turner. As she explained it, even "if all the barriers were lifted, Negroes, after having the experience of equal opportunity, would still choose to live together." Why, asked Warren, "because there was nothing to prove?" "That's right," replied Turner. "The melting pot," she explained, "has had a pretty homogenous and uninteresting flavor to me. It has become a gray mass of mediocrity, and I reject the melting-pot idea if it means that everybody has to come down to the same standard." Warren stood vindicated. He had suddenly, unexpectedly, found his own vision of southern society articulated by a student demonstrator. He also found confirmation of the view, best articulated by

James Baldwin, that blacks did not want to enter the burning house of white America but rather serve as "the regenerator[s]" of that America, working not "merely for integration into white society but for the redemption of society—a repudiation, and a transcendence, of white values."[28]

CHAPTER TEN

The Demonstrators

"MY THANKS ARE LATE coming but they're warm as can be for your book," exclaimed Eudora Welty to Robert Penn Warren on August 22, 1965. "It's so good, and I've read it with care, deep interest, profound admiration, and I may say some anguish—for you, us, the subject." The subject, of course, was civil rights. Warren's book *Who Speaks for the Negro?* had just hit bookshelves, to mixed reviews. The *New York Times* declared the book "fascinating," "good at dramatizing" tensions within black leadership, and "superbly candid" for its emphasis on black disunity, or "individualism." *Newsweek* pronounced the book "important" but ultimately "disappointing," in large part due to "Warren's own pervasive presence" in the narrative. "The book is, in good part, a plotting of Warren's own inner progress," wrote *Newsweek*, "from well-intentioned, paternal Southern conservative to his current position of troubled moderate whose basic attitude is still paternalistic, but whose ideological children have all grown up and left home."[1]

Welty was more positive. Warren had visited her at her home in Jackson while traveling for the book in February 1964. They had known one another for almost thirty years; he was one of the first readers of her stories in the 1930s, following her as she placed seven in the *Southern Review*, a literary journal that he ran with fellow Fugitive Cleanth Brooks at Louisiana State University in Baton Rouge.

Born in 1909, Welty was four years younger than Warren and already one of the South's most respected writers, having written four collections of short stories, a novel, a novella, and an extended monologue titled *The Ponder Heart* by 1954. She had a pleasant, endearing face; short hair; and big eyes, and she found wonder in southern culture, black and white. During the 1930s, for example, she traveled through "the eighty-two counties of Mississippi" taking pictures that she would eventually publish as a book, later describing the volume "not as a social document" but as "a family album" in which African Americans played a prominent—if separate—part. She documented whites and blacks at home, at work, at the state fair, and at other places. She attended the "Negro State Fair Parade" and photographed a black float, including it alongside a photo of a white "Church float" from the (white) State Fair Parade. Neither race appeared any better off financially in Welty's photographs; all were victims of the Depression in threadbare clothes, broken-down shoes, sitting on dilapidated porches, their homes equally unpainted and ramshackle.[2]

One thing that distinguished the races in Welty's album was culture. For example, she "asked for and received permission" to attend a black church service at a "Holiness Church" in Jackson, sat in the front row, and took pictures of the congregation mid-worship. She photographed the black Sunday school teacher and her class, the preacher, and members of the church. She then accepted an invitation from Maude Thompson of the black Parish Street Baptist Church in Jackson to photograph participants in a "Bird Pageant" to raise money for a new piano. "The pictures of the Bird Pageant," recalled Welty, "were made at the invitation, and under the direction, of its originator, Maude Thompson." They showcased the participants in elaborate bird costumes but did not cover the actual show, for Welty left her camera outside. "I would not have dared to interfere," she recalled, "and my regret is that I could not, without worse interfering with what was beautiful and original, have taken pictures during the Pageant itself." That something black might be "beautiful and original" spoke to Welty's view of race, a bifurcated lens that appreciated the artistic value of uniquely black cultural traditions, even if those traditions were reinforced by segregation. "Had I no shame as a white person for what message might lie in my pictures of black persons?" she queried. "No, I was too busy imagining myself into their lives to be open to any generalities. I wished no more to indict anybody, to prove or disprove anything by my pictures, than I would have wished to do harm to the people in them, or have expected any harm from them to come to me."[3]

Welty's respect for African American culture made her views of civil rights complicated. In 1963, she delivered a talk at Millsaps College in Jackson and expressly asked that African Americans be allowed to attend, a move that took some courage, even as it garnered praise from faculty and staff at neighboring black Tougaloo College. Yet, Welty proved no romantic, hailing Warren for "warning" readers against succumbing to "sentimentality" when assessing the black struggle. "The other night I read parts of it [*Who Speaks for the Negro?*] again," she confessed to Warren in August 1965, "so much having taken place since—Malcolm X dead, Martin Luther King become a messiah—not to speak of all the rest." Malcolm X had been shot in New York six months earlier, and King had led a widely publicized march from Selma to Montgomery in March, an event that only boosted his national profile. Welty mulled over these events, wondering whether the push for civil rights had become an abstraction, a national drama choreographed by media-savvy leaders who spouted "generalities" about the South but took little time to consider the complex interrelationships and intra-politics of local communities and local people.[4]

Already, she had written two pieces on civil rights that sought to bring the political drama to earth, grounding it in the rich soil of lived experience. The first had taken on the murder of NAACP officer Medgar Evers in Mississippi two years earlier, an event that Welty engaged by composing a hypothetical portrait of Evers's killer, a white salesman and ex-Marine named Byron De La Beckwith, who she imagined to be frustrated, marginalized, and confused—not a particularly eloquent or representative spokesman for the white South. In a second piece on civil rights, Welty posed the question whether southern writers should enlist their talents to further political causes or, as she termed it, "crusade," a question she answered in the negative. To Welty, crusaders spoke in "generalities," not specifics, while novelists focused on the messy, inner lives of individuals trapped in circumstances that were beyond their control.

Of course, this too was a type of politics—an approach that lent itself less to radical reform than a reevaluation of the status quo, and perhaps a critique of reform itself. As if to illustrate this point, Welty penned a short story with the expressly political title "The Demonstrators" in 1965, not long after reading Warren's *Who Speaks for the Negro?*[5]

Published in the *New Yorker* on November 26, 1966, "The Demonstrators" opens with a scene on a Saturday night "near eleven o'clock," in a small fictional town named Holden, Mississippi, where the town's doctor, Richard Strickland is approached by a distraught "Negro child" after having treated his old "Latin, civics, and English" teacher for a seizure. The child leads him to a dimly lit house, its dooryard "packed with a standing crowd" of African Americans. Inside, a "young, very black-skinned woman" lies in bed with a "wound below the breast." Strickland fails to notice that the woman is in fact his maid, focusing instead on the puncture wound and sarcastically asking a crowd of women gathered around the victim whether there was "too much excitement to send for the doctor a little earlier?" He then orders boiling water and queries the women about the injury, asking whether an "icepick" had caused the puncture, which they confirm.[6]

As the doctor tries to learn what has transpired, an "old woman" smokes a pipe and an infant sits "on the splintery floor" with "a spoon stuck pipelike" in its mouth, oblivious to the fact that "guinea pigs" are "running underfoot, not only in this room but on the other side of the wall, in the kitchen where the water finally got boiled." Amidst this chaotic scene, the doctor realizes that the victim is his maid, "Ruby Gaddy," and that her attacker was "Dove Collins," another black resident of Holden who he had "sewed up" on prior occasions, usually after weekend brawls. Strickland knows most of the onlookers in the room, including the pipe-smoking woman, Lucille, who had worked for his mother. Upon leaving Lucille in charge of watching Ruby, Strickland steps out of the house only to notice many of his own family's clothes hung on the porch to dry, including "his mother's gardening dress, his sister Annie's golf dress, his wife's favorite duster that she liked to wear to the breakfast table, and more dresses, less substantial." The dresses, which his mother and/or wife had presumably given to their black help, remind the doctor of "a child's drawing of angels," a dramatic counterpoint to the "house of murder" where Gaddy lies dying, and a reference to whites as providers and protectors of their black servants. Strickland emerges as precisely such an angel himself, a white professional who provides succor to blacks, much like his father had. "The doctor was the son of a doctor," wrote Welty, "practicing in his father's office; all the older patients, like Miss Marcia Pope—and like Lucille and Oree—spoke of his father, and some confused the young doctor with the old; but not they." As a young man, Strickland had married "the prettiest girl in the Delta" and owned the "only practice in town," but he had not gone on to live a particularly happy life. "His father and his mother both were dead," wrote Welty, "his sister had married and moved away," and "a year ago his child had died. Then, back in the summer, he and his wife had separated, by her wish." Part of the reason for this was the death of their child, Sylvia, who had succumbed to pneumonia "at the age of thirteen" but had never been truly well. "She had never sat up or spoken" due to an injury "at birth," prompting his wife to dedicate much of her time to the child, "tending her, lifting her, feeding her, everything." "What do you do after giving all your devotion to something that cannot be helped, and that has been taken away?" Strickland asks himself. "You give all your devotion to something else that cannot be helped." Presumably, Holden gives his to African Americans, who in turn give Strickland a sense of purpose, and peace, essentially serving as substitutes for the family that he has lost. After treating Ruby, for example, Strickland "sat bent at the wheel of the car" and experiences a "feeling of well-being" that brings him "to the point of tears." In contrast to Strickland, who is grief-stricken and alone, the African Americans of Holden appear happy and well-adjusted, as attested to by laughter in the yard amidst Ruby's suffering, and their close-knit community centered around a church, "where the sounds of music and dancing came from habitually on many another night besides Sunday." Even death itself promises entry into "the gates of joy," as a black preacher declares upon arrival at the house to read Ruby her last rites.[7]

Once she established Strickland's close, even spiritual connection to Holden's black community, Welty delivered a surprise twist, a flashback to a civil rights worker who Strickland had invited into his home that summer. "Last June," reminisced the doctor, "there had come along a student, one of the civil-rights workers, calling at his office with a letter of introduction." Strickland had invited him home for dinner and asked him about a story in a civil rights newspaper that told of activists being forced to pick cotton in Mississippi in June by local whites. "What's this I read in your own paper, Philip?" queried the doctor, "it said some of your outfit over in the next county were forced at gunpoint to go into the field at hundred-degree temperature and pick cotton. Well, that didn't happen—there isn't any cotton in June."[8]

The activist concedes the doctor's point but dismisses its relevance. "They won't know the difference where the paper is read," he declares brazenly. "We are dramatizing your hostility." The line echoed a claim that Martin Luther King, Jr., had made in *Why We Can't Wait*, his memoir of Birmingham in 1963, where he defended the use of direct action tactics in order to "dramatize" the injustices of Jim Crow and "to create such a crisis and foster such a tension that a community which has constantly refused to negotiate is forced to confront the issue." Welty found this Machiavellian, siding with Robert Penn Warren's observations that nonviolent protest was ultimately a "tactical" maneuver to provoke white violence, not an expression of morality or ethics. "You're not justified in putting a false front on things, in my opinion," declares Strickland to the demonstrator, "even for a good cause." The activist disagrees. "It's a way of reaching people," he argues. "Don't forget—what they might have done to us is even worse." It was a troubling point, one that seemed to call into question the ethics not simply of the demonstrator in the story but demonstrators generally, including perhaps Martin Luther King, Jr.[9]

Welty ended her story with Strickland discovering Dove, Ruby's assailant, bloody in the street. Dove begs Strickland to "hide" him, which Strickland does, but the black killer subsequently passes away in the doctor's office. "Two Dead, One Ice Pick. Freak Episode at Negro Church," reads the local paper's headline, carefully noting that "No Racial Content [Was] Espied," a jab at media interest in civil rights–related, white-on-black crimes. Holden's mayor confirms this conclusion, noting that the "incident" was not believed to "carry racial significance." According to local black minister Percy

McAtee, "no outside agitators were involved." Such references suggested that Welty felt comfortable poking fun at northern coverage of racial violence in the South, coverage that focused much less on black-on-black violence than white-on-black crime. "We stood there a while and flipped some bottle caps down at him and threw his cap down after him right over his face and didn't get a stir out of him," explains one "official of the congregation." "The way he acted," continues the official, "we figured he was dead. We would not have gone off and left him if we had known he was able to subsequently crawl up the hill." Here, even blacks treat the death of one of their own nonchalantly, underscoring Welty's point that black-on-black violence simply did not matter as much as whites targeting black victims. Welty then made sure to note that Dove and Ruby were in a "common-law" relationship, a nod to white arguments that blacks ascribed to a looser code of morality, and that the ice pick used in the killings "had been found in the grounds of the new $100,000.00 Negro school," an allusion to efforts by whites in the South to provide blacks with better accommodations lest they demand integration. One white character, "County Sheriff Vince Lasseter," even notes that "that's one they can't pin the blame on us for. That's how they treat their own kind. Please take note our conscience is clear."[10]

Heartfelt and sardonic at the same time, Welty's story underscored many of the same points that Warren had made in *Who Speaks for the Negro?* Among them was the idea that close personal relationships existed between the races in the South, including relationships that tended to transcend the ostensibly oppressive conditions of racial segregation. Also, Welty complicated the stock narrative of the civil rights "movement," nudging it away from King's romantic portrayal of an indigenous uprising led by long-suffering blacks to a more complicated, even postmodern portrait of an unprincipled charade orchestrated by dishonest, interloping whites.

As political as "The Demonstrators" appeared to be, Welty herself shied from political pronouncements, refusing to acknowledge a stake in the racial politics churning tornado-like around her Mississippi. "Must the novelist crusade?" she asked rhetorically at Mississippi's Millsaps College in December 1964, a year before "The Demonstrators" came out, concluding cryptically that "writing fiction places the novelist and the crusader on opposite sides," a point that only made sense if one understood crusaders to be northern civil rights activists and novelists to be southern defenders of the status quo. Otherwise, the distinction was flimsy. After all, novelists throughout American history had crusaded for social reform: Harriet Beecher Stowe against slavery, Upton Sinclair against usury, John Steinbeck against poverty, and black writers Ralph Ellison, James Baldwin, and Richard Wright against racism. Welty did not mention such writers, of course, arguing instead that "the zeal to reform has never done fiction much good." Better, she contended, if writers simply washed their hands of politics and focused on interpersonal relationships, like the relationships forged between blacks and whites in the Jim Crow South. "It can be said at once," she wrote, "that we are all agreed upon the most important point: that morality as shown through human relationships is the whole heart of fiction, and the serious writer has never lived who dealt with anything else." Of course, serious writers had dealt with other things, but Welty downplayed this view, siding with Warren on the idea that interpersonal relationships characterized the Jim Crow South, softening the edges of its repressive legal system. For Welty, the morality of human relationships transcended the immorality of racial segregation, an argument that coincided closely with arguments in favor of the plural South, a system that could only be understood if one junked abstract slogans about equality and justice and delved into the nettled, interlocking paths of the briar patch.[11]

This, however, took patience, attention to nuance, and time—something that northern "demonstrators" had little use for. The "crusader's message is prompted by crisis," Welty argued, and therefore "has to be delivered on time." Ironically, she herself worried about time, even writing the editor of the *New Yorker* to push for rapid publication of "The Demonstrators," hoping that it would coincide with reflections on mass protests in Selma, Alabama, earlier that year. The magazine had sat on the story for almost twelve months, causing Welty to worry that it might appear dated since it referenced "events from real life" that "could be pin-pointed as to month or year," namely the appearance of hundreds of northern volunteers in rural Mississippi in the summer of 1964.[12]

Two of those volunteers, Andrew Goodman and Michael Schwerner, had been murdered by white racists, along with a black activist named James Chaney. Welty reflected on the murders during her talk at Millsaps, noting that the tragedy of the deaths warranted quiet, contemplative grieving, not activism and protest. "To deplore a thing as hideous as the murder of the three civil rights workers," Welty commented, "demands the quiet in which to absorb it." Such a view called into question the tactics espoused by black leaders like Martin Luther King, Jr., who had argued for the dramatization of white violence as a critical means of winning support for civil rights. Welty's efforts to distinguish herself, a genuine "novelist," from such tactics hinted less at aesthetics than politics, including larger doubts about the movement's message. "Nothing was ever learned in a crowd," she argued in 1965, "or by addressing or trying to please a crowd." This, of course, was a jab at King, whose many public addresses had influenced thousands of Americans. As Welty saw it, King was a sanctimonious "messiah" who needed to be counterbalanced by thoughtful representations of the South, its cultural complexity, and its close interracial relationships. "No matter how fast society around us changes," she observed, "what remains is that there is a relationship in progress between ourselves and other people; this was the case when the world seemed stable, too. There are relationships of the blood, of the passions and the affections, of thought and spirit and deed. There is the relationship between the races. How can one kind of relationship be set apart from the others? Like the great root system of an old and long-established growing plant, they are all tangled up together; to separate them you would have to cleave the plant itself from top to bottom."[13]

Particularly destructive, Welty believed, were efforts by civil rights activists and the media to portray white southerners as violent and savage. Certainly, there were violent elements in the region; she understood this, but she did not ascribe to the view that all white southerners were violent and full of hate. After conceding that black/white relationships were intertwined and complicated, she demanded sympathy—for whites. "We in the South are a hated people these days," she lamented, "we were hated first for actual and particular reasons, and now we may be hated still more in some vast un-particularized way. I believe there must be such a thing as sentimental hate. Our people hate back." To counter such hate, Welty proposed that southerners "write with love. Not in self-defense, not in hate, not in the mood of instruction, not in rebuttal, in any kind of militance, or in apology, but with love." Writing "with love," to Welty, meant countering King's tactic of nonviolent dramatizations with sympathetic portrayals of white southerners, stories featuring "characters and plots" that "in honesty and with honesty reveal them (ourselves) to us, in whatever situation we live through in our own times."[14]

Welty's portrayal of Dr. Strickland in "The Demonstrators" exemplified this. As the civil rights volunteer emerges a manipulative liar, Strickland exudes a genuine warmth and sense of well-being that comes from his relationship, and his service, to Holden's black community. Indeed, Strickland appears as a more sensitive, sympathetic character than the demonstrator, who is clearly on a "crusade." If Welty's story was not a "crusade" for segregation, it was certainly a counterpoint to the simplistic civil rights narrative projected by black "messiah" Martin Luther King, Jr. Published in one of the nation's most esteemed literary magazines, "The Demonstrators" aimed to score a point of sympathy for the white South just as white southerners felt the blame for the murder of Schwerner, Chaney, and Goodman. Such civil rights killings, Welty seemed to argue, would have drawn much less national interest, in all likelihood no national interest, if the killers and victims had all been black . . . like Dove and Ruby.

CHAPTER ELEVEN

Mockingbirds

NOT A MONTH after the *New Yorker* accepted "The Demonstrators" for publication, another southern writer—Harper Lee—wrote to a prominent newspaper editor in Richmond, Virginia, named James Jackson Kilpatrick, complaining that her novel, *To Kill a Mockingbird*, had been misunderstood. First published in 1960, *Mockingbird* boasted over 3 million copies sold, far beyond anything Robert Penn Warren, Eudora Welty, Flannery O'Connor, or even William Faulkner had achieved. *Mockingbird* also preceded "The Demonstrators" by six years. Long before Welty sat down to pen a story about a white doctor who cared for blacks, in other words, Lee had told a similar story of another white professional, a lawyer, who defended a black client against a rape allegation in a fictional town called Maycomb, Alabama.[1]

Lee explained the idea behind her lawyer, Atticus Finch, to Kilpatrick in January 1966, after hearing that a local schoolboard in Hanover County, Virginia, had banned her book. Located just north of Richmond, Hanover County had deemed Lee's book "immoral" for espousing racial integration, an odd claim given that the book, according to Lee, did no such thing. "Surely," she fumed, "it is plain to the simplest intelligence" that *Mockingbird* was not immoral but rather expressed in plain language "a code of honor and conduct, Christian in its ethic that is the heritage of all Southerners."[2]

The code was the same unwritten code of manners that Flannery O'Connor had extolled, a set of mutually accepted rules that governed race relations in the region, softening the harsh edges of segregation. Few, however, understood this. Not only did Hanover County's schoolboard mistake *Mockingbird* as a paean to civil rights, but many readers in the North and West also read her southern lawyer protagonist as a forward-thinking progressive who risked "social ostracism" by representing a black client. Yet, that wasn't who he was, a point Lee had made more clear in an earlier draft of the story, one that she had delivered to her editor, Tay Hohoff, at J. B. Lippincott in New York in 1957. The manuscript told the story of a young woman—Jean Louise Finch—who lives in New York but returns home to rural Alabama only to learn that her father, Atticus —who she reveres for being kind to blacks—had joined the Citizens' Councils and come out publicly against *Brown v. Board of Education.* Jean Louise is shocked, but after some reflection comes to realize that *Brown* and the emerging civil rights movement had effected an ugly transformation in her father and her town—putting its white and black communities at odds and shattering their old bonds. In one scene, for example, Atticus agrees to represent a black driver guilty of accidentally killing a white pedestrian, but does so only to keep NAACP attorneys, or "buzzards" as he calls them, off the case. Atticus's anger at the NAACP surprises Jean Louise, who recalls that before *Brown*, Atticus would have represented the very same client simply out of the "goodness" of his heart.[3]

Later, Jean Louise visits Calpurnia, the black maid who had raised her and her brother, Jem, after their mother died, only to learn that Calpurnia has lost her "compassion" for whites, including Jean Louise. "Cal, Cal, Cal," laments Jean Louise in anguish when Calpurnia greets her with a "haughty" air at her house. "I'm your baby, have you forgotten me? Why are you shutting me out? What are you doing to me?" Rather than embrace her old ward, Calpurnia blasts Jean Louise with an impersonal, unfamiliar venom, disparaging her by demanding, "what are you all doing to us?"[4]

Calpurnia's anger and Atticus's resentment both lead Jean Louise to wonder, "what was this blight that had come down over the people that she loved?" Of course, it turned out to be *Brown*, just the type of abstract, "higher law" idealism that the North had long imposed on the South, the same idealism that Robert Penn Warren complained of in his meditations on civil rights in 1956. Indeed, striking parallels emerge between *Watchman* and Warren's 1956 book, *Segregation: The Inner Conflict*, almost as if Lee had read Warren's memoir—which came out roughly six months before Lee completed her manuscript. For example, Warren recounted a meeting with a Citizens' Council leader who spouted many of the same ideas that a Citizens' Council speaker does in *Watchman*. Likewise, notions of race-mixing, civilizational decline, and so on appear. Warren recoiled at this rhetoric, as did Jean Louise, who goes on to advance a more sensible argument for opposing the Supreme Court that—somewhat uncannily—echoes Warren. For example, Warren argued in *Segregation: The Inner Conflict* that *Brown* represented an assault on "constitutionality," moving the nation "one more step toward the power state, a cunningly calculated step" that expanded federal power under the guise of advancing a "moral issue." Jean Louise makes a similar argument to Atticus, complaining that "to meet the real needs of a small portion of the population, the Court set up something horrible," a precedent that "rubbed out" states' rights and left the nation without "much check on the Court."[5]

More similarities stand out as well, like when Warren suggested that *Brown* had worsened race relations in the region, a point that Lee confirmed when Jean Louise visits Calpurnia only to find that she has "forgotten" about Jean Louise, lumping her together with "white folks." "It was not always like this," laments Jean Louise after Calpurnia snubs her. "She loved us, I swear she loved us." Now, however, that love is gone. "She didn't see me," complains Jean Louise, "she saw white folks." Calpurnia's replacement, Atticus's sister Alexandra, confirms the new paradigm when she explains to Jean Louise that "nobody in Maycomb goes to see Negroes anymore," not after the NAACP had "filled 'em with poison till it runs out of their ears."[6]

Even though Maycomb's whites suspect their black neighbors of being corrupted by outside activists, Lee agreed with Warren that there was a fifth column of decency in the South, a substantial cadre of whites who were themselves sympathetic to the black plight, a point Lee confirmed by noting that "the woods are full of people" like Jean Louise, who feels compassion for African Americans. However, such southerners felt constrained by a cultural aversion to collective efforts at reform, preferring to focus on their relationships with "individuals."[7]

While the parallels between Lee's manuscript and Warren's *Inner Conflict* may have been accidental, merely common sentiments felt by educated white southerners generally, Hohoff rejected the draft. Perhaps she felt the story redundant, too similar to Warren's recent piece, or simply not interesting enough to sell. Instead, she urged Lee to recast her tale in the impoverished, pre–civil rights 1930s, when Atticus and Calpurnia got along and Calpurnia cared unselfishly for "Scout" and Jem as children. The request pressed Lee to shift the narrator's perspective from a twenty-six-year-old liberal living in New York City to a child who knew nothing but Jim Crow. The resulting manuscript, which Lee titled *To Kill a Mockingbird*, yielded a less bitter Atticus, a less venomous Calpurnia, and a more innocent, endearing South.[8]

Lee centered her story around the alleged rape of a white woman, Mayella Ewell, by a black man, Tom Robinson, who came to be represented at trial by Atticus Finch, now a much younger attorney who decides early on that Robinson is innocent of all charges and that Mayella has falsely accused him of rape after getting caught trying to seduce him by her father. Although Robinson emerges as an obvious mockingbird (someone innocent who should not be killed), Lee sprinkled her story with other innocents as well, none more prominent than Atticus himself, whose last name also connotes a harmless songbird. As Lee told it, Finch was representative of the white southern elite, a descendant of a slave-owning cotton planter who "knew his people" and was "related by blood or marriage to nearly every family in town," a stark counterpoint to Zora Neale Hurston's Jim Meserve. Conveniently, Atticus had suffered loss, his wife, whose death presses him to rely heavily on his black maid, Calpurnia, to raise his two children. Although Atticus and Calpurnia interact daily, they refrain from physical intimacy, enabling Lee to make a point about the close bonds that existed between whites and blacks in the South, a notion underscored by Calpurnia's own name, an allusion to Julius Caesar's third and final wife. A quasi-wife to Atticus, Calpurnia loves him and the children but remains Platonic, as does Atticus, his own name an allusion to the ancient Greek region of Attica, home to Socrates, Aristotle, and, of course, Plato.[9]

That the South embodied a classical, if unequal society was an argument that whites had long made, not least the Nashville Agrarians in the 1920s. However, Lee went out of her way to cast this society in an endearing light, peppering it with quirky characters like the mysterious "Boo Radley," a neighbor who rarely leaves his house; the Averys, whose house burns down; Miss Rachel, who is elderly and single; and Mrs. Henry Lafayette Dubose, a dowager rumored to keep "a CSA pistol concealed among her numerous shawls and wraps." By contrast, the villains of the story turn out to be the Ewells, a particularly lazy, low-class, "contentious" family who are widely considered to be the "disgrace of Maycomb," not unlike the white trash in Flannery O'Connor's short story "Revelation." Blacks inhabit the story primarily as servants—not just Finch's Calpurnia but also "a Negro girl" who works for Mrs. Dubose and Calpurnia's son Zeebo, a garbage man. While Calpurnia uses the n-word to refer to lower-status blacks, Atticus chastises Scout for saying it, telling her it is "common," again an allusion to his decent nature.[10]

Finch's respectful attitude toward African Americans continues through his representation of Tom Robinson, a member of Calpurnia's church who hails from "clean-living folks" and stands in stark contrast to Mayella Ewell, who emerges as a lascivious, treacherous figure. Finch comes to see his representation of Robinson as a matter of honor, noting that if he did not represent the black defendant, then he "couldn't hold up my head in town . . . couldn't represent this county in the legislature," and as he explained to his children, "couldn't even tell you or Jem not to do something again." In a startling sentence, Finch likens the defense of Robinson to the South's fight in the Civil War, noting that "simply because we were licked a hundred years before we started is no reason for us not to try to win," a hint that the true meaning of the war was not the preservation of slavery so much as the upholding of a code of chivalric honor that had existed in the antebellum period. "This time we aren't fighting the Yankees," explains Atticus to Scout, "we're fighting our friends. But remember this, no matter how bitter things get, they're still our friends and this is still our home." Much like Warren, Lee portrayed the South's struggle as an inner conflict, a battle between the best elements of the region, what Warren called its "fifth column of decency," and its baser elements, its proponents of violence and hate, its "Ewells."[11]

The best elements emerged, in Lee's telling, as the mockingbirds of the story—and perhaps of the civil rights era. Atticus proved to be one, a "feeble" man with an innocent bird's name, "nearly blind in his left eye," who is older than most parents in town and who plays checkers and the "Jews-Harp" instead of football and hunting. He gives Scout and Jem air rifles, telling them that "it's a sin to kill a mockingbird" on account that "they don't do one thing but sing their hearts out for us," the only time, in Scout's memory, that she "ever heard Atticus say it was a sin to do something." The link between sin and mockingbirds underscored the moral message of the novel, which obscured the sin of segregation by focusing on individuals or groups who were compassionate, sympathetic, and adhered to a high level of personal standards or manners. Clearly, this applied to Tom Robinson, whose death the local paper compares "to the senseless slaughter of songbirds by hunters and children," and it also applied to Atticus Finch, an upstanding white gentlemen who defends a black client.[12]

To further drive home her point, Lee made Finch a natural marksman, "the deadest shot in Maycomb County," who refuses to use his capacity for violence for any reason save to help the innocent. "If your father's anything," explains a neighbor to Jem and Scout, "he's civilized in his heart. Marksmanship's a gift from God, a talent—oh, you have to practice to make it perfect, but shooting's different from playing the piano or the like." At first blush a harmless, half-blind checker-player, Atticus suddenly proves to be a born killer, a white southerner capable of just the type of violence that northerners associated with southern whites generally. However, Finch curbs his violent tendencies, subordinating them to a higher code of civility and honor. As "Miss Maudie" explains to Jem and Scout, "I think maybe he [Atticus] put his gun down when he realized that God had given him an unfair advantage over most living things. I guess he decided he wouldn't shoot till he had to, and he had to today." In a scene that shocks the children, Finch shoots a rabid dog in the street "with movements so swift they seemed simultaneous," killing the dog before he even knew "what hit him." As Scout moves to inform her friends of the shooting, Jem stops her, cautioning that a celebration of Atticus's violent capabilities would only diminish his stature. "Don't say anything about it, Scout," Jem declares. "Atticus is a gentleman, just like me!"[13]

The motif of the gentleman recurs throughout the book, tracing a code of conduct that, to Lee's mind, characterized the best elements of the white South. For example, when Jem and Scout are tempted to retaliate against Mrs. Dubose for insulting their father, Atticus replies, "just hold your head high and be a gentleman. Whatever she says to you, it's your job not to let her make you mad." A clear line divides the emotionally controlled Finches from the town's angry, lower-class whites: "ignorant, trashy people" who resent anyone "favoring Negroes over and above themselves." Atticus, by contrast, confesses to liking blacks after Scout asks him whether he was a "nigger lover." "I certainly am," declares Atticus, "I do my best to love everybody."[14]

Just as Welty critiqued northern liberals in "The Demonstrators," so did Lee in *Mockingbird*, though her jabs were more subtle. For example, at one point Scout declares that "helping ourselves to someone's scuppernongs was part of our ethical culture," a subtle dig at the "ethical culture" school of thought founded by Felix Adler in 1877, a Jewish thinker from New York who declared that morality need not be tethered to religion, and that religion had in fact failed to address the pressing moral issues of the day. Lee also featured a discussion among Maycomb's leading ladies about northern approaches to racial matters during which a Mrs. Grace Merriweather declares that Yankee liberals were "born hypocrites." "At least we don't have that sin [hypocrisy] on our shoulders down here," proclaims Merriweather. "People up there set 'em free, but you don't see 'em settin' at the table with 'em. At least we don't have the deceit to say to 'em yes you're as good as we are but stay away from us. Down here we just say you live your way and we'll live ours." In keeping with this pluralist observation, Lee presented the black South as a separate society, one that whites needed permission to enter. This becomes apparent when Calpurnia takes Scout and Jem to her church in the black section of Maycomb, the "Quarters," where they are promptly confronted by a "bullet-headed" woman with "strange almond-shaped eyes" named Lula, who demands to know "why you bringin' white chillum to nigger church." Calpurnia responds by saying that the children were her "comp'ny" to which Lula blurts, "you ain't got no business bringin' white chillum here—they got their church, we got our'n." After Calpurnia prevails, the children quickly confront a very different atmosphere to what they are accustomed, including "no sign of piano, organ, hymn-books, church programs—the familiar ecclesiastical impedimenta we saw every Sunday," but rather a congregation who sang hymns by "linin'," or repeating spoken-word verses announced by the minister, a practice common in African American churches in the South. Meanwhile, the children are shocked to learn that Calpurnia speaks "colored-folks talk" when she is around other African Americans, not the "white-folks talk" that they are used to hearing from her. "That Calpurnia leads a modest double life never dawned on me," muses Scout, reflecting on the discernible contrasts between the white and black worlds of Maycomb.[15]

Comfortable in their own part of town, "the Quarters," Maycomb's black community does not come across as a particularly beleaguered group. They are poor, to be sure, but so are Maycomb's whites, including the Finches. Atticus's practice has suffered during the Depression, a point he makes to Scout by noting that "professional people were poor because the farmers were poor," and "nickels and dimes were hard to come by for doctors and dentists and lawyers" like himself.[16]

The same could not be said for the town's mixed-race residents. "They're real sad," proclaims Jem, referencing a family of mixed-race children fathered by a white drunk named Dolphus Raymond. "They don't belong anywhere," explains Jem. "Colored folks won't have 'em because they're half white; white folks won't have 'em 'cause they're colored, so they're just in-betweens, don't belong anywhere." This was the same argument that Faulkner had made in *Absalom, Absalom!* and Warren had made in *Band of Angels*, where Amantha Starr's primary challenge is not that she finds herself a slave after her father's death but that she is of mixed-race heritage and does not truly feel like she belongs.[17]

Although committed to racial separation, Finch's status within the black community soars when he rises to defend Tom Robinson, "a faithful member" of Calpurnia's church, a point underscored by Reverend Sykes, who confesses to Jem and Scout that "this church has no better friend than your daddy." Meanwhile, Atticus contemplates the possibility that a white mob might seize Robinson and kill him before his trial, a question that allows the lawyer to distinguish the civilized white people of Maycomb from lower-class whites, including that "Old Sarum bunch," the Cunninghams, who are known to binge drink and "get shinnied up." "We don't have mobs and that nonsense in Maycomb," explains Atticus to Scout and Jem, further noting that the Ku Klux Klan boasts no support in the town and had actually been shamed out of existence by a local Jewish businessman named Sam Levy. "Way back about nineteen-twenty there was a Klan," Atticus tells his children. "They paraded by Mr. Sam Levy's house one night, but Sam just stood on his porch and told 'em things had come to a pretty pass, he'd sold 'em the very sheets on their backs. Sam made 'em so ashamed of themselves they went away." Finch's story diminishes the Klan's reputation, even as it extols Maycomb's tolerance for diversity, in this case its acceptance of Jews. "The Levy family met all criteria for being Fine Folks," remembers Scout, "they did the best they could with the sense they had, and they had been living on the same plot of ground in Maycomb for five generations." Despite their longstanding tenure in Maycomb, in other words, the Levys remained distinct—but respected—scions of the plural South. As Scout's teacher Miss Gates explains to her, "There are no better people in the world than Jews . . . They contribute to every society they live in, and most of all, they are a deeply religious people." This was a clear parallel to arguments made by Warren and, of course, Zora Neale Hurston, who hailed Jews as exemplars of a minority that bore special cultural gifts.[18]

In stark contrast to "Fine Folks" like the Levys were the Ewells, "the disgrace of Maycomb for three generations," people who "lived like animals" and had "never done an honest day's work" but were nevertheless granted certain dispensations because their depravity was immutable. "There are ways of keeping them in school by force," explains Atticus, "but it's silly to force people like the Ewells into a new environment." Reforming the Ewells, Lee implied, was impossible. Just as Finch emerges as an iconic version of the southern gentleman, so too do the Ewells become caricatures of implacable reprobates who exist beyond the reaches of the law. "Every town the size of Maycomb had families like the Ewells," recalls Scout.

"No truant officers could keep their numerous offspring in school; no public health officer could free them from congenital defects, various worms, and the diseases indigenous to filthy surroundings." The Ewells occupy a rung of Maycomb's social ladder even lower than its blacks, their livelihood gleaned in large part by scavenging the town's dump "every day" for food and reusable items, a dump presided over by Calpurnia's eldest son, Zeebo, the town's "garbage collector," who Calpurnia has taught to read from the Bible and Blackstone's *Commentaries.*[19]

More complicated are the Cunninghams, a farm family whose son Walter had "hookworms" from going "barefooted in barnyards and hog wallows" but who otherwise "never took anything they can't pay back." Although poor, the Cunninghams work hard, refusing to accept public money. However, they also constitute a menacing presence, threatening violent retaliation against any perceived slights by blacks against whites. For example, Mr. Cunningham's sinister side emerges on the night prior to Tom Robinson's trial, when he joins a mob of white men aiming to seize Robinson and kill him. In one of the novel's most improbable scenes, Scout confronts the mob and engages Cunningham on the topic of his son, prompting the man to abandon the mission. "I'll tell him you said hey, little lady," promises Cunningham, "then he straightened up and waved a big paw. 'Let's clear out,' he called. 'Let's get going, boys.'"[20]

Lee's inclusion of a lynch mob in *Mockingbird* introduced the question of white vigilante violence, precisely the kind of violence that had killed Emmett Till. In Lee's telling, however, Scout humanizes the killers, softening them to a point that even a young girl could dissuade them from murder. As Atticus explains to Jem, "a mob's always made up of people, no matter what. Mr. Cunningham was part of a mob last night, but he was still a man." Precisely for this reason, Scout's innocent, childlike appeal is able to stop the murder. "That proves something," argues Atticus, "that a gang of wild animals *can* be stopped, simply because they're still human." Atticus concludes that precisely because mobs are composed of average folks, appeals to higher principles, including southern manners, could move them. "Hmp," he declares, "maybe we need a police force of children . . . you children last night made Walter Cunningham stand in my shoes for a minute. That was enough."[21]

Scout's improbable presence is not the only force for good in the white community; so too is Atticus, who decides to guard Robinson's cell, and Braxton Underwood, the editor of the *Maycomb Tribune*, who "covered" Atticus with a "double-barreled shotgun" from his newspaper's window. Of course, neither helps Robinson in his trial, particularly after a jury made up entirely of "farmers," some of whom "looked vaguely like dressed-up Cunninghams," are selected to decide his fate. Atticus tries to explain to the jury that Tom had taken pity on Mayella Ewell and agreed to help her complete chores around her home. Mayella, however, had developed designs on Tom and tried to seduce him, a violation of the cardinal rule of Jim Crow, namely the prohibition against interracial intimacy, or what Atticus terms "a rigid and time-honored code of our society, a code so severe that whoever breaks it is hounded from our midst as unfit to live with." Rather than critique the code, Atticus blasts Mayella for flouting it. "She is the victim of cruel poverty and ignorance," he declares, "but I cannot pity her: she is white. She knew full well the enormity of her offense, but because her desires were stronger than the code she was breaking, she persisted in breaking it." This, to Atticus, was unacceptable. "She did something that in our society is unspeakable," he proclaims, "[she] kissed a black man." Her father's subsequent response, which was to call the sheriff and accuse Robinson of rape, was, Atticus continues, actually understandable. "We do know in part what Mr. Ewell did," declares Finch; "he did what any God-fearing, persevering, respectable white man would do under the circumstances—he swore out a warrant."[22]

Finch's argument showcased Lee's complex take on Jim Crow, her sense that it embodied an ancient "code," violations of which led to tragedy. However, African Americans were also due respect and fair treatment under the law. "We know all men are not created equal," proclaims Atticus. "Some people are born smarter than others, some people have more opportunity because they're born with it, some men make more money than others." However, "there is one way in this country in which all men are created equal," he continues; "our courts are the great levelers, and in our courts all men are created equal," a point similar to the one that Warren had made in his 1929 essay "The Briar Patch."[23]

While the farmer-filled jury delivers a guilty verdict, the black spectators in the court room stand as Atticus walks out, hailing him; meanwhile, black families across Maycomb inundate the Finches with "enough food to bury the family," bringing Atticus to tears. Not only does Maycomb's black population celebrate Atticus's work for Robinson but so too does the town's best white citizens. "We're so rarely called on to be Christians," explains Miss Maudie to Jem and Scout, "but when we are, we've got men like Atticus to go for us." Of course, Atticus remains conservative in his views on race, confident that Jim Crow would have protected Robinson had Mayella Ewell not violated it. The only laws that needed changing, argues Atticus, are minor ones, including rules of evidence in capital cases. "He said he didn't have any quarrel with the rape statute, none whatever, but he did have deep misgivings when the state asked for and the jury gave a death penalty on purely circumstantial evidence." The problem with juries extended, in Atticus's mind, to their composition. They excluded women (something the Supreme Court would not fix until 1975 in *Taylor v. Louisiana*) and educated townspeople who weren't "interested" in serving, or were "afraid" that they might have to decide a case against one of their neighbors. "Why don't people like us and Miss Maudie ever sit on juries?" asks Jem, providing Atticus with a chance to explain that "we generally get the juries that we deserve." "What if—say, Mr. Link Deas had to decide the amount of damages to award, say, Miss Maudie," Finch continues, "when Miss Rachel ran over her with a car. Link wouldn't like the thought of losing either lady's business at his store, would he? So he tells Judge Taylor that he can't serve on the jury because he doesn't have anybody to keep store for him while he's gone." The tendency of juries to be made up of lower-class, uneducated whites was a dubious assertion that Lee made to underscore class divisions in the Deep South, a point illustrated by Jem, who argues that "there's four kinds of folks in the world. There's the ordinary kind like us and the neighbors, there's the kind like the Cunninghams out in the woods, the kind like the Ewells down at the dump, and the Negroes." This, of course, was the same point that Ruby Turpin had made in Flannery O'Connor's short story "Revelation."[24]

To underscore the importance of class in the South, Lee had Scout argue that "there's just one kind of folks. Folks," a point that prompts Jem to unravel one of the driving questions of the first half of the book, namely the distinction between the upstanding elements of the white community and the debased, white-trash Ewells. "If there's just one kind of folks," posits Jem, "why can't they get along with each other? If they're all alike, why do they go out of their way to despise each other?" This child's question implied that the white South was at odds with itself, prompting Jem to draw a distinction between southerners who possess "background" and southerners who do not. Those who possess "background," argues Jem, were educated. "Background doesn't mean Old Family" he suggests, but rather "how long your family's been readin' and writin'." Such folks, in turn, made up the "handful" of whites in Maycomb who "say that fair play is not marked White Only" and that "a fair trial is for everybody, not just us," all points of view shared by individuals "with background." Jem's ruminations on background lead him, oddly, to a revelation about their mysterious neighbor Boo Radley. "Scout," he claims, "I think I'm beginning to understand something. I think I'm beginning to understand why Boo Radley's stayed shut up in the house all the time . . . it's because he wants to stay inside."[25]

Boo Radley's significance becomes clear at the end of the novel, when he emerges to save Scout and Jem from an attack by Bob Ewell on Halloween night. Ewell stalks the children and assaults them with a knife, only to be thwarted and then killed by Boo, who seizes the knife and stabs Ewell. Throughout, Lee describes Radley in ghostlike terms, including his nickname "Boo," as well as his "sickly white hands," "colorless" eyes, and the fact that "he drifted" when he walked. Radley's appearance on Halloween raises the question whether he, too, may in fact have been wearing a costume, a mask for something deeper, more symbolic—something haunting the town. Lee hinted at what this might be on the night of Bob Ewell's death—just after Radley "drifted" home—when Atticus sits by Jem's bed and reads Robert Franc Schulkers's *The Gray Ghost*, a children's story from the 1920s about a young protagonist named "Stoner's Boy" who embarks on a series of misadventures with his friends. In *Ghost*, Stoner's Boy is falsely accused of vandalizing a rival gang's clubhouse, only to be vindicated at the end of the book, leading Atticus to tell Scout, in *Mockingbird*'s final scene, that "most people" are nice "when you finally see them."[26]

The line appeared to be a nod to Radley, who emerges as a hero at the end of *Mockingbird.* However, the story evoked more than just the adventures of a children's hero. For anyone familiar with the Civil War, the real "Gray Ghost" was Colonel John Singleton Mosby, a Confederate guerrilla who became known for his surprise attacks on Union forces. Born in Powhatan County, Virginia, in 1833, Mosby attended the University of Virginia, studied classics, and then practiced law before volunteering in the Confederate Army, eventually becoming legendary for his ability to operate behind enemy lines, mounting surprise raids and then disappearing—like a ghost.[27]

Mosby proved one of the "most-popular Confederate heroes" of the South, a popularity that surged in the 1950s when CBS dedicated a television series to his life. "Once each week for thirty minutes," notes historian James A. Ramage, "in thirty-nine episodes, Mosby thrilled families throughout the nation with his daring and cunning raids against the Union army." Even if Lee had not been a Civil War buff, in other words, she likely knew, and knew that her readers knew, Mosby's story, which was televised nationally from 1957 to 1958 just as she wrote *Mockingbird.* In fact, *The Gray Ghost* drew criticism in September 1957 when Arkansas governor Orval Faubus moved to block the integration of Little Rock's Central High School, prompting President Dwight D. Eisenhower to send in federal troops. CBS executives feared that it might prove awkward to "have a Confederate raider humiliating the Union cavalry each week on television" as Faubus flaunted the federal government, leading it to devolve decisions about airing the program to local stations. Only one station, in Boston, cut the show. Most embraced it, generating a huge "ratings success" and an audience of "21 million" viewers.[28]

Atticus Finch's interest in *The Gray Ghost* during the final scene of *To Kill a Mockingbird* was no accident. Like *Mockingbird* itself, *Gray Ghost* was a children's story that evoked the legend of a Confederate hero who fought an insurgent war against the North, a war that Atticus actually claimed was being refought in the dispute over Tom Robinson. Of course, for Atticus the war was not about reinstating slavery so much as defeating the South's worst forces, its violent, uneducated, base elements, replacing them with the honor, decency, and mutual respect that he, and Harper Lee, believed to characterize the best of the region. That Atticus picks up *Gray Ghost* on the night Bob Ewell attempts to kill his children invited readers to draw a link between him and Mosby, a southern hero who fought a principled, guerilla war against the North.[29]

If Atticus was one version of Mosby, an heroic embodiment of southern ideals who was not afraid to defend a black man in public, Radley was another, a silent southerner who believed in the good but was too afraid to get involved, preferring to remain behind closed doors. Even Radley's real name, "Arthur," evoked the chivalric ideal, as did his conduct when he kills Ewell to save Scout and Jem, vindicating those with "background" over the white "trash" that "you have to shoot before you can say hidy to 'em."[30]

Both Atticus and Sheriff Tate refuse to link Radley to the crime, even though he has a legitimate defense of protecting the children, for fear that it would be a "sin" to take "the one man who's done you and this town a great service an' drag him with his shy ways into the limelight." This was the second mention of sin in the book, the first having referenced the killing of mockingbirds. Radley, of course, emerges as the third mockingbird, a ghostly representative of the silent, or what Robert Penn Warren called "secret," South that believed in right and wrong but remained out of view. Scout underscores this, explaining to Finch that to arrest Radley would be "sort of like shootin' a mockingbird, wouldn't it?"[31]

By identifying Radley as a "mockingbird," Lee suggested that her story was not simply about the railroading of Tom Robinson, a mockingbird, but also the railroading of the decent elements of the white South, Radley and Finch. For example, Lee downplayed the racial oppression inherent in Jim Crow by focusing on problems with the law of sentencing, not segregation. If anything, segregation emerged as a useful arrangement, a system that would have saved Tom Robinson from prosecution had Mayella Ewell only adhered to it. Robinson's problems were further exacerbated by the close proximity between his and the Ewells' home near the dump, a problem that would not have arisen had he resided where he belonged, in the "Quarters."

Published in 1960, *Mockingbird* garnered generally positive reviews, though none picked up on Lee's rehabilitation of white southerners or her subtle defense of segregation. Writing for the *New*

York Times, Frank H. Lyell noted that Atticus represented "the embodiment of fearless integrity, magnanimity, and common sense," a sympathetic character who defied "the current lust for morbid, grotesque tales of Southern depravity." Lee's book, claimed Lyell, amounted to a "level-headed plea for interracial understanding." Author Herbert Mitgang took the book to be an exploration of the "opening of the eyes of Southern childhood to the dreary facts of Negro-white injustices." Mitgang read the book as a lesson in the evils of racial oppression, noting that Atticus is "deeply concerned with imparting a sense of justice to his children," particularly the "accepted injustice" that characterized the Southern "way of life." Phoebe Adams reviewed the book for the *Atlantic Monthly*, commenting that Atticus was a "liberal, honest man" who defended "a Negro accused of raping a white girl" while raising his children with "angelic cleverness," ultimately yielding "pleasant, undemanding reading."[32]

That Lee chose to voice her position on the book six years later, after a Virginia schoolboard banned it, underscored her understanding of the work not as a manifesto for the civil rights movement but as a defense of the South. Lee's invocation of honor and heritage implied that the book was not about racial integration or rights so much as something inherited from Dixie's past, an unwritten "code," as she put it, governing interracial conduct in the region. Lee's lead character Atticus Finch invokes such a code when explaining to his daughter why the South fought the Civil War and argues that the very same code compels him to defend Tom Robinson. If it was a sin to kill a mockingbird under the theory that it caused no harm, so too was it a sin to kill a finch. Genteel, sympathetic, and respectful to blacks, Atticus shared little in common with the demagogues and thugs who had come to characterize the region during the weeks and months that Lee spent writing her novel, such as populists like Orval Faubus and murderers like J. W. Milam and Roy Bryant, the killers of Emmett Till.[33]

CHAPTER TWELVE

The Cantos

JAMES JACKSON KILPATRICK, balding and bespectacled, looked out the window of his North Fourth Street office in Richmond and winced. Few understood the symbolic importance of Atticus Finch better than he, editor of Richmond's *News Leader* and the recipient of Harper Lee's hotly worded letter in January 1966. An Okie by birth, Kilpatrick had spent his professional career in Virginia, moving to Richmond shortly after graduating from the University of Missouri and rising rapidly through the *News Leader*'s ranks from cub reporter to lead editor. He made fast friends with prominent Virginians, including the state's most renowned senator, Harry F. Byrd, who applauded the young journalist's commitment to southern traditions, including segregation. However, Kilpatrick rejected the lowbrow racism and violence of the Ku Klux Klan. Like Harper Lee, he saw segregation through the lens of mutual harmony and pluralism. Recounting his own childhood in Oklahoma, Kilpatrick recalled that blacks "had their lives; we had ours," and interactions between the two, though common, were governed by established norms. "There were certain things one did," explained Kilpatrick, "and there were certain things one did not do." For example, "a proper white child obeyed the family Negroes, ate with them, bothered them, teased them, loved them, lived with them, [and] learned from them." However, "one did not intrude upon their lives, or ask about Negro institutions, or bring a Negro child in the front door." At once separate and unequal, race relations in the South were also characterized by "an oddly intimate remoteness," as Kilpatrick put it, an arrangement much like the one enjoyed by Atticus and Calpurnia that facilitated the perpetuation of what Kilpatrick termed a "dual society" preferable to the integrated chaos of the North. "In plain fact," Kilpatrick argued, "the relationship between white and Negro in the segregated South, in the country and in the city, has been far closer, more honest, less constrained, than such relations generally have been in the integrated North."[1]

Much like *Mockingbird* lent Jim Crow a coat of respectability, so too did Kilpatrick seek to maintain a spirit of gentility and cultural sophistication at the *News Leader*, even to the point of humiliating less-educated whites. Upon hearing that Harper Lee had been censored in Hanover County, for example, Kilpatrick indicted the schoolboard for possessing "the kind of small-bore stupidity" that had plagued the South since 1954, a stupidity that, in Kilpatrick's view, "deserves to be roundly condemned."[2]

Kilpatrick had battled local morons for over a decade, working hard to demonstrate that a commitment to segregation need not amount to a rejection of the mind, including literature and the arts. In 1958, for example, Kilpatrick reached out to Ezra Pound, one of the world's most renowned poets, and asked him to contribute to the *News Leader* as a foreign correspondent. The move was audacious. Originally from Ohio, Pound had left the United States for Europe in 1908 at age twenty-two, eventually settling in London, where he proceeded to promote young, largely unknown artists who struck him as talented. Among Pound's finds were James Joyce, T. S. Eliot, and Ernest Hemingway, all of whom would go on to become legends of Anglo-American letters. Pound's own work garnered attention as well, beginning with a collection of verse in 1912 that defied the stuffy, late-nineteenth-century style of British imperial voices like Alfred Lord Tennyson and Rudyard Kipling, an achievement that vaulted him into the van of a new movement called "Imagism" for its simple, direct description of quotidian scenes. One of Pound's most celebrated rhymes, for example, described a run-of-the-mill subway stop: "The apparition of these faces in the crowd," he wrote simply, "petals on a wet, black bough."[3]

Edgy and irreverent, Pound also became interested in politics, concluding by the 1920s that World War I had been caused largely by the machinations of global financial elites, particularly bankers. While this was not a particularly offensive idea, Pound laced his attack on finance capitalism with an ugly anti-Semitism rooted in stereotypes about usury that would stay with him through the 1920s and into the 1930s as he left London and relocated to Italy, where he began radio broadcasts supporting fascist leader Benito Mussolini. Although Mussolini enjoyed the support of Italy's wealthy class, he also celebrated a romantic notion of the Italian people that appealed to Pound, a sense that Italians were an exalted group defined by ancient traditions, a shared culture—including literature—and close ties to the land. Mussolini, like Pound, blamed Italy's problems on foreign and internal enemies, including Jews, who were then portrayed as ethnically, racially, and/or culturally different from Italians.[4]

Pound broadcast profascist programs on Italian radio through World War II. Meanwhile, he composed a massive, Italian-inspired poem called *The Cantos*, which ranged over economic, political, and cultural terrain. Modeled after Dante's *Inferno*, *The Cantos* departed from Pound's earlier, simpler works by invoking obscure allusions to classical mythology, Chinese philosophy, and American history, including references to Thomas Jefferson and Andrew Jackson. Divided into discrete parts and written in a disjointed, almost conversational style, *The Cantos*' mashup of obscure, erudite references and unvarnished, unrhyming verse garnered literary attention even as his radio broadcasts—which riffed on many of the same themes—drew the ire of the U.S. Army, who arrested him promptly after the war and threatened him with execution, a fate that Pound avoided thanks in part to the intervention of Ernest Hemingway, his old friend, and Allen Tate, chair of poetry at the Library of Congress.[5]

Tate, of course, was an Agrarian. Born in Kentucky in 1899, he had studied under John Crowe Ransom at Vanderbilt, befriended Robert Penn Warren, joined the Fugitive poetry group, and contributed to *I'll Take My Stand*, the Agrarian manifesto that featured Warren's essay defending segregation, "The Briar Patch." Tate found in Pound much that resonated with the Fugitives, including a facility for "beautiful, flowing" prose and an erudite knack for far-ranging "juxtapositions of the ancient, the Renaissance, and the modern worlds." Tate also found a shared love of the land and antipathy to modern life, hailing Pound as "a powerful reactionary" who opposed the same finance capitalism that the Agrarians had long railed against, an artist of lost causes who devoted himself "to those ages when the myths were not merely pretty, but true" and leveled those myths "against the ugly specimens of modern life that have defeated them." Tate overlooked Pound's anti-Semitic, fascist sympathies, arguing that poetry should be assessed on its stylistic merits alone, independent of politics, a point of view that he shared with fellow Agrarian John Crowe Ransom, who elevated this philosophy to the level of theory in a 1941 book titled, simply, *The New Criticism.* Hailed by literary scholars and English professors nationwide, the New Criticism enjoyed a rapid rise to prominence in the 1950s and 1960s, eventually coming to dominate American letters by the 1970s, pressing students to focus more on mechanics than ethics, on rhyme, meter, setting, and plot over and above political or cultural context.[6]

Ironically, it all hailed from Nashville. New Criticism's ascension to literary prominence was fueled not just by the works of Crowe and Tate but also by that of Robert Penn Warren and Cleanth Brooks, who wrote two textbooks—*Understanding Poetry* and *Understanding Fiction*—that eschewed context for mechanics and were adopted by high-school and college teachers across the country. Despite—and perhaps because of—their success, the New Critics drew their own detractors, however, some of whom argued that the movement's emphasis on style was a ruse, an attempt to deflect criticism of their conservative, reactionary themes by focusing on abstractions like metaphor and simile. The Fugitives' defense of segregation in *I'll Take My Stand* factored in here, as did Tate's own work, the most acclaimed example of which was a poem called "Ode to the Confederate Dead," which painted the southern cause in tragic, wistful terms, lamenting the loss of a generation of young southern men, reminiscing over the "furious murmur of their chivalry," and imploring the reader to remember them, "row after row," lying forgotten beneath "the leaves crying like an old man in a storm."[7]

Of course, sympathy for the South's past did not mean that Tate or his Vanderbilt friends endorsed fascism. They did not. The Fugitives' interest in local, decentralized rule led them to decry centralizations of power, a cornerstone of fascist thought, and they loathed populist leaders like Mussolini. Robert Penn Warren began writing *All the King's Men* while visiting Italy under Mussolini in 1939, recoiling at the similarities between the Italian dictator and Huey Long. Warren also rejected anti-Semitism, even penning a Civil War novel about a sympathetic Jewish protagonist who immigrated to the United States from Germany only to find himself fighting Confederates in Virginia.[8]

However, Warren liked Pound. In 1949, he joined Tate in lobbying successfully for Pound to receive the prominent Bollingen Prize for poetry. The prize came from the Library of Congress (where Tate held a chair and Warren was a fellow) and was designed to honor the best of American poetry, an honor that many thought should not be bestowed on Pound, whose anti-Semitic, profascist rants had raised the ire of the federal government during the war. The only reason Pound escaped federal prison was his own eccentricity, a condition so severe that a cadre of military psychiatrists declared him incompetent to stand trial, prompting the federal government to commit him to a mental institution in Washington, D.C., called St. Elizabeth's, where he accepted the Bollingen Prize in 1949 and stayed until he was finally released in 1958.[9]

Kilpatrick learned of Pound's séjour at St. Elizabeth's after a series of prominent magazines—*Esquire*, *The New Republic*, and *The Nation*—published articles calling for his release. In 1958, Harvard English professor Archibald MacLeish convinced attorney Thurmond Arnold to file a petition on Pound's behalf declaring that no further psychiatric treatment was necessary, or at least not likely to do any good, resulting in his release. Unfazed by the aura of fascism, racism, and mental illness that surrounded the poet, Kilpatrick invited Pound to Richmond, where the wordsmith impressed the editor with his roving command of Western literature and art. "His mind is a river that holds ten thousand years of sand," noted Kilpatrick, admiring Pound's mastery of Western letters, including Dante's *Divine Comedy*, and his enlistment of those letters in a critique of modernity. "He is the last statesman of a lost cause," hailed Kilpatrick, "of a cause lost a thousand years ago—and most of his enemies are dust." Kilpatrick promptly hired the poet as a foreign correspondent, giving him wide discretion in what to report, including anything from politics to poetry. Kilpatrick dismissed Pound's anti-Semitism, noting that his anti-Jewish views—though real—would never "inspire the faintest urge in anyone to put a torch to a synagogue," for "a less effective rabble-rouser could not be conceived: the rabble would not understand a word that he says."[10]

Neither did readers in Richmond. Pound's communiques from Europe proved almost unintelligible. He rambled about "the interests of the Rothschild," a prominent Jewish banking family; Franklin Delano Roosevelt, who he called "F. D. Sowbelly"; and Brigitte Bardot, a French actress. He blasted socialism as "a synonym for imbecility" and hailed "Andy Jackson['s]" quixotic, nineteenth-century campaign against the national bank, leaving Kilpatrick frustrated as to what, precisely, he was paying for. In a last ditch attempt to rehabilitate his correspondent, Kilpatrick encouraged Pound to simply write about American tourists abroad or Italian landscapes. Pound refused. The Bollingen Prize winner proved unwilling, or unable, to write clear sentences, leading Kilpatrick to terminate the relationship.[11]

Kilpatrick's dalliance with Pound was quixotic, to be sure, but coincided with a larger effort on his part to elevate the intellectual stature of the *News Leader*, and the South generally, in the 1950s. His most successful effort in this regard was the recovery of an eighteenth-century theory of constitutional law that would have made Pound proud, a concept called "interposition" that vested states with the power to override the Supreme Court. Kilpatrick invoked the idea to elevate the conversation about *Brown*, realizing that naked appeals to white supremacy were unlikely to sway the nation in the South's favor, displaying precisely the kind of "small-bore stupidity" that characterized Hanover County's attack on Harper Lee. Instead, Kilpatrick hailed interposition, a theory inspired by James Madison and Thomas Jefferson that presumed states retained the sovereignty to "interpose" their views of the Constitution against the Supreme Court, essentially nullifying the federal government.[12]

The doctrine was almost as obscure as Pound's *Cantos* but caught the attention of public officials and elected leaders across the South. First was Virginia senator Harry F. Byrd, Kilpatrick's friend, who read about it in the *News Leader* and declared it a fitting legal cornerstone for a larger campaign of "massive resistance" against the

Court. Next were state legislatures, six of whom promptly adopted "interposition resolutions" to signal their opposition to the Supreme Court, then southern senators and representatives in Congress, who made interposition the cornerstone of a "manifesto" pledging legal resistance to *Brown* on March 12, 1956.[13]

But it remained a windmill. The idea that individual states could openly defy the federal government fell afoul of established law that had been cemented, unequivocally, by the Civil War. Anyone who understood legal history would have realized this, including perhaps Kilpatrick. But he and those who followed him seemed to sense that the campaign to save segregation desperately needed poetry, a language that did not sound barbaric or racist but instead evoked the refinement of Jefferson, the stateliness of Madison, and the learned language of the law. Even if the South lost, in other words, it needed to lose with dignity, not dressed in a sheet and holding a noose. Looked at this way, Kilpatrick's editorials on behalf of interposition were themselves *Cantos*, erudite gibberish that took a set of base ideas and made them soar.

Yet not all Virginians approved. One detractor was an attorney in Richmond who watched Kilpatrick's campaign with great interest and disapproval. Lewis F. Powell, Jr., one of Richmond's ablest lawyers, understood interposition as simply a fancy word for nullification, the idea that states could openly defy the federal government, something that was not allowed by the Constitution. Powell was twenty years Kilpatrick's senior, rail thin, and far more learned in law than the Richmond journalist. He had graduated from Washington and Lee University's law school in 1930, the same year that the Agrarian manifesto *I'll Take My Stand* was published, and had risen rapidly through Richmond society, even gaining a seat on the city's schoolboard in 1950. Roughly the same age as Robert Penn Warren and Allen Tate, Powell saw nothing ostensibly wrong with segregated schools. He grew up in the same dual society that Kilpatrick and the Fugitives did, "lived with black servants and played with black children," adopted the notion that segregation promoted black "development," and was genuinely "shocked" at the Supreme Court's opinion in *Brown*.[14]

However, Powell did not believe that states could simply flout the Supreme Court. Instead, he felt that the South faced two choices:

abolish its public schools, which would be "catastrophic," or comply narrowly with the ruling, removing any overt mention of race from southern state law while relying on local discretion, social pressure, and residential segregation to maintain southern schools more or less as they were pre-*Brown.* While on Richmond's schoolboard, for example, Powell approved a general plan proposed by the governor that removed overt racial prohibitions from school attendance but provided state officials with the discretion to "assign" students to schools based on a variety of factors, some of which could be used as proxies for race in the event that black students put up by the NAACP might try to enter white schools. Powell also endorsed the construction of schools in overcrowded black areas to alleviate the threat that they might be sent to underenrolled white schools, a position that he rationalized as part of a larger effort to stave off integration. In some cases, Powell even conceded that token numbers of black students might prudently be enrolled in white schools, if for no other reason than to cement Richmond's compliance with *Brown.*[15]

Kilpatrick dismissed Powell's approach. On January 16, 1956, he met Powell in a one-on-one debate at Richmond's exclusive Commonwealth Club, a stately red-brick structure on West Franklin Street and wheeled out all the arguments that he had been making in the *News Leader*'s editorial column in favor of interposition, recalling that it was first articulated by James Madison and Thomas Jefferson. Powell countered with a devastating review of Supreme Court precedent, declaring it the final arbiter of the Constitution, meanwhile reminding Kilpatrick of Richmond's humiliating demise during the Civil War. The South's decision to secede from the union, argued Powell, had been interposition's epitaph.[16]

Kilpatrick, and Virginia, did not listen. Two weeks after Powell engaged the popular editor at the Commonwealth Club, the state legislature voted unanimously to endorse interposition. Powell promptly sent a letter to Kilpatrick congratulating him on his victory, even as he wrote Virginia governor Thomas B. Stanley imploring him to veto the bill—to no avail. The governor signed the law and led Virginia, and the South, into massive resistance against the Supreme Court, a quixotic campaign that for a brief moment elevated James Jackson Kilpatrick to the apex of southern politics.[17]

But Powell would be vindicated. The decision to declare interposition in Virginia in 1956 led, by 1958, to disaster. Schoolboards in Charlottesville, Norfolk, and Warren County closed their schools, rousing the ire of white parents who promptly organized against massive resistance, a trend that continued as white business leaders blamed interposition for a decline in northern investment to the Old Dominion. Powell worked behind the scenes to shore up this link, even as southerners recoiled at the public humiliation of Arkansas governor Orval Faubus for refusing a direct order from President Dwight D. Eisenhower to protect black students in 1957, prompting the deployment of federal troops to his city. The Supreme Court piled on one year later, declaring in no uncertain terms that it and not the states remained the final arbiter of the Constitution.[18]

Kilpatrick complained to friends in January 1960 that massive resistance was over. Any hope of defying the Supreme Court, he conceded, was futile. Just as Ezra Pound had failed to deliver for the *News Leader*, so too had interposition failed to deliver for the South, leading Kilpatrick to jettison his defiant gestures and adopt a chastened, more cautious outlook. Prohibition consoled him. Likening *Brown*'s integration mandate to the federal government's failed effort to foist temperance on the nation, Kilpatrick called for a gradual campaign of political resistance, an effort to win the hearts and minds of Americans in the North and West against civil rights. Once the South developed enough allies, he hoped, Congress might thwart enforcement of the Court's decisions or permit a realignment of the Court itself.[19]

Kilpatrick's change in tone led him, ironically, back to Powell. The two would come to agree that legal subterfuges were unlikely to help the South, while national opinion might be swayed on behalf of the region. However, the two also realized that before the South could connect with voters in the North and West, the region needed to develop a cogent, reasoned response to the civil rights movement. Just like Robert Penn Warren, William Faulkner, Flannery O'Connor, Eudora Welty, and Harper Lee, both Powell and Kilpatrick knew that engaging the movement was necessary lest the narrative of events be written entirely by blacks, a concern that led them to seek out chinks in the movement's veneer of moral superiority while at the same time countering black arguments that white southerners were congenitally violent and racist. Kilpatrick led. In 1963, he engaged James Baldwin in an essay noting that "it was a shock to many good-hearted white persons to be told bluntly by Mr. Baldwin, in *The Fire Next Time*, that the Negro is not interested in adopting the white man's cultural, social, religious, or moral values—that the Negro wants nothing from the white man but his power." Kilpatrick balked at this, conceding that even if white music was "banal" and white religion "a sort of Rotarianism remote from Galilee," black culture was no better. "The felony rate among Negroes regularly runs almost three times the national average," he lamented, and "the same bleak picture obtains in the area of illegitimacy." While such numbers bore links to structural causes—poverty, discrimination, and so on—Kilpatrick leveled them at poor moral character, arguing that African Americans should work to improve their standards rather than protest in the streets, a campaign that had led to "riot, civil disobedience, and wild disorder."[20]

No one deserved more blame for this disorder, continued Kilpatrick, than Martin Luther King, Jr., who had cynically manipulated protests to make southern whites look bad. "To understand Dr. King's approach to the demonstration process," Kilpatrick wrote on March 30, 1965, "it is necessary only to read closely his recent book, *Why We Can't Wait*," a memoir of the movement's campaign in Birmingham, Alabama. "Here Dr. King spells it out," argued Kilpatrick, "with impersonal detachment, just how these things work: Committees must be organized, and schedules must be arranged of persons to be arrested; the police must be provoked into acts of brutality, calculated to look good on television." Kilpatrick's reading of King's memoir portrayed the black leader as a puppeteer of violence, someone who cynically manipulated white racists in order to generate dramatic images of brutality capable of stirring northern sympathy.[21]

Powell joined. He quoted King's Birmingham memoir to note that the minister's doctrine of "civil disobedience" was nothing less than a "heresy" which threatened to "weaken the foundations of our system of government." Powell focused on a portion of the memoir that included the "much publicized" letter King had written from Birmingham Jail, which invoked the concept of a "higher law" superior to written law, complaining, "if the decision to break the law really turns on individual conscience, it is hard to see in law how

Dr. King is any better off than former Governor Ross Barnett of Mississippi, who also believed deeply in his cause and was willing to go to jail." This was a point that Warren, Faulkner, O'Connor, and Welty had all made, arguing that extremists on both sides of the racial divide—whether diehard segregationists or civil rights activists—were obscuring the more reasonable, peace-loving elements in the South. "As the use of disobedience tactics has expanded," argued Powell, "the relationship between the act of protest and the law protested has become increasingly attenuated." To illustrate, the Virginia attorney cited a protest organized by James Farmer and CORE at the 1964 World's Fair in New York. The protest had occurred just after Farmer was interviewed by Warren for *Who Speaks for the Negro?* and involved a group of demonstrators who threatened massive disruptions of the fair, including the shutdown of freeways leading to the event, a move that many found confusing since there was no obvious link between the fair and racial inequality, either North or South. According to Farmer, however, CORE picketed the fair not because they had any problem with the event itself but rather to dramatize "the contrast between the glittering world of fantasy and the real world of brutality, bigotry and poverty," a position that Powell found untenable.[22]

Like Welty, Powell showed little interest in black efforts at "dramatizing hostility." "If valid breach of peace and trespass laws may be violated at will," he argued, "there would soon be little left of law and order." To establish this point, he cited "riots in Harlem, Rochester, Philadelphia, Chicago and Watts," all of which had suffered through violent periods of black unrest beginning in the summer of 1964 and continuing through 1967. For Powell, 1967 was "a year of crises in which the symptoms of incipient revolution are all too evident," a "revolution" stoked by a rising cadre of "militant leaders" including H. Rap Brown and Stokely Carmichael.[23]

Carmichael, of course, had been interviewed by Robert Penn Warren in 1964 and had since grown more radical. After participating in the Selma campaign in Alabama in 1965, Carmichael had become tired of nonviolence and begun to argue for armed self-defense, a philosophy that rejected King's tactics of peaceful protest. He denounced nonviolence and called for "Black Power" in Greenwood, Mississippi, in 1966, only to be followed by other young black leaders, including H. Rap Brown, a Louisiana native and graduate of Southern University who also endorsed armed resistance to white oppression. Brown suggested that urban riots were to be praised as black resistance, a point for which Powell had little patience. Powell joined Kilpatrick in complaining that King had opened a Pandora's Box of problems by calling for defiance of the law, a box that needed to be forcefully shut. "Is it possible for the masses," asked Powell, "especially the economically deprived and emotionally inflamed—to draw fine distinctions between 'just' and 'unjust' laws or between various methods of disobedience? Can we reasonably expect throngs in the streets to understand and observe subtle differences between peaceful protest, disorderly conduct, and mob violence?"[24] As Powell saw it, King was not a moral leader so much as a "prophet of civil disobedience" guilty of planting seeds of unrest by advancing specious theories, among them the notion that some laws were "just," others "unjust," and that "each person" could "determine for himself which laws [were] 'unjust'" at which point they were "morally bound—to violate the 'unjust' laws." To Powell, Brown and Carmichael were part of a logical, if frightening progression, heirs to the early, seemingly innocuous demonstrations led by King.[25]

Precisely because he felt that King threatened disorder and chaos, Powell questioned his influence. As Powell saw it, the minister had "enchanted" many Americans, including "naïve" liberals, "clergymen and campus intellectuals" who failed to grasp the impracticality of his ideas. "There seemed to be a curious unawareness," argued Powell, "that once lawlessness is tolerated and justified it feeds upon itself and leads either to revolution or violent repressive measures." Ignoring structural causes of the riots like police brutality, unemployment, substandard housing, and segregation, Powell located the source of the explosions in irresponsible rhetoric, thereby recasting King as a morally questionable harbinger of crime and anarchy. "He is arm-in-arm with Carmichael," Powell stated, "in slandering his own government," even as he "is now urging 'massive civil disobedience' for the purpose of 'dislocating' northern cities," including "disruptive demonstrations," "weekly school boycotts," "blocking plant gates," and "disrupting governmental operations with sit-in demonstrations in federal buildings."[26]

Although Powell downplayed the poverty and discrimination that still plagued African American communities, his argument struck a chord with elected officials in the North and West. After all, King had made increasingly radical statements about the direction of the civil rights struggle, moving away from simple requests to end overt discrimination and toward more complex questions of fighting poverty, ending the war in Vietnam, and redistributing wealth. King also laced much of his talk with calls for a stronger, more centralized federal government, an entity better equipped to deal with state and local resistance. "State, municipal, and county laws and practices negate constitutional mandates," declared King in 1964, "as blatantly as if each community were an independent medieval duchy." To deal with this, he called for a "broad-based and gigantic Bill of Rights for the Disadvantaged" to be administered by the federal government that would guarantee "full employment," provide a "social-work apparatus on a large scale," and "incorporate in its planning some compensatory consideration" for slavery and segregation.[27]

Powell saw danger in such moves, precisely the kind of government-creep that Warren had warned about in *All the King's Men.* Even if King was right that blacks had suffered disproportionately, their plight was no justification for radically altering the political makeup of the United States, a makeup that Powell believed preserved liberty. This link between localism and liberty was central to his political philosophy, something that he shared with the Agrarians. They too feared a federal leviathan and were perfectly willing to sacrifice the type of social equality that King professed in order to preserve localism and limited government.

Powell never gained a chance to confront King on these points. Four months after he declared King a harbinger of lawlessness, the black minister traveled to Memphis for a major campaign on behalf of the city's sanitation workers. The reverend would not, however, live to see the end of the protest. On April 4, 1968, a white racist named James Earl Ray shot King on the balcony of the Lorraine Motel. The bullet pierced King's jaw and lodged itself in his shoulder, killing the civil rights leader almost instantly.

As the nation mourned, Powell's star rose. King's murder prompted unrest in over one hundred cities across the country, including violent uprisings in Chicago, the District of Columbia, and

Baltimore that prompted the federal government to send in troops. Newscasts of burning neighborhoods lent credence to Powell's fear that America was teetering on the brink of chaos, leading prominent government officials and Republican Party leaders to view him as a sensible, even prescient advocate for stability and order. Not long after King's assassination, Powell received a call from Richard M. Nixon, the newly elected president of the United States, asking him if he wanted to serve on the U.S. Supreme Court. He said no. Two years later he got another call with the same question and said yes.

James Jackson Kilpatrick applauded. On November 23, 1971, he drafted a glowing endorsement of Powell in his new nationally syndicated column, "A Conservative View," exclaiming that Powell was a "great lawyer" and "one of the finest and most decent human beings to reach the national stage" in his "lifetime." Declaring that he and Powell shared a "friendship of 25 years," Kilpatrick argued that the nominee's "gifts" included "clarity, order, and reason," and that he was a "scholar" who "loves the law." Powell was moved. He wrote a note thanking Kilpatrick for his support, noting that "your column, published last week in the Richmond *News Leader* and syndicated across the country, is by far the most generous thing ever written about me."[28]

CHAPTER THIRTEEN

Regents v. Bakke

That Lewis Powell found himself on the Supreme Court of the United States was uncanny but not shocking. President Richard M. Nixon had expressed an interest in appointing a southerner to the Court following his election in 1968, part of a larger campaign to roll back some of the left-leaning decisions of the Warren Court and also to build southern support for the Republican Party. Nixon hoped that he might pick up votes in Dixie, particularly among educated, business-minded suburbanites who were being lured from small towns to booming "Sunbelt" cities like Charlotte, Atlanta, and Houston, changing the demographics of the region. Long dominated by rural politicians like Harry F. Byrd in Virginia, southern states began to rewrite their voting districts in the 1960s to comply with a Supreme Court decision called *Baker v. Carr*, a 1962 opinion that required regular reapportionment based on population shifts. Suddenly, southern cities and suburbs gained sizable legislative majorities, even as the region's rural demagogues found themselves haranguing empty barns.[1]

Nixon noticed. Not only did his staff pay close attention to suburban southerners in composing his political strategy, but he himself could relate to their concerns. Although born in Yorba Linda, California, in 1913, Nixon had won an academic scholarship to Duke University to study law in 1934. For three years, he lived in the segregated South, rubbing shoulders with a small group of educated, aspiring southerners who bore more in common with Lewis F. Powell, Jr. (who graduated a few years before Nixon just up the road at Washington and Lee), and Harper Lee (who attended law school not too long after him at the University of Alabama), than George Wallace or Ross Barnett. Nixon's time in the South, he later confessed, gave him an appreciation for white southern perspectives that he would not otherwise have had.[2]

Of course, even if Duke had taught Nixon nothing, electoral shifts favoring middle-class whites put a very different demographic on the Republican radar, even better explaining why a California president might have looked for a professionally distinguished, politically moderate southern judge. Nixon first nominated a South Carolina circuit judge named Clement Haynsworth, who boasted a reputation for civility and competence that rivaled Powell's. However, Haynsworth met with Senate opposition due to a partisan squabble over an earlier Lyndon B. Johnson nominee, prompting Nixon to approach Powell, who by that time had gained national recognition as president of the American Bar Association (ABA). Powell, however, declined, causing Nixon to tap a third southern lawyer, Fifth Circuit judge G. Harrold Carswell, a fellow Dukie who subsequently drew criticism for his unreconstructed views of race and a lackluster resume.[3]

Nixon went back to Powell. Although reluctant to join in 1969, Powell agreed in 1971. By that time, he had grown increasingly concerned, even alarmed, that the United States was in crisis. On June 26, 1970, for example, Powell wrote Nixon directly to warn him that the United States needed to work harder to counter left-wing propaganda, reminding the world that America guaranteed its people more freedom than the Soviet Union or China. "Much of the world," Powell explained to Nixon, "has come to believe the lies that it is America—not the Communist superpowers—which is repressive, militaristic and imperialistic," forgetting that "there is a significant difference between totalitarianism and a free democracy." Totalitarianism weighed on Powell much like it did on Robert Penn Warren and the Agrarians, prompting Powell to recommend that the president "appoint a select nonpartisan commission" to develop "an adequate political warfare strategy for the United States." "Political warfare," as Powell described it, meant a "war of words and ideas," essentially a propaganda campaign like the one James Jackson Kilpatrick had advocated years before, aimed at selling American values both at home and abroad. Preexisting efforts to convey American values like the United States Information Agency struck Powell as insufficient, even though the agency boasted a cadre of high-profile southern members, including William Faulkner. Powell counseled the president to do more, warning that "millions" of Americans had "accepted Communist propaganda in varying degrees," reams of it "parroted daily in much of the communications media, on the campus, in literature, by the arts and theater, and on the public platform."[4]

Powell reiterated these fears one month later at a gathering of business leaders in South Carolina, the text of which he also sent to the president. In it, Powell conceded that there was inequality in America but argued that the poor in the United States fared better than their peers abroad. "There is still some poverty in America," he lamented, "but the fact is that we enjoy the highest standard of living on a national basis known to history, and many who are regarded as poverty-stricken in this country would be prosperous indeed compared with standards which prevail in most of the world." Taking a global view of poverty, Powell found Americans to be relatively well-off and disregarded arguments for legal reform like those advanced by Martin Luther King, Jr. To Powell's mind, procedural reforms guaranteeing the poor better access to the political system and the courts, like indigent defense, remained one of the few areas of law that needed to be tweaked in order to address concerns about poverty—a position that Robert Penn Warren had taken in "The Briar Patch" in 1929 and that Atticus Finch had taken in *Mockingbird*. Beyond that, Powell argued, America's political system was superlative and calls for radical change unwarranted.[5]

Powell's faith in America fueled his aversion to demonstrators. As he saw it, the American left, including "black militant revolutionary groups" along with white radicals belonging to Students for a Democratic Society, aimed not to end poverty and fight racism so much as to "destroy America." Of particular concern to Powell was the left's attack on legal process, on "majority rule, checks and balances, due process and the rule of law itself," a critique that he had made of King. That Powell saw a continuity between the civil rights movement's direct action phase and the New Left's "ideological assault on the fundamentals of our system" was telling, an indicator that between the time the White House first asked him to join the Court in 1969 and his decision to say yes in 1971, he had developed a personal commitment to countering what he perceived to be an increasingly radical turn in American politics.[6]

One problem with that politics, argued Powell, was its insistence that America was still racist and needed to compensate African Americans for past harm, a position that Powell found unwarranted. "We have witnessed racial injustice in the past," he maintained in his speech to southern industrialists in 1970, "as has every country with significant racial diversity. But contrary to the guilt-ridden views of those who talk about reparations for past injustice," he continued, "a people can fairly be judged only by their record—not that of earlier generations." It was a clear rejection of the argument that whites owed blacks for slavery, a claim that King had made in his 1964 book *Why We Can't Wait*, arguing that the federal government "must incorporate in its planning some compensatory consideration for the handicaps" that blacks had "inherited from the past." Powell disagreed, stressing that the law had done all it could for blacks by removing overtly racist classifications and guaranteeing the vote. "Racism, in all shapes and forms," exhorted Powell, "is now prohibited by laws which provide the most sweeping civil liberties ever enacted by any country for the benefits of a minority race. Racial prejudices in the hearts of men cannot be legislated out of existence," he continued. "They will pass only as human beings learn to respect and deserve to be respected by others," a point that Robert Penn Warren had made in Rome in 1957 and William Faulkner one year earlier. "We should stop being silent Americans," Powell declared in 1970; "all of us should speak strongly for what is good in this great country."[7]

Of course, this is what southern writers like Warren, Faulkner, Eudora Welty, Harper Lee, and Flannery O'Connor had been doing for over a decade. Now Powell brought their perspective to the Supreme Court, a move that became apparent soon after his confirmation when the Court agreed to consider a Texas challenge to public school funding. The plaintiffs, who happened to be poor Mexican Americans, lived in "school districts with low property valuations," prompting them to argue that funding schools through local property taxes led to gross inequalities in education, violating the Constitution's guarantee of equal protection. In Texas, for example, students who happened to live in wealthy school districts received an average of $585 per pupil while students in poor districts averaged only $60 per pupil. The resulting difference in educational quality, argued the plaintiffs, was substantial and unjustified.[8]

Powell seized the case as an opportunity to demonstrate that one of the advantages of preserving inequality in school funding was that it kept schools tied to local communities, thereby inhibiting centralized state "control." Altering school funding, he warned, threatened to bring about "national control of education," a move that he likened to totalitarianism. "I would abhor such control for all the obvious reasons," complained Powell, noting that he had "in mind the irresistible impulse of politicians to manipulate public education for their own power and ideology—e.g., Hitler, Mussolini, and all Communist dictators." Powell's fear of government-creep echoed concerns that Warren had made in 1957, that Harper Lee had made in her first draft of *To Kill a Mockingbird*, and that Zora Neale Hurston had made not long after *Brown*, in 1955.[9]

But Powell went farther, even finding inequality to have some benefit. "Each locality," Powell argued in *San Antonio v. Rodriguez*, "is free to tailor local programs to local needs," an arrangement that lent itself to a multiplicity of educational approaches, or what he called "pluralism." "Pluralism," he wrote, "affords some opportunity for experimentation, innovation, and a healthy competition for educational excellence," meaning that even if some school districts received less money, they could always develop new ways of teaching, perhaps even arriving at more effective forms of pedagogy. This was a little obtuse, of course, for teachers with fewer resources would probably not turn down more money if they could get it. However, Powell's defense of inequality echoed Warren's critique of *Brown*, a centralized, big-government effort to achieve racial equality that Warren found to be an assault on "variety and pluralism," a point he had made to Ralph Ellison in Rome.[10]

Powell's endorsement of inequality in *Rodriguez* laid the foundation for a string of cases that he would use to insert southern pluralist views—that is, views that respected diversity but also tolerated inequality—into Supreme Court jurisprudence. For example, Powell rejected the idea that the Constitution guaranteed equal opportunity, something that "generations of southern conservatives" had rejected as "patent nonsense," in part because it demanded massive exertions of state power to create level playing fields that were, on their face, just as difficult to guarantee as equal outcomes. Powell also rejected the idea that segregation in the North was somehow less pernicious than segregation in the South, a point that Warren had made in 1956, and that James Baldwin had confirmed in 1964.[11]

Powell called out the North and West for hypocrisy on October 12, 1972, when the Court heard a case styled *Keyes v. School District No. 1*, which was brought by African American parents in Denver, Colorado, complaining that the city's public schools were unconstitutionally segregated. Although Colorado prohibited segregation as a matter of law, the plaintiffs alleged that the Denver schoolboard had nevertheless worked to keep black and Hispanic students contained in predominantly segregated schools through a variety of deliberate means, including "the manipulation of student attendance zones," the invocation of "a neighborhood school policy," and the "selection" of sites for new schools in neighborhoods that the board knew would yield segregated results. Denver was far from Birmingham or Selma, to be sure, but the plaintiffs hoped the Court might extend their southern rulings to states in the North and West.[12]

Writing for the majority, Justice William Brennan seemed amenable to this idea but only in cases where deliberate efforts to preserve segregation could be shown. So long as plaintiffs could demonstrate a "purpose or intent to segregate," argued Brennan, then "de facto" districts that did not openly endorse segregation could be treated as "de jure" districts that did, and federal courts could order a variety of remedial measures to achieve racial balance, like busing. However, in cases where segregation occurred accidentally, due to longstanding residential patterns or demographic shifts from one neighborhood to another, for example, the Court found no constitutional foul.[13]

In a startling concurrence, Powell declared that the de facto/de jure distinction should be abandoned and all school districts, whether intentionally segregated or not, treated the same. Rather than "perpetuate the *de jure/de facto* distinction," argued Powell, "I would hold, quite simply, that where segregated public schools exist within a school district to a substantial degree, there is a *prima facie* case that the duly constituted public authorities (I will usually refer to them collectively as the 'school board') are sufficiently responsible to warrant imposing upon them a nationally applicable burden to demonstrate they nevertheless are operating a genuinely integrated school system." This was a surprise. Powell's claim that de facto segregation was just as bad as de jure appeared, on its face, to be a remarkably progressive position, an effort to hold school districts accountable whether they had intentionally segregated minority students or not.[14]

However, Powell had long rejected the de jure/de facto distinction, most notably in a case out of Charlotte, North Carolina, in 1970, when he and Virginia attorney general Andrew Miller had filed a brief arguing that intrusive efforts like busing went far beyond what *Brown v. Board of Education* had originally intended. As Powell saw it, *Brown* demanded an end to overtly segregationist law, nothing more. Further inquiries into the status of segregated schools, he argued, whether they were intentionally segregated or not, struck him as ill-advised, likely to drive white parents out of urban districts and into distant suburbs, as had already happened in Richmond. Powell argued forcefully that courts should allow urban school districts considerable freedom in determining how, precisely, integration should be achieved. Districts that ended up with predominantly black schools due to housing patterns, he maintained, should not be burdened with draconian mandates that they achieve racial balance. "Overzealousness in pursuit of any single goal is untrue to the tradition of equity and to the 'balance' and 'flexibility' which this Court has always respected," noted Powell in *Keyes*. According to him, the Constitution did "not require that school authorities undertake widespread student transportation solely for the sake of maximizing integration." Better to retain some segregation, he maintained, than subject children to arduous commutes in the name of "racial balance," a goal that *Brown* had never envisioned.[15]

A trace of Confederate resentment laced Powell's words. Southerners had long argued that the North's outrage over southern segregation was hypocritical, and that just as much segregation existed above the Mason-Dixon line as below. To Powell, "the same voices which denounced the evils of segregated schools in the South" were to blame for "complacently" ignoring segregation in the North, ultimately making less "comparable" progress toward integration in cities like Denver. This was precisely the portrait of the North's false "treasury of virtue" against which Robert Penn Warren had long railed. Now Powell rounded out the picture, noting that "public schools are creatures of the State, and whether the segregation is state-created or state-assisted or merely state-perpetuated should be irrelevant to constitutional principle." Northern claims to moral superiority, in other words, were hypocritical since northern communities were just as implicated in creating segregated conditions as their southern counterparts. "The Court today does move for the first time," argued Powell, "toward breaking down past sectional disparities," opening the door to a larger revelation that the South was really no different from the rest of the country when it came to racism, and that "the history of state-imposed segregation is more widespread in our country than the *de jure/de facto* distinction has traditionally cared to recognize." This was an argument for redemption, for returning the South to the national fold as a region that was no more guilty of racial injustice than anyplace else.[16]

Powell's concurring opinion in *Keyes* wrote into law a topic that had been surfacing in southern literature for some time, namely that the Jim Crow South was morally no more contemptible than the presumably more liberal, egalitarian North, a move that absolved Dixie of any special duty to make up for its explicitly racist past. That a Supreme Court justice would do this, declaring de facto segregation no different from de jure, indicated that a rethinking of the South's level of responsibility for racial inequality was underway, now impacting the interpretation of the Constitution itself.[17]

Powell's position in *Keyes* gained credence in 1974 when he joined a majority opinion in *Milliken v. Bradley*, which prohibited federal judges from merging school districts in order to prevent white flight. This case came from another northern city, Detroit, and was also brought by African American plaintiffs who argued that the city's school district had deliberately taken measures to segregate black students. Thanks to white flight, however, the only practical solution was to merge the city district with adjoining suburban districts in the "three-county metropolitan area." Unless such a "metropolitan plan" were imposed, argued the plaintiffs, Detroit would be left with "an all-black school system immediately surrounded by practically all-white suburban school systems, with an overwhelmingly white majority population in the total metropolitan area." While this was true, Chief Justice Warren Burger held that school district lines constituted a "deeply rooted" American commitment to "local control" and could not be "casually ignored or treated as a mere administrative convenience." To support this point, Burger cited Powell, invoking the Virginian's holding in *San Antonio v. Rodriguez* that "local control over the educational process affords citizens an opportunity to participate in decision-making, permits the structuring of school programs to fit local needs, and encourages 'experimentation, innovation, and a healthy competition for educational excellence.'" While *Rodriguez* had only implicitly involved the question of race—it was decided primarily on the grounds of wealth—*Milliken* made the racial connection explicit. By citing Powell, Burger could claim that the neighborhood school remained one of the last bastions of local community control in America—a value that outweighed the problem of segregation—a position that southerners like Warren, Welty, O'Connor, and Lee had long extolled.[18]

Burger's invocation of Powell in *Milliken* suggested that views long-endorsed by white southerners were becoming more representative of national opinion, and that *Brown*'s influence was fading. While Chief Justice Earl Warren had invoked federal power to intervene in local affairs and fight racism, local affairs were now being cited as a firewall to racial reform. Of course, the landscape was different—overt classifications were a thing of the past—but the question remained whether state action had not orchestrated segregation in the North—just as it had in the South—albeit in more subtle ways. Justice William O. Douglas seemed to think it had. In an eloquent dissent, Douglas outlined all the various ways that government action had contributed to school segregation in the North, including the enforcement of covenants barring blacks from white neighborhoods, the construction of public housing "to build black ghettos," and the diligent maintenance of school district lines between them. All of these factors, which scholars would eventually come to identify as "structural racism," could, argued Douglas, easily have led Burger to endorse Detroit's metropolitan plan.[19]

But he did not. Instead of citing Douglas, Burger cited Powell, thereby consecrating arguments that the Virginian had long made, including the importance of local ties to local schools, the inevitability—nay utility—of inequality, and the dispassionate observation that the migration of families from one district to another to avoid integration was simply part of the "American scene," not something that courts could, or should, be able to stop. To Douglas, this was nothing short of a Confederate coup. As he put it, Burger's opinion took the nation "back to the period that antedated the 'separate but equal' regime of *Plessy v. Ferguson*," a time when public schools were at once segregated and unequal. Douglas implicated Powell directly in this shift, noting that his opinion in *Rodriguez* had sanctioned the very arrangement by which "the poorer school districts must pay their own way," a position that—when coupled with the residential segregation caused by white flight—meant public schools could be both racially separate and unequal. "So far as equal protection is concerned," fumed Douglas, "we are in a dramatic retreat from the 7-to-1 decision in 1896 that blacks could be segregated in public facilities, provided they received equal treatment."[20]

Powell had prevailed. His rulings had successfully protected unequal funding between districts in *Rodriguez*, absolved the South of moral guilt in *Keyes*, and now helped provide the rationale for holding school district lines constitutionally insurmountable in *Milliken*. Further, he had done so with the full cooperation of a majority of his colleagues on the Court and arguably a majority of the voting public as well. Although *Milliken*, *Keyes*, and *Rodriguez* all drew criticism from civil rights circles, few mainstream politicians—including the president or Congress—disagreed with the decisions.[21]

And there was more. Powell's most influential stamp on the question of integration and schools came four years after *Milliken*, in a challenge to affirmative action plans in university admissions. The case was filed by a white plaintiff named Allan Bakke, who had been denied admission to the University of California at Davis Medical School. Convinced of his eligibility, Bakke blamed his rejection on a policy that reserved sixteen out of one hundred available entry positions to minorities, including African Americans, Mexican Americans, Asian Americans, and American Indians. While average scores for minority admits hovered around the 35th percentile on the Medical College Admissions Test, Bakke's score neared the 90th percentile, fueling his frustration that lower-scoring minorities had been admitted before him.[22]

Conservatives on the Court, like William Rehnquist, sided immediately with Bakke, arguing that the racial set-asides endorsed by UC Davis were discriminatory. In a joint opinion, Justices John Paul Stevens, Burger, Potter Stewart, and Rehnquist agreed that UC Davis's quota system violated Title VI of the 1964 Civil Rights Act, which banned racial discrimination by any institution that received federal funds. While the act had been written to ameliorate conditions in the American South, conservatives on the Court believed that the law applied to any institution that singled out individuals by race. Whether the victims of such policies were minorities or not, they argued, quotas like the one at the UC Davis Medical School represented an arbitrary and therefore illegitimate racial classification.[23]

Liberals Brennan, Byron White, Harry S. Blackmun, and Thurgood Marshall all disagreed, siding with the school officials. To them, the UC Davis program was race conscious but not discriminatory. Unlike segregation statutes in the American South, they argued, Davis's affirmative action plan did not operate "to stigmatize or single out any discrete and insular, or even any identifiable, nonminority group." On the contrary, it aimed to remedy "past societal discrimination" against blacks, including the legacies of slavery and segregation, a goal that the four justices found compelling. "It is inconceivable," argued Brennan, "that Congress intended to encourage voluntary efforts to eliminate the evil of racial discrimination while at the same time forbidding the voluntary use of race-conscious remedies to cure acknowledged or obvious statutory violations." Justice Marshall, who of course had argued *Brown* on behalf of the NAACP, fleshed out what precisely these violations were in a separate opinion that covered the legal history of slavery, Reconstruction, and Jim Crow, noting that black life expectancy was shorter than white, black infant mortality rates were "nearly twice that for whites," and the "percentage of Negroes who live in families with incomes below the poverty line is nearly four times greater than that of whites." All of these factors, coupled with America's history of racial discrimination—South and North—led Marshall to conclude that "meaningful equality remains a distant dream for the Negro."[24]

Powell balked. To his mind, discrimination against African Americans was hardly the stark tableau of oppression and abuse that Marshall had painted. "There is no principled basis for deciding which groups would merit 'heightened judicial solicitude,'" Powell argued, since the United States was "a Nation of minorities," many of whom "had to struggle—and to some extent struggles still." Although Powell recognized that the 14th Amendment had been written expressly for "members of the Negro race," he argued that its language was sufficiently neutral to embrace a broader assemblage of minorities, including Asians, Hispanics, and even whites. To demonstrate, Powell parsed out several different racial groups that the Supreme Court had recognized in past opinions, noting "as the Nation filled with the stock of many lands," so too was the 14th Amendment extended to include Chinese Americans, Japanese Americans, Mexican Americans, and even "Celtic Irishmen" in a case styled *Strauder v. West Virginia* and "Austrian resident aliens," in *Truax v. Raich*. Building on these last two, Powell wondered why separate white ethnic groups could not also be considered protected minorities, like blacks. Noting that the petitioner in *Bakke* had "identified Blacks, Chicanos, Orientals, & American Indians," he then posed the question, "Why not Italians, Irish, Greeks, etc." To his mind, such groups also amounted to "racial 'classification[s]'" and were therefore "suspect." "I see no basis," he wrote in his preconference notes, "for viewing a 'minority' vs 'white' classification in a different light."[25] "Our cases," continued Powell, "hold that a racial classification can be sustained only if the state interest is compelling, and no less intrusive means are available."[26]

Powell's emphasis on white minorities marked a dramatic departure from Brennan's and Marshall's focus on blacks, but was not completely out of step with the times. The question of white minorities had captured the minds of many in the 1970s, as Italian, Greek, Polish, and other immigrant groups worked to reclaim their distinct cultural roots. Representatives of such groups demonstrated a concerted interest in the *Bakke* decision, even filing a set of amicus briefs on behalf of the Italian-American Foundation, the Polish American Congress, the American Jewish Committee, the Hellenic Bar Association of Illinois, and the Ukrainian Congress Committee of America. All argued that African Americans were not the only minority to have suffered discrimination in the United States, nor were whites a monolithic bloc that should automatically be held guilty for slavery and segregation. On the contrary, they maintained, quota systems that set aside places for black students were themselves forms of discrimination that the Constitution forbade.[27]

Powell accepted such white ethnic views, holding that "the white majority" was itself "composed of various minority groups, most of which can lay claim to a history of prior discrimination at the hands of the State and private individuals." Among these groups were Greeks and Italians, who had both filed briefs; the Irish, who had been recognized by the Court in the past; and, somewhat remarkably, even "white Anglo-Saxon Protestants," who may not have suffered the same discrimination as other groups but still constituted a separate, white "minority." That Powell viewed all of these entities as ethnically dissimilar revealed a larger sense on his part that there was, ultimately, no such thing as a white "majority" nor was there a compelling reason to compensate African Americans for past harm.[28]

Powell's insensitivity to the ordeals of slavery and Jim Crow stunned Brennan and Marshall but dovetailed nicely with Powell's southern upbringing, a past steeped in oral histories of black indolence and white suffering under Yankee oppression during the Civil War and Reconstruction. Powell even went so far as to reference this period in *Bakke*, noting that the "the clock of our liberties . . . cannot be turned back to 1868," the year the 14th Amendment was imposed on the South, a time when white southerners decried federal Reconstruction as a campaign of oppression aimed at punishing white rebels. North Carolina native and president Andrew Johnson impugned Reconstruction as a government effort to treat African Americans as "special wards" of the state, a critique that Powell invoked again in *Bakke*. "It is far too late," wrote Powell in 1978, "to argue that the guarantee of equal protection to all persons permits the recognition of special wards entitled to a degree of protection greater than that accorded others," a clear rejection of UC Davis's admissions policy and of black claims to compensation for past discrimination generally.[29]

Powell's invocation of Reconstruction to deride affirmative action suggested that he saw a parallel between the 1970s and the 1870s, the end of Reconstruction, and that he viewed himself as a type of redeemer, a figure who, like Andrew Johnson, sought to bring the nation back together by calling for an end to radical efforts aimed at helping blacks. During his administration, for example, Johnson had so firmly supported the South that Republicans impeached him, including among their gripes his rejection of black suffrage, his resistance to military Reconstruction, and his decision to pardon Confederate officers. That Powell quoted Johnson in *Bakke* was telling, a confirmation of arguments that he had been making for some time against the civil rights movement and in support of the position that the law had done all it could for African Americans. Now he used his influence on the Court to firmly close the door on black demands for further concessions, stating explicitly that the Constitution provided no remedy for generalized claims of "societal discrimination."[30]

Thurgood Marshall, who had dedicated much of his professional life to enlisting the federal government in the cause of racial equality, seethed. "It is more than a little ironic," noted Marshall, "that, after several hundred years of class-based discrimination against Negroes, the Court is unwilling to hold that a class-based remedy for that discrimination is permissible." To Powell's argument that America was made up of minorities who had all suffered, Marshall scoffed. "The experience of Negroes in America has been different in kind, not just in degree, from that of other ethnic groups," he argued. For this reason, African Americans deserved "greater protection under the Fourteenth Amendment where it is necessary to remedy the effects of past discrimination." Although Powell proved impervious to Marshall's entreaties, other members of the Court felt his anger. As Justice Brennan remembered it, Marshall "had been extremely sensitive the entire Term regarding the Court's approach to the Bakke issue" and was "livid over LFP's opinion which he regarded as racist." Even Brennan expressed shock at Powell's allusion to blacks as "special wards," a pejorative term that "harkened back to the insensitivity, if not racism," of the Reconstruction-era South.[31]

Yet Marshall did not dissent entirely from Powell's opinion. If the first part made him boil, the end appealed to him. There, Powell made the argument that even though race could not be considered for purposes of addressing past harm, it could be considered as a relevant attribute of a student's identity, much like past educational experience, regional origin, or cultural heritage. According to Powell, so long as admissions programs did not aim to compensate applicants for past repression, "racial or ethnic origin" could be taken into account, as could "geographic" origin and whether applicants were "culturally advantaged or disadvantaged." The ultimate goal of this, he explained, was to recognize "diversity." Citing 1st Amendment protections of academic freedom, Powell claimed that some schools might legitimately choose to admit diverse classes with students from different backgrounds, income levels, and even racial groups for reasons that had to do with their particular pedagogic mission. "A farm boy from Idaho can bring something to Harvard College that a Bostonian cannot offer," argued Powell. "Similarly, a black student can usually bring something that a white person cannot offer." This was not a uniquely southern view, to be sure, nor was it Powell's alone—the plaintiffs had argued as much in their brief. However, Powell's endorsement of diversity at the same time as he invoked the South's struggle to end Reconstruction raised the intriguing possibility that he was elevating a particular form of diversity to the national stage, a version hostile to aggressive government efforts aimed at achieving equality, like affirmative action, the name given to federal programs aimed at compensating minorities for past and present discrimination.[32]

Donald Davidson, one of the Nashville Agrarians, had enlisted diversity in a manner similar to Powell's in a book called *The Attack on Leviathan*, which was first published in 1938 but reprinted in 1962. "The history of the American establishment," argued Davidson, "implies, if it does not enforce, diversity rather than uniformity," including a landscape shaped by "diverse racial, social, political, and environmental influences." Davidson pitted diversity against what he called "Northeastern imperialism," or centralized efforts to manipulate the "Federal mechanism" in the interest of achieving national goals like industrialism, even if those goals came at the expense of "manners, morals, and human happiness." To counter the federal "leviathan," as he put it, Davidson called for the "power to safeguard educational systems against the rule of external interests" and the power "for the South to preserve its bi-racial social system." The latter, of course, had been dismantled by *Brown*, but the former still seemed very much in play: either schools like UC Davis would be brought under the short leash of federal mandates or they could be allowed to chart their own course under the rubric of diversity, free from the "rule of external interests."[33]

Critics missed Powell's alignment with Davidson, not to mention the link between *Bakke*, *Rodriguez*, and *Keyes*, all of which recognized pluralism but resisted centralized governmental attempts to address inequality. As Powell put it in a handwritten set of preconference notes on October 13, 1977, allowing schools to consider race for purposes of diversity was not warranted as a means of compensating blacks for slavery or segregation but was warranted as an acknowledgment that the United States was a "uniquely pluralist society," a point that Davidson had long since made.[34]

Powell's enthusiasm for pluralism obscured the manner in which diversity could serve decidedly illiberal purposes. For example, diversity had been invoked at Harvard in the 1920s not to include blacks but to stem fears that Jewish applicants were outscoring their gentile counterparts and dominating admissions. Administrators and alumni alike feared that Harvard's traditional student stock, white Anglo-Saxon Protestants, might find themselves a minority at the school, their cultural influence on campus weakened by large numbers of studious, high-achieving Jews. To compensate, Harvard's admissions committee developed a plan to deemphasize test scores and admit students based on other factors, including region of origin, effectively diluting the number of Jewish applicants from the Northeast with WASPs from the West, Midwest, and South. Harvard continued to expand this white-centric "concept of diversity" following World War II, looking not simply at geographic diversity but also at different backgrounds and a wider variety of "talents and aspirations."[35]

The Harvard plan suited Powell nicely, underscoring his argument that diversity had nothing to do with affirmative action for blacks and that whites were not a unified, monolithic bloc. Harvard's plan also coincided with Powell's aversion to quotas, which confused some who saw little real difference in an admissions plan that set aside a predetermined number of seats for minorities and one that simply allowed admissions committees to take race into account as one of many factors that applicants brought to the table.

However, the question of quotas actually went to the core of the issue of diversity, or rather the type of diversity that Powell endorsed. In an article cited by the American Jewish Committee's amicus brief in *Bakke*, sociologist Nathan Glazer warned that quotas might actually reduce the freedom of institutions to assemble incoming classes. As he explained it, an endorsement of quotas by the Supreme Court could lead the federal government to "fasten a quota for race and minorities on every medical school in the country, and on every institution of higher education that is within its reach, which is almost all of them." This, in turn, would hamstring admissions committees as the federal government could simply threaten to revoke federal funding from those institutions that did not meet numeric "benchmark[s]" establishing "racial balance." Instead, Glazer suggested that schools be allowed to take race into account as simply one of "many factors," precisely the position that Powell settled on.[36]

Glazer raised the possibility that Powell's endorsement of diversity was not simply relevant to integrating classrooms but rather to providing institutions the freedom to assemble classes in whatever manner they saw fit. Harvard had argued for precisely such freedom in its amicus brief, positing that "educators need substantial freedom to search for better solutions to difficult educational problems." Powell agreed with this and consequently did not endorse a blanket requirement that all schools seek diversity in the same way. For example, he found that some schools provided diversity simply because they adhered to a particular educational vision, a position that led him to endorse private religious schools that aimed for ideological homogeneity, not diversity, in their classrooms. "Parochial schools," argued Powell in 1977, "have provided an educational alternative for millions of young Americans," often encouraging "wholesome competition with our public schools." This competition, he observed, helped create a disaggregated educational landscape that promoted "pluralism and diversity" by providing applicants with dramatically different educational choices, even if some of those choices did not promote diversity within classrooms.[37]

Private nonsectarian schools also played an important role in Powell's vision of diversity, not least because they provided, as he put it in 1967, the "major remaining barrier to maximum integration —socially, racially, and economically" in America. This was a startling comment, but it illuminated Powell's view of pluralism, which included space for a disaggregated landscape of institutions and ideas, free from centralized control. Although Powell accepted *Brown*, for example, he clung fast to Donald Davidson's view that the federal government remained a leviathan bent on rendering all students—and all people—the same. "Maximum integration," Powell argued, should not be avoided for reasons that had to do with maintaining white supremacy but because integration contributed to the centralization of state power by diminishing irregularity and dissent. This was true not just of racial integration, he argued, but social and economic integration as well. He viewed all three to be parts of the same problem, a move toward what he termed the "mass production" of "thoughts and ideas."[38]

Behind Powell's fear of the mass production of ideas, of course, lay a larger worry about the centralization of state power, a concern that had occupied Robert Penn Warren, Ralph Ellison, Harper Lee, and Zora Neale Hurston, all of whom endorsed pluralism and diversity within institutions and between them, a point that Powell wrote into constitutional law. For example, he wrote a dissent in a challenge to the Mississippi University for Women's exclusion of men, arguing that excluding men allowed the institution to promote the goal of diversity. Same-sex education, argued Powell, provided "an element of diversity that has characterized much of American education and enriched much of American life." "A distinctive feature of America's tradition," explained Powell in *Mississippi University for Women v. Hogan*, "has been respect for diversity. This has been characteristic of the people from numerous lands who have built our country. It is the essence of our democratic system." To bolster this point, Powell cited New England's "Seven Sister" colleges—Mount Holyoke, Vassar, Smith, Wellesley, Radcliffe, Bryn Mawr, and Barnard—explaining that such schools produced a "disproportionate number of women leaders" in part because the large number of female faculty provided a "motivation for women students." While the gender demographics of all-female colleges were less diverse than at coeducational institutions, the simple existence of an all-female option, argued Powell, provided "an element of diversity."[39]

Not surprisingly, Powell also found pluralism amidst the dramatically unequal funding patterns of public schools, a point he had made in *San Antonio v. Rodriguez.* This had little to do with improving the classroom experience. Schools that found themselves in poor districts obviously did not choose—or want—to receive less money. However, Powell found no problem with a landscape that incorporated relatively broad ranges of inequality in terms of funding, student body composition, and curricula. To him, such incongruities were actually a good thing, byproducts of America's core identity as a "pluralistic society" that stood apart from nations defined by government "orthodoxy." Countering such orthodoxy was to Powell part of the larger struggle against totalitarianism, a struggle that he believed possessed inherent value, independent of compensatory justice.[40]

By invoking pluralism, in other words, Powell expressed his long-held conviction that the United States was not, nor necessarily should be, assimilationist. Further, he made it clear that America's racial past distinguished it among nations. While African Americans did not deserve any special treatment for past discrimination or persistent racism, they remained an integral part of America's "uniquely pluralistic society," a society whose diversity—both within and between institutions—helped keep it free. This link between race and diversity, not race and equality, made Powell's pluralism southern. No one else on the Court understood what precisely he had meant by decoupling diversity from affirmative action in his lone concurring opinion, nor did subsequent critics of the decision. To them, Powell's decision represented a moderate, nonideological compromise between the right and left wings of the Court. One critic hailed Powell's invocation of white minorities as an "amazing feat of making all parties reasonably happy." Journalist Edwin M. Yoder congratulated Powell on his "common-law craftsmanship," declaring his *Bakke* opinion "magisterial" and "a truly distinguished example of the Court at its best."[41]

Others saw in Powell's ruling more than simply an aim to compromise. They perceived a genuine shift in his otherwise conservative southern views in favor of black rights. As John Herbers put it for the *New York Times*, *Bakke* meant that "the great majority of affirmative action programs, public and private, will continue." Herbers placed hope in the fact that *Bakke* might allow for future efforts to help minorities, forming a type of "legal concrete" upon which "further affirmative action programs can be made." The U.S. Commission on Civil Rights agreed, as did Attorney General Griffin Bell and President Jimmy Carter, both of whom celebrated the ruling as a "great gain for affirmative action."[42]

Some even charged Powell with trying to hide support for affirmative action in the rhetoric of diversity. For example, Yale law professor Guido Calabresi derided Powell's invocation of diversity as a ruse, a sleight of hand aimed ultimately at hiding his interest in compensating blacks for past discrimination. "After stating that no advantage can be given to individuals solely because they belong to groups that have suffered past discrimination," complained Calabresi, "Justice Powell, in effect, permitted such advantage, at least in University admissions." The Yale professor accused Powell of engaging in a deliberate "subterfuge" by veiling "reparation[s]" in the trappings of diversity. It would have been better, Calabresi argued, had Powell simply conceded that "special consideration for blacks" was constitutionally permissible "so long as they, as a group, remain subject to generalized disadvantages, since redress of these on a societal level remains a legal object of the Civil War amendments."[43]

Of course, Powell rejected the notion that the Civil War amendments called for further aid to blacks in America, a point he made clear in *Bakke* by stating that "it was no longer possible to peg the guarantees of the Fourteenth Amendment to the struggle for equality of one racial minority" since the United States had itself become "a Nation of minorities." Calabresi missed this, along with Powell's larger fear that the civil rights movement's flouting of legal process had opened the door to totalitarian rule. The law professor's ignorance of the justice's positions led him to misinterpret Powell's motives, blinding him to the possibility that the Virginian actually did believe in diversity as a standalone principle, a guarantor of liberty rather than a "ruse" for equality.[44]

While Calabresi impugned Powell's honesty, others impugned Powell's ability. Harvard law professor Alan Dershowitz and Lauren Hanft declared that Powell "erred seriously" in relying on Harvard's admissions plan in *Bakke*, not least because it had "in fact been deliberately manipulated for the specific purpose of perpetuating religious and ethnic discrimination in college admissions." The authors referred, of course, to Harvard's invocation of diversity as a means of curtailing Jewish enrollment in the 1920s. However, they failed to recognize that Powell did not necessarily see a problem with curtailing Jewish enrollment, particularly not if it meant accepting "culturally" different white Protestant "minorities" from other parts of the nation. If Harvard wanted to admit such students for the purpose of achieving diversity, that was its choice.[45]

Conversely, overwhelmingly WASP institutions could, in Powell's view, accept Jewish students with lower scores to achieve diversity, just as predominantly Jewish schools could, if they wished, deny WASPs admittance in the interest of preserving Jewish identity. No anti-Semite, Powell actually saw an analogy between Judaism and the South, a point he made at a prayer breakfast in San Francisco in 1972, not long after joining the Court. In what he termed a "lay sermon," Powell lamented the decline of "those values the individual once gained from respect for authority and from responsible participation in a larger community life." Echoing Warren and the Agrarians, Powell complained that Americans were increasingly being "cut adrift from the type of humanizing authority which in the past shaped the character of the people," an authority that could be found not in the state but "more personal forms" such as "the home, church, school, and community." To illustrate, Powell invoked an example of what he believed to be the ideal community, a place where individuals retained their sense of identity and humanity against the depersonalizing forces of the modern era: the East European village, or shtetl. "This sense of belonging was portrayed nostalgically in the film *Fiddler on the Roof*," exclaimed Powell. "Those who saw it will remember the village of Anatoepka in the last faint traces of sunset on Sabbath eve." *Fiddler on the Roof* was based on a story by Sholem Aleichem, a Russian Jew who immigrated to America after a wave of violent pogroms swept Ukraine. In the tale, a father named Tevye struggles to maintain his Judaic traditions in the face of hostile forces, including Russia's anti-Semitic Czarist government and his daughters' modern desires to marry outside their faith. "There was the picture of Tevye," explained Powell nostalgically, "the father, blessing his family, close together around their wooden dining room table. They sang what must have been ancient Hebrew hymns, transmitted from family to family through untold generations."[46]

Powell's invocation of *Fiddler on the Roof* proved an adroit way of raising the same concerns about assimilation and cultural loss that southerners like Warren, Hurston, and Lee had long raised—also by invoking Judaism—in the 1950s and 1960s. In fact, Powell's talk served as a reminder that southerners had actually become interested in preserving their respective racial cultures long before their northern peers, an interest that dated back to the Nashville Agrarians four decades earlier. In his sermon on Russian Jews, Powell bridged the Agrarian vision of close-knit local communities with the new northern ethnic resurgence, foreshadowing a quiet redemption between North and South on the question of race.

Dershowitz and Hanft missed this, and in so doing made the same mistake that Calabresi did, misinterpreting Powell as a closet liberal who invoked diversity as a "pretext" for affirmative action. This was wrong. Powell was neither liberal nor in favor of affirmative action. He believed, like the Agrarians had believed, in decentralized, disaggregated rule, arguing that such rule prevented the encroachment of Donald Davidson's leviathan, a term he used to describe a society "organized under a single, complex, but strong and highly centralized national government." Powell feared such a society as well, a fear that led him to embrace the plural South, with its quiet, rural, biracial shtetls.[47]

CHAPTER FOURTEEN

The Last Lynching

Four months after *Bakke* was decided, President Jimmy Carter signed a resolution restoring Jefferson Davis's citizenship to the Union. Like most high-ranking Confederate officers, Davis had lost the right to vote after the Civil War, part of his punishment for rebelling against the United States. Now, Carter welcomed him home, declaring that it was time to "clear away the guilts and enmities and recriminations of the past," a nod toward a new era of national acceptance of the once-recalcitrant South. Of course, Carter himself hailed from that South, a farm in southwest Georgia in the heart of the region's conservative plantation-belt. Yet, he cast himself not as a Confederate holdout but a moral, Christian, small-town farmer, noncomplicit in the South's history of violence and racial injustice. Promising "a government as good as our people," Carter ambled humbly onto the national stage, a peaceful man of strong moral fiber, precisely the kind of individual that Harper Lee might have cast in one of her novels, a benevolent southerner with positive, unassailable, moral values.[1]

Carter's repatriation of Davis coincided with a growing sentiment among white southern leaders and intellectuals that the region had transcended its racialized past and was now ready to rejoin the nation, perhaps even lead it. As literary critic Michael Kreyling put it, southerners in the 1970s aimed to "decentralize race and to substitute community," arguing that the Civil War was not fought simply to preserve white supremacy or to maintain slavery but to combat the North's "materialistic, acquisitive society," which compromised small-town sensibilities and led to the "dehumanization" of average folks. Robert Penn Warren, William Faulkner, Flannery O'Connor, Eudora Welty, and Harper Lee had all advanced this position in their fiction. Now Warren returned to his desk, sounding a similar chord in an essay commemorating Carter's decision to restore Jefferson Davis's citizenship, using the move to laud the "heroism and honor" of the Old South while praising Davis as a man for whom "honor" was a "guiding star," unlike the mercenary "pragmatism" of modern America where "the sky hums with traffic, and eight-lane highways stinking of high-test rip across hypothetical state lines, and half the citizens don't know or care where they were born just so they can get somewhere fast." In a voice remarkably reminiscent of his days as a Nashville Agrarian in the 1920s, Warren lamented mass culture and industrialization as "technologically and philosophically devoted to the depersonalization of men," a sentiment that had been simmering in southern literary circles for decades. Now such views came bubbling to the surface of the national culture as the president of the United States, a southerner, repatriated Jefferson Davis, a southerner, mere months after Supreme Court Justice Lewis F. Powell, Jr., also a southerner, invoked the first Reconstruction to counter the Second.[2]

All celebrated the end of assimilation as a national ideal, praising the rise of racial and ethnic pluralism, a campaign that they decoupled from black calls for aggressive government programs aimed at compensating African Americans for past discrimination. Southern whites like Lewis Powell and Jimmy Carter joined northern whites in extolling white ethnicity, deftly penciling themselves into a larger tableau of white ethnic/immigrant particularism, in part to counter black demands for reparations, in part to recast the South as home to an embattled white minority uniquely suited to speak for the restoration of traditional, small-town values against a menacing federal leviathan. This latter claim, a rereading of the South as a bastion of local liberty and an ensuing case for a type of multiculturalism independent of any effort to achieve racial equality, proved the hallmark of a new era.

To illustrate, Jimmy Carter traveled to South Bend, Indiana, in

1976 only to announce that the federal government should refrain from interfering with the "ethnic purity" of urban, immigrant neighborhoods in the North. Although Carter did not quibble with *Brown*, he nevertheless promised that he would not "use the Federal Government's authority deliberately to circumvent the natural inclination of people to live in ethnically homogenous neighborhoods." This shocked some, particularly those who assumed that Carter was on board with civil rights. However, Carter's empathy for Irish and Italian Americans in South Bend coincided with the same type of pluralist thinking that Powell had promoted in *Rodriguez*, *Keyes*, and *Bakke*, the notion that certain neighborhoods might prefer culturally homogenous populations, and that diversity between such neighborhoods was worth preserving, even if it meant upholding things like school district lines that inadvertently perpetuated segregation and inequality. Carter embraced this, indicating that "bad effects" could come from "injecting" a "diametrically opposite kind of family" or a "different kind of person into a neighborhood."[3]

Critics, including former civil rights activist and Carter ally Andrew Young, declared the candidate's statement a "disaster," prompting the white farmer to apologize. However, Carter did not amend his views so much as his terms, junking "ethnic purity" for "ethnic character" and "ethnic heritage." Echoing Warren, Welty, and Lee, Carter confessed that "people have a tendency—and it is an unshakable tendency—to want to share common social clubs, common churches, [and] common restaurants," meaning, of course, that he saw "nothing wrong with a heterogenous type American population," and that there was nothing wrong with "a lower-status neighborhood that is black primarily or Latin American primarily or Polish primarily or of Germanic descent primarily."[4]

President Carter joined Powell in elevating such arguments to the national level. As Carter saw it, neighborhoods that happened to be segregated along residential lines were fine, and the federal government should play no role in realigning them to achieve racial balance. He promised voters, for example, that he would not invoke his presidential authority or influence to "move people of a different ethnic background into a neighborhood just to change its character." This had obvious implications for the rapid resegregation of

American cities due to white flight, a dilemma that some hoped might be solved by locating subsidized, low-income housing in suburban districts. Carter opposed this, declaring that he did not support the construction of "high-rise, very low-cost housing" in neighborhoods with "expensive homes."[5]

Carter's sense that ethnic neighborhoods warranted preservation and that government action should not be used to disrupt community ties coincided closely with the line of reasoning followed by Powell on the Supreme Court. In decisions like *Rodriguez* and *Keyes*, Powell had made it clear that the achievement of racial balance was secondary to the preservation of local communities, and that preserving such communities promoted pluralism, if also inequality. Precisely this faith in America's "uniquely pluralist society" informed Powell's decision in *Bakke*, which celebrated diversity but shut the door on federal causes of action aimed at compensating blacks for past discrimination, a position that black activist and Supreme Court justice Thurgood Marshall lamented as a clear blow to civil rights.

Yet, white southerners discounted voices like Marshall's in the late 1960s and 1970s, praising instead African Americans who expressed an aversion to integration and a pride in uniquely black cultural formations. For example, Warren wrote a paean to black activist James Farmer in the *New York Review of Books*, extolling Farmer's rejection of Martin Luther King, Jr.'s doctrine of nonviolence in lieu of Black Power in the late 1960s. While many white intellectuals found the rise of Black Power unsettling, Warren found it refreshing, noting that the move away from nonviolence marked a shift in the nexus of civil rights away from black elites and toward the grassroots. "The chances for violence increase" with the "development of a mass base," explained Warren, casting black violence as an inevitable outcome of the popularization of black protest. "For a mass base," he argued, "involves the ignorant, the unemployed, the unemployable, and the alienated, who have no comprehension of a doctrine of nonviolence, only their 'own fierce indignation.'" Casting King as an elitist who did not represent the majority of African Americans, Warren hinted that iterations of Black Power had always been present in the black South, a sensibility that grew more energized as the movement progressed. Of course, this was precisely the point that Stokely Carmichael had made during his conversation with Warren in 1964, two years before Carmichael rolled out the slogan "Black Power" in Greenwood, Mississippi. During that early talk, Warren had gotten the black activist to concede that even at its apex, King's doctrine of nonviolence was not simply an aspirational tactic but also an elite effort to demonstrate to whites the superiority of black discipline and resolve.[6]

Although King's self-righteous articulations of black moral superiority rankled Warren, the southern writer admired Farmer, particularly his frank claims that the victories of the early civil rights demonstrations "'inspired a renewed search for black identity,' the quickening of a desire for a 'valid' visibility." This implied a move toward more pronounced articulations of blackness that would later be advertised by leaders like Carmichael, which Warren respected. "As the movement in general, and CORE in particular, broadened the base," he suggested, "the emphasis on integration, which had been largely rooted in the Negro middle class, was shifted to an emphasis on race and nationalism, which had been the traditional appeal of the Negro masses." Such an upsurge in mass interest in identity, continued Warren, had always been latent among the majority of blacks in the South and marked a welcome turn toward pluralism among black elites. To "accept" their "blackness," he argued, African Americans needed to move "from an early simplistic idea of integration to the idea of a fluid, pluralistic society with the maximum range for individual choices."[7]

Sounding a chord that went back to his novel *Band of Angels*, Warren took the emergence of Black Power as a positive endorsement of a new black consciousness, free from the assimilationist ethos of *Brown*. Warren also took Black Power as an incentive to probe his own sense of identity and the complicated relationship between that identity and the South's history of racial violence, something that he did in a 1974 poem entitled "The Ballad of Mr. Dutcher and the Last Lynching in Gupton." The verse tells the story of a mysterious white man with a "gray" face, a "gray coat," and a "small gray house" who harbors a strange secret, "as though there was something he knew but knew that you'd never know what it was he knew." As it turns out, the man is adept at lynching blacks, a revelation that emerges one "hot" afternoon when "some fool nigger, wall-eyed drunk and with a four-hit hand-gun, tried to stick up a liquor store." The offender tries to escape but is apprehended, providing Mr. Dutcher with an opportunity to hang him, which he does.[8]

Warren's poem was startling. For one, his invocation of the word "nigger" in 1974 was controversial, even offensive. Warren himself had derided the term in *Who Speaks for the Negro?* priding himself on the fact that his father had not allowed the word in their house. "If one of the children in our house had used the word nigger," remembered Warren in 1965, "the roof would have fallen in." Yet out it came in 1974. Warren could certainly have argued that this was an effort to convey historical accuracy about life in Gupton, but that only begged the question: why invoke a lynching in the nondescript hamlet of Gupton—in 1974?[9]

The answer appeared to lie in Warren's theory of identity, which he also related to racial violence. For example, the identity of the poem's main character, Mr. Dutcher, turned out to be closely bound up with his relationship to race, and in particular his special race-related skill: lynching. Thus, he ceased to become "gray" only when he snuffed out a "black" man, thereby making him decidedly "white," his birthplace the "big white oak" from which the African American is hung. "But isn't a man entitled," concludes Warren's poem, "to something he can call truly his own—even to his pride in that one talent kept, against the advice of Jesus, wrapped in a napkin, and death to hide?" While Warren had never endorsed lynching, his poem proved an odd corollary to the racial politics of the early 1970s, in particular militant assertions of Black Power. Warren's verse seemed to imply that white violence had forged white identity, and that violence had always played a role in identity formation, whether white or black. Just as blacks were beginning to publicly and militantly define themselves against whites, in other words, so too did Warren feel comfortable publicly drawing characters who defined themselves militantly against blacks, in essence acknowledging the role that white violence had played in forging white identity in the South. This painted a very different picture of racial/ethnic difference than the one advanced by white ethnics in the North, who tended to argue that their unique identities stemmed from their places of origin, not their violent interactions with other ethnic groups. Warren suggested, by contrast, that southern identity was forged in southern conflict, and that conflict, as a social phenomenon, helped forge racial and ethnic difference. Violence in America could not simply be written off as a byproduct of "social dislocation, poverty, or illiteracy," he suggested, "but was in fact a creative/destructive force that had helped shape the landscape of southern, and by extension American, culture."[10]

Warren had made a similar point in *Who Speaks for the Negro?* where he recalled "an oak tree" with a "rotten and raveled length of rope hanging from a bare bough," beside the "decrepit, shoe-box-size jail" in Guthrie, Kentucky, his hometown. The rope was the remnant of a lynching, a practice that men at the time "mysteriously" had to do but that Warren doubted he could do, for he lacked the courage. "I remember, too, that I got the idea that this was something men might do," he recalled, "might mysteriously have to do, put a rope around a man's neck and pull him up and watch him struggle; and I knew, in shame and inferiority, that I wouldn't ever be man enough to do that." It was an odd statement, suggesting that the extra-legal killing of blacks conferred some kind of manhood on its perpetrators, a manifestation of southern honor steeped in violence. For Warren, the allusion to extra-legal killings reinscribed his larger theory that southern violence had helped maintain the lines of racial difference and, by extension, racial diversity in the region. No guilt-stricken liberal, Warren seemed to acknowledge that with expressions of identity came expressions of violence, and that just as the legacy of white violence in the South had to be acknowledged as a contributor to white identity, so too did militant articulations of Black Power need to be acknowledged as inevitable, even necessary, expressions of black identity. If the rise of Black Power left northern liberals feeling disappointed and excluded, in other words, Black Power—and its rejection of nonviolence—made Warren feel vindicated, demonstrating that black calls for integration were contrived by elites and that the black masses, like all masses, ultimately enlisted violence in their cultural formation.[11]

That southern culture and southern diversity were forged in a violent dialectic between white and black, not geographic origin, religious tradition, or linguistic genealogy, reemerged once again in Warren's writings in 1975 when he published yet another racially ambivalent/offensive poem entitled "Old Nigger on One-Mule Cart Encountered Late at Night When Driving Home from Party in the Back Country." This verse, published in the prominent *New Yorker*, also featured the highly offensive n-word and told the story of a white man who leaves a party "in July, in Louisiana" after dancing with a beautiful young woman, only to encounter on the "wrong side of the road," a "fool-nigger" driving a mule with a wagon filled with "rusted bed springs." The narrator barely avoids a violent crash, possibly even his own death, but not before seeing the black man's face, which Warren described in Edvard Munch-ian terms, replete with "bulging" eyes that gleamed "white" in the dark and a mouth "Wide open, the shape of an O, for the scream / That does not come." This near-death experience with a black caricature enabled Warren to suggest that white and black in the South existed in violent contradistinction to one another, one driving a modern automobile and the other a primitive wagon, one coming from a day of leisure and the other toil, but both capable of killing the other, the near aversion of which proved a defining, identity-affirming moment. "Brother, Rebuker, my Philosopher past all Casuistry," queries Warren's narrator after nearly avoiding the head-on collision, "will you be with me when I arrive and leave my own cart of junk / Unfended from the storm of starlight . . . / To enter, by a bare field, a shack unlit?" Suddenly placing himself in the black man's position, Warren suggested that their material disparity, the car versus the cart, the leisure versus the toil, only obscured a more complex dialectic between blacks and whites in the South, one in which blacks served not simply as "Rebuker[s]" but also, oddly, as "Brother[s]," who helped to orient individual identity within the cultural constellation of the region. In his final line, for example, Warren cast the black/white dialectic as a relationship both rife with danger and with meaning, a critical part of what enabled the South to resist the alienating forces of northern mass culture and industrialism, a point that Warren made by concluding his poem with a reference to Arcturus, the brightest star in the northern hemisphere: "Can I see Arcturus from where I stand?" He suggests that the entire episode signified a parable of southern identity, or rather the orientation of that identity vis-à-vis violence, inequality, and race.[12]

Old allies approved. Cleanth Brooks, one of the original Nashville Agrarians, praised Warren's mule cart poem, noting in a letter to Warren dated April 3, 1975, that "I like very much indeed 'Old Nigger' etc. I think the final section is superb. It repeats one of your big themes but does so in its own way and with a special richness of tonality. Indeed, this section represents you at your very best." Over half a century had passed since Brooks had joined Warren in their Nashville revolt, a time that might have allowed for some evolution in their thinking. After all, *I'll Take My Stand* had been pilloried, Warren had publicly disavowed his "Briar Patch" essay, and the South had undergone a Second Reconstruction. Yet, just as Warren's celebration of Jefferson Davis and recovery of the n-word in recent poems evinced a rebel spark, so too did Brooks's salute to Warren's uncomfortable poem hint at a return to old Confederate battle positions, a celebration of the South that was at once agrarian, plural, and unequal.[13]

Ironically, the very faith that Warren and Brooks retained in the South's unreconstructed past led them to advance an early, ambitious, multicultural portrait of American letters, a project that they attempted in a two-volume textbook cowritten by Yale professor and literary scholar R. W. B. Lewis entitled *American Literature: The Makers and the Making*. Published in 1973, the book comprised one of the first literary anthologies in America to include a significant amount of work by black authors, a topic that Warren and Brooks began discussing in the summer of 1970, when Warren wrote Brooks encouraging the inclusion of a "black section" in the text. Volume 1 of the anthology extended from the colonial era to 1865 and included two black writers, David Walker and Frederick Douglass, along with a subsection entitled "Folk Songs of the Black People," which canonized spirituals like "Swing Low, Sweet Chariot" and "Go Down, Moses." To Warren and Brooks, such songs reflected the "genius" of the black race, a genius that enabled them to make a case for an independent black culture forged in slavery that had nevertheless generated contributions of significant cultural value to the American scene. Citing Melville Herskovits, for example, Warren and Brooks acknowledged evidence of a "cultural continuity" between Africa and the black South, an extremely controversial topic in the 1970s as some tried to argue that slaves had lost all cultural ties to their African origins while others lobbied for an Afrocentric approach to black history, locating modern black cultural practices in African soil. Warren and Brooks acknowledged both perspectives, noting that "researchers have more and more emphasized the idea that African elements did survive, in the spirituals as in other forms of black music in America." To establish this point, they cited James Weldon Johnson, the very black intellectual who had worked with Guy B. Johnson at UNC in the 1930s on black folklore. However, Warren and Brooks also recognized that African Americans had improvised, sometimes by inventing their own modes of expression, sometimes by modifying white influences in the New World. "The slaves, usually long out of Africa and speaking only English," wrote Brooks and Warren, "had developed their own new culture out of whatever had been preserved from [their] racial past, whatever might be called racial temperament and sensibility, and what had been assimilated from the surrounding white world." Warren and Brooks found no problem attributing literary significance to such black cultural innovations. In fact, they even elevated some black art forms over white, noting for example that white "spirituals" struck them as "generally dull," while black spirituals boasted "a language marked by great originality and power." Referencing James Weldon Johnson again, they noted that "even the phrases that have come to be accepted as the titles are often of suggestiveness and poetic beauty: 'Go Down Moses,' 'Joshua Fit de Battle ob Jerico,' [and] 'Swing Low Sweet Chariot.'" Praising the "dramatic and poetic quality" of such compositions, along with the fact that they were "highly organized" as "literary compositions," Warren and Brooks held Negro spirituals in high regard and deemed them significant enough to represent a separate, valuable black culture, what they called the "genius of the race," a term resonant with Zora Neale Hurston's views of racial culture in *Herod the Great.*[14]

Volume 2 of *Makers and the Making* contained even more African American voices, including a section on black literature from Reconstruction to the Harlem Renaissance that included Booker T. Washington, W. E. B. Du Bois, and James Weldon Johnson, and a second section on the Harlem Renaissance, with excerpts from Langston Hughes, Jean Toomer, Countee Cullen, and Zora Neale Hurston. Hurston's inclusion in the anthology was notable for two reasons. One, she was the only black woman to make the collection, and, two, her work had been largely forgotten since the publication of *Seraph on the Suwanee* in 1948, leaving her destitute and alone in Florida until her death in 1960. Despite her descent into obscurity, however, Warren and Brooks found her early work on black folklore in the South compelling enough to include in their canon-making survey, leading them to incorporate excerpts from her autobiography, *Dust Tracks on a Road*, and her ethnographic account of black communities in the South, *Mules and Men*, in their textbook. This was two years before Hurston enjoyed a national resurgence of interest thanks to an article in *Ms.* magazine in 1975.[15]

While modern critics could certainly fault Warren and Brooks for not giving African Americans more credit for "making" American literature, they proved ahead of their time in recognizing and incorporating black artists, including obscure ones like Hurston. Not until the 1980s would serious discussions about the exclusion and inclusion of minorities in literary canons explode on college campuses, at least some of that debate fueled by negative reactions to the Nashville Agrarians' early emphasis on reading texts separate from their historical and political context. Yet it was Warren's and Brooks's tie to the New Criticism that made their inclusion of black voices particularly notable, suggesting that they acted not out of political pressure but out of a genuine sense that African Americans had in fact contributed works of literary significance to American letters, independent of politics. They even went so far as to acknowledge the formation of a distinct black culture in the American South and to theorize questions of black southern dialect. "The dialect of the spirituals," wrote Warren and Brooks in their textbook, "is not to be accounted for as simply a malformation or corruption of the pronunciation of standard English." On the contrary, they argued, it was "a rather old-fashioned English, filled with seventeenth and eighteenth century standard forms that, with the passage of time, have become obsolete." To demonstrate, they noted that certain words associated with black vernacular speech actually boasted nineteenth-century English roots, including "wud" for "with," "de" for "the," "yer" for "your," and "dan" for "than," yielding sentences like "let him kiss me wud de kisses of his mouth; for yer love is better dan wine," culled from a version of the "Song of Solomon" in Sussex, England, in 1860.[16]

That black southerners spoke a form of ancient English corroborated Warren's longstanding view that Jim Crow had served as a type of cultural greenhouse, or incubator, and was not simply a system of racial repression. Warren had made this argument in his "Briar Patch" essay four decades earlier, even as the ensuing years brought with them a dramatic surge in prointegration assimilationist thought, including the recommendations of Gunnar Myrdal in *American Dilemma* that black institutions and traditions be destroyed. By 1978, Myrdal was mum, and the Fugitives, like Jefferson Davis, were returning to the national stage. Just as Warren, Lewis, and Brooks began to speak once again of separate racial cultures and talents, elevating black writers like Hurston to the pantheon of the "Makers" of American literature, so too were they joined by an emerging cadre of black voices, including southern black writers who were themselves interested in recovering the work of writers like Hurston as well.

This was new. During the 1930s and 1940s, black critics like Alain Locke, Sterling A. Brown, and Richard Wright had all criticized Hurston for writing in black dialect, a "socially unconscious" move that only corroborated white stereotypes of black folk. By the 1950s, Hurston's conservative views, including her critique of *Brown*, further alienated her from black literary circles, leading her to a life of relative isolation in Florida. That Warren and Brooks sought to resurrect her in 1970 could conceivably have been viewed, particularly from the standpoint of older critics, as simply a white effort to focus on the lowest echelons of black life. However, the rise of Black Power, Black Studies, and a political aesthetic that came to be known as the Black Arts Movement (BAM) brought with it a renewed interest in black folklore, precisely because it was not integrated into white, mainstream culture. A young African American writer helped pioneer this move after visiting Hurston's unmarked grave in 1973 and then publishing a widely read article about her for *Ms.* magazine in 1975, two years after Brooks and Warren had published Hurston in their anthology. The writer's name was Alice Walker.[17]

CHAPTER FIFTEEN
Beyond the Peacock

Alice Walker was only sixteen years old when Zora Neale Hurston died in 1960, but she followed Hurston's path, publishing a novel in 1970 about a black family that persevered through three generations of poverty and racial discrimination in the South. Although this would not be her best known work—that would be *The Color Purple*, which appeared in 1982—it would establish Walker as an African American author who embraced her southern roots. Born and raised in Georgia, Walker used her fiction to demonstrate Jim Crow's cruelty, particularly its destructive impact on African American families and women. However, she also recognized that a complex black culture had evolved in the southern states, a rich "cultural inheritance" as she put it, that she not only identified with but felt was "superior" to white culture.[1]

Walker first became interested in Hurston in 1970, when she was researching a story that involved voodoo, leading her to Hurston's book on southern folklore, *Mules and Men.* Declaring it a "perfect book," Walker praised its focus on the lives of "regular people from the South," that is, regular black people whose stories had been largely forgotten, even by the descendants of such people now living in the North. "No matter how they tried to remain cool toward all Zora revealed," wrote Walker of her northern family with rural Georgia roots, "in the end they could not hold back the smiles, the laughter, the joy over who she was showing them to be: descendants of an inventive, joyous, courageous, and outrageous people." To Walker, Hurston was important because she did not tell stories merely of racial subjugation but also of "racial health; a sense of black people as complete, complex, undiminished human beings, a sense that is lacking in so much black writing and literature." Hurston gained this sensibility, continued Walker, precisely because she came of age in an entirely black community, free from whites. "Zora grew up in a community of black people," Walker wrote, "who had enormous respect for themselves and for their ability to govern themselves."[2]

Yet Hurston had been largely forgotten. Walker remembered a college professor had mentioned Hurston briefly, but her books were out of print and most of the reviews of her work were "misleading, deliberately belittling, inaccurate, and generally irresponsible." Walker could only find one critic willing to sing Hurston's praises, a young white scholar named Robert Hemenway, whose indignation that Hurston had died in obscurity inspired Walker to visit Eatonville herself and find her grave in 1973. Of course, Warren and Brooks had already decided to include Hurston in their anthology, *American Literature: The Makers and the Making*, but this was an undergraduate textbook, not a source that professional writers like Walker, or readers of writers like Walker, were likely to consult. Therefore, Walker—not Warren or Brooks—got credit for resurrecting Hurston's legacy in an article for *Ms.* magazine in 1975, a piece that declared her one of the "most significant unread authors in America."[3]

Walker's piece sparked a flurry of interest in Hurston, leading others to gain inspiration from her work, including rising stars in black letters like Toni Morrison, Maya Angelou, Gloria Naylor, and Jamaica Kinkaid, as well as literary critics like Henry Louis Gates, Jr., a young African American studies professor at Yale. Gates credited his interest in Hurston to Walker's 1975 article, commending her not only for reviving Hurston's reputation but for providing a counterpoint to the perception, popularized by Gunnar Myrdal and others, that black culture was pathological and that African Americans' best hope was to assimilate into white society. Such a view, argued Gates, had become rampant in scholarly circles, perpetuated by white liberals, white conservatives, and even blacks themselves, including "almost all of the N.A.A.C.P.'s desegregation briefs." Gates found Hurston more inspiring than the NAACP's argument in *Brown*, not least because she imagined well-adjusted, self-sustaining black communities that had little interaction, much less integration, with whites. Gates commended Hurston for countering the notion that "racism had reduced black people to mere ciphers, to beings who react only to an omnipresent racial oppression, whose culture is 'deprived' where different, and whose psyches are in the main 'pathological.'"[4]

Gates relied on Hurston's work to compose an entirely black theory of literary interpretation, arguably one of the highest indications that a uniquely black culture existed in the United States, a project that he would first publish the results of in 1983 under the title "The 'Blackness of Blackness': A Critique of the Sign and the Signifying Monkey." The Signifying Monkey, according to Gates, was a recurring trope in African American linguistic culture, an allusion to the indirect, or "figurative," use of language as a means of achieving instrumental ends, whether it be negotiating relationships, upstaging rivals, or subverting authority. Hurston, to Gates, was particularly adept at this, and the first black author to use signifying "as a vehicle of liberation" for black women. Hurston's novel *Their Eyes Were Watching God*, Gates argued, was the "paradigmatic signifying text," in part because its protagonist, Janie, "gains her voice, as it were, in her husband's store not only by engaging with the assembled men in the ritual of signifying (which her husband had expressly forbidden her to do) but also by openly signifying upon her husband's impotency." As Gates saw it, Hurston was not employing a "minstrel technique" as Richard Wright had once complained; she was actually furthering a nuanced linguistic practice unique to black culture in the South. Although Warren, Brooks, and Lewis had also extolled Hurston for her recovery of black culture in their anthology, Gates delved deeper into the theoretical implications of what that culture might entail, arguably presenting a comprehensive literary theory whole-cloth out of black life. Gates's study provided intellectual heft to claims by Warren and others that a complex, linguistic culture had evolved in segregated black communities in the Jim Crow South, a byproduct of the region's racial pluralism.[5]

Yet not all interpretations of that pluralism were positive. Questions of whether black culture came from Africa or from the South led to heated debates within policy and academic circles. For example, anthropologists Sidney W. Mintz and Richard Price both noted in a widely disseminated paper in 1973 that "for many years the controversy about the proper theories and methods to be used in the study of African-American culture centered on 'the Negro family.'" One prominent example of this was a report composed by Undersecretary of Labor Daniel Patrick Moynihan in 1965, which identified non-nuclear black "family structure[s]" as a "fundamental problem" facing African Americans in the United States, a problem characterized by absentee fathers, domineering mothers, and dislocated children condemned to suffer a perpetual "cycle of poverty and disadvantage." Thanks to protracted racism, agued Moynihan, black families had collapsed, men had left, and woman had assumed the dominant role in making decisions and raising children. Critical to breaking this cycle was nudging African Americans toward a more nuclear model exemplified by gainfully employed fathers, stay-at-home mothers, small numbers of children, and little outside interference from distant relatives or kin. Until this was accomplished, Moynihan maintained, African Americans were doomed to suffer a "tangle of pathology" that would prevent them from advancing materially whether they confronted actual discrimination or not.[6]

Ironically, proponents of southern pluralism disagreed. Writing for the majority in a case styled *Moore v. East Cleveland*, Lewis F. Powell, Jr., proclaimed that an ordinance banning extended families from living under the same roof was an unconstitutional violation of the 14th Amendment. As Powell explained it, many families tolerated unconventional arrangements, a simple fact of life in the South. "I confess to being strongly 'result oriented' in this case," noted Powell in a memo dated September 16, 1976. "The ordinance is an extreme example of the idiocy of the city council, if one may assume that it knew what it was doing. Grandparents, children, and grandchildren have resided together, I suppose, from the beginning of man's existence. It is a manner of family living often both necessary and beneficial." Powell could find "no way to identify purposes for this exclusion of lineal descendants from the family dwelling unit that bears any relation to legitimate government objectives." In what would become the Court's controlling opinion, Powell discounted the nuclear family as the only legitimate way to assess a valid household, noting that many in the South lived with their extended kin. Further, he found no validity to the city council's claim that barring extended families either "reduces traffic congestion" or "minimizes the burden on the schools."[7] Both obscured the real reason for the bill, which was to discourage poor blacks from living in East Cleveland. During conference, Powell noted that East Cleveland had "experienced a change in the 60's from all-white to virtually all-black."[8]

Ironically, the voters who supported the family restriction in East Cleveland were black, not white. However, the blacks who endorsed the ban were middle class, not poor. Powell's vindication of family patterns more common among the black poor than black elites coincided with a general unease among white southerners when it came to the upper echelons of black communities. Robert Penn Warren expressed a similar unease in his review of James Farmer's memoir, which impugned Martin Luther King, Jr., as an elitist, as did Warren and Brooks in their literary anthology, which celebrated Zora Neale Hurston, Negro spirituals, and the black folk. All seemed more comfortable reading black America through the lens of black poverty, perhaps because the black poor tended to best exhibit the very cultural traits that white southerners ascribed to African Americans generally. Class, in other words, undergirded their assumptions about race.

Conversely, efforts to ameliorate class inequality struck southern pluralists as threats to diversity. This explains, for example, why Powell struck down East Cleveland's ban on extended families even as he upheld the structural inequalities that had contributed to East Cleveland's white flight. That Powell could condone such flight, which he did in *Rodriguez*, *Milliken*, and *Keyes*, underscored his southern pluralist sensibility. Although blacks could not expect aggressive state efforts to achieve economic parity, they deserved respect for their diversity. Herein lay a defining aspect of southern pluralism, an endorsement of cultural difference that coincided with a concomitant rejection of state efforts to change the structural conditions that may have contributed to that difference. Such logic, in the end, animated Powell's opinion in both *Moore* and *Bakke*, helping to explain why he endorsed diversity but rejected progressive/aggressive efforts to bring about racial justice.

Alice Walker took a different approach. "There are rich people who own houses to live in and poor people who do not . . . and this is wrong," she wrote in 1975. "Literary separatism, fashionable now among blacks as it has always been among whites, is easier to practice than to change a fact like this." Recognizing that celebrations of African American identity had "always" been popular among southern whites, Walker cautioned against the type of thinking that animated Powell's opinions. To her mind, a "just society" would not include the kind of stark distinctions between rich and poor that had traditionally characterized the South, but rather would feature economic and political equality as well as diversity. "What a black Southern writer inherits as a natural right," observed Walker, "is a sense of community," not entirely unlike the sense of community that white writers felt but different in its conjunction with "an abiding love of justice." Justice, to Walker, meant racial equality in a distributive, material sense, an initiative dedicated to ameliorating poverty and expanding economic opportunity, not just praising diversity.[9]

To dramatize her point, Walker invoked a white southern writer who hailed from her hometown of Milledgeville, Georgia: Flannery O'Connor. Walker took her mother to Milledgeville in 1974, first visiting their old home, a decaying "sharefarmer shack," and then O'Connor's stately residence, Andalusia, which was "neatly kept," with "peacocks strutting about in the sun." In a piece entitled "Beyond the Peacock," Walker confessed to feeling "fury" at the pristine condition of O'Connor's home, particularly when compared to the "rotting" state of her own, reading the contrast as evidence of racial injustice generally in the South. "Her house becomes—in an instant—the symbol of my own disinheritance," recalled Walker, who recounted a childhood rent with "misery," including memories of her "shabby segregated school that was once the state prison and that had, on the second floor, the large circular print of the electric chair that had stood there." Such gross inequalities, she argued, did not just offend the sensibilities of African Americans in the South but had a larger "damaging" effect on their "psyche." Echoing the NAACP's argument in *Brown* two decades earlier, Walker lamented that "an unjust society" threatens "the soul of the sensitive person" with "deformity."[10]

However, Walker did not beat a drum for integration. She celebrated the demise of formal Jim Crow, to be sure, but harbored no particular interest in abandoning black history or identity for a chance to integrate into the white mainstream. "When I consider the enormity of the white man's crimes against humanity," wrote Walker in 1982, "I think—in perfect harmony with my sister of long ago: *Let the earth marinate in poisons. Let the bombs cover the ground like rain. For nothing short of total destruction will ever teach them anything.*" It was an apocalyptic vision, to be sure, far beyond anything James Baldwin had envisioned in *The Fire Next Time.* Not just a burning house, Walker imagined a planetary cataclysm. "If we have any true love for the stars, planets, the rest of Creation," implored Walker, "we must do everything we can to keep white men away from them," for whites had "never met any new creature without exploiting, abusing, or destroying it."[11]

By contrast, African Americans were, in Walker's eyes, an "inventive, joyous, courageous, and outrageous people, loving drama, appreciating wit, and, most of all, relishing the pleasure of each other's loquacious and *bodacious* company." Rather than contracting a sense of inferiority from the Jim Crow South, Walker demonstrated the opposite, a sense of moral and spiritual superiority—not completely unlike that expressed by James Baldwin, Ralph Ellison, Zora Neale Hurston, Richard Wright, and even Martin Luther King, Jr. To further convey the complexity and richness of the black experience in the South, Walker began work on a novel about a black family living in rural Georgia that suffers all the negative aspects of Jim Crow—poverty, lack of education, little opportunity, and so on—but still manages to prevail. Set in the 1930s, the same decade as Lee's *To Kill a Mockingbird*, the novel tells the story of a poor African American woman named Celie who endures abuse at the hands of her stepfather and her husband, only to find love with a woman, "Shug," her husband's mistress. During the course of the story, whites appear intermittently as violent and cruel caricatures, in one case killing Celie's father for being successful, then abusing Celie's daughter-in-law for refusing to work as a maid, and finally jailing

Celie's daughter-in-law for defending herself against a white assault.[12]

However, the novel's main purpose was not to excoriate whites. The book, *The Color Purple*, focused mainly on blacks, featuring characters who transcended their grim conditions and lived complex, meaningful lives. For example, Celie finds a significant relationship with Shug, despite her abuse at the hands of her husband and stepfather, completely independent of white contact. Meanwhile, Celie's sister, Nettie also finds love while serving as a missionary in Africa, free from white interaction. Both persevere in carving out their own destinies, free from the aid of white characters like Lee's Atticus Finch or Welty's Dr. Strickland.

Published in 1982, *The Color Purple* won the Pulitzer Prize in 1983 and was subsequently made into a celebrated film in 1985. One of the most significant contributions to southern literature in the 1980s, the book marked a larger sea-change in southern letters, a move away from the benign portraits of the South's dual society that had been painted by Robert Penn Warren, William Faulkner, Flannery O'Connor, Harper Lee, and Eudora Welty, to more critical examinations of racial inequality. A new generation of African American writers pioneered this move, led by Walker, Ernest J. Gaines, Gloria Naylor, Toni Morrison, and Maya Angelou, all of whom focused on the daily humiliations and abuses suffered by African Americans under Jim Crow, not their harmonious relations with white benefactors.[13]

Such new black voices eclipsed older white ones, fusing an appreciation for pluralism, in particular black culture, with an equal commitment to equality. Walker, Gaines, Morrison, and Angelou all conveyed the realities of black life in a way that both countered white southern versions of Jim Crow as a harmonious dual society and pushed for racial reform—not unlike what Richard Wright had attempted with his memoir, *Black Boy*, in 1945. Walker wrote and spoke publicly in much the same vein that Wright once had, lambasting white authors like Flannery O'Connor and calling for social change.[14]

Yet, here lurked a conundrum. Even as Walker called for an end to inequality, she feared that were blacks to actually "rise" through the ranks of southern society, so too would they "converge" with, and become like, their white peers. Referring to O'Connor's story

"Everything That Rises Must Converge," for example, Walker conceded O'Connor's point that as the South proceeded to become more "progressive," so too would it become "culturally bland, physically ravished, and where the people are concerned, well, you wouldn't be able to tell one racial group from another. Everybody would want the same things, like the same things, and everybody would be reduced to wearing, symbolically, the same green-and-purple hats." This, of course, was O'Connor's argument about civil rights, and it went to the heart of Walker's work as well. If, for example, whites were as contemptible as Walker said, and if equality would make whites and blacks indistinguishable from one another, why work for it? Why not relish in the moral and spiritual superiority of the black experience, even if that meant occupying a less materially comfortable realm?[15]

Walker did not pursue the question, perhaps because she shared Richard Wright's view that equality trumped diversity. Or, perhaps she was not completely serious about O'Connor's story in the first place; perhaps she envisioned a way for both equality and diversity to coexist. By the close of the 1980s, this appeared to be a growing sentiment. Tensions between diversity and equality, and arguments for a form of pluralism that hinged on inequality, were largely forgotten. Few critics challenged the critical assessment of Jim Crow voiced by Walker, Angelou, Morrison, and others, marking a larger consensus that southern segregation amounted to discrimination, plain and simple, not pluralism. Meanwhile, white writers fell silent. Harper Lee refused to do interviews. Eudora Welty wrote no more of civil rights or demonstrators, and Warren lost interest in black politics. Even James Jackson Kilpatrick, the notorious segregationist who had wooed Ezra Pound and placed the theory of interposition at the heart of massive resistance, recanted his old views, noting in a 1980 coffee-table book called *The American South: Four Seasons of the Land* that "until the 1950s, most of our people lived in a Southern bayou, clogged by prejudice and by tradition and moral blindness. An impenetrable mat had formed. The submerged mass had to be cut away, and we are better for having the channel cleared. Some racism remains—you never can clean out hyacinths entirely—but our public waterways are freer than they used to be."[16]

Meanwhile diversity, the concept that Lewis F. Powell, Jr., had elevated to a compelling constitutional interest in *Bakke*, found an unlikely home. As Duke law professor Paul Carrington put it, Powell's invocation of diversity became adopted as "the *nom de guerre*" of an "aggressive movement" aimed at countering American pretensions to liberal, democratic ideals, arguing instead for an indictment of the United States as "oppressive, imperialist, patriarchal, hegemonic, and in need of replacement, or at least transformation." Georgia State professor Benjamin Baez concurred, noting that Powell's invocation of diversity came to represent not just "the appreciation and celebration of difference—in culture, ethnicity, gender, race, and sexual orientation" but also "a critique of the dominance of the Western tradition in the undergraduate curriculum." At least part of this sentiment came from the very "New Left" that Powell had publicly reviled in the 1960s, including Tom Hayden, a founding member of the Students for a Democratic Society (SDS), whom Powell loathed. Hayden joined a larger movement that advocated curricular changes at American universities, in particular the incorporation of marginalized voices into the humanities curriculum, a contested debate that took its name from a Canadian policy, forged in discussions between English- and French-speaking factions in Quebec, called "multiculturalism" in the 1970s and 1980s. Multiculturalism proved a compelling slogan for educational reformers in the United States, an idea that many linked to diversity.[17]

For example, some argued for a "particularist," or separatist, version of diversity, one that traced black culture all the way back to Africa. Georgia native Molefi Kete Asante (née Arthur Lee Smith, Jr.) argued for such an approach, emphasizing black ties to Africa, its history, culture, and politics. Black educator Asa Hilliard joined, proposing a series of "African-American Baseline Essays" that located the origins of Western civilization in Africa and taught students that the ancient Greeks had stolen their foundational ideas from Egypt. Meanwhile, civil rights veteran Jesse Jackson incorporated a particularist sensibility into his politics, arguing successfully in 1988 for the redesignation of blacks as "African-Americans," reasoning that the term "Negroes" did not adequately "describe the historical location of the African-American community."[18]

Less Afrocentric proponents of multiculturalism also emerged, focusing not on places of origin so much as adaptations and contributions to American culture, including African American culture in the South. This prong best explained the work of Zora Neale Hurston, as well as that of Alice Walker and Henry Louis Gates, Jr., who argued that "pluralism sees cultures as porous, dynamic, and interactive, rather than the fixed property of particular ethnic groups." Although clear tensions arose between the extreme factions of the pluralist and separatist wings of multiculturalism, the two prongs often merged under the messy rubric of diversity. In 1987, for example, both New York and California "materially increased the time allotted to non-European cultures" in public schools. Meanwhile, at the college level, institutions like Florida State University required that undergraduates "take one liberal arts course that looks at race, gender or ethnicity within Western culture and another that focuses solely on a different, non-European culture."[19]

Conservatives recoiled at such moves, arguing that they traded academic rigor for political expediency, even as they undermined America's melting-pot ideal. The same year that Powell retired from the Supreme Court in 1987, for example, Yale professor Allan Bloom attacked multiculturalism on college campuses, arguing that it threatened to undermine the "shared goals or vision of the public good" which had once united Americans across geographic and class lines. Pulitzer Prize–winning historian Arthur M. Schlesinger, Jr., agreed, arguing that "the ethnic revolt against the melting pot" ideal had taken the form of a "denial of the idea of a common culture and a single society," spelling "serious trouble" for the country.[20]

Of course, missing from such attacks on multiculturalism was any sense of the sustained battle that white southerners had long waged against monocultural, assimilationist notions of the United States. Even though Powell did not endorse the SDS, for example, he still believed that America was a "uniquely pluralist" society and that different racial groups, including African Americans, possessed different perspectives and contributed different insights, a view that undergirded his opinion in *Bakke* and that coincided with the old Agrarian "expression of dissatisfaction with the culture, or pseudoculture that has accompanied the diffusion of industrialism," as Nashville Agrarian Donald Davidson put it in 1938. Southern intellectuals like Robert Penn Warren, Zora Neale Hurston, Richard

Wright, William Faulkner, Flannery O'Connor, Ralph Ellison, Eudora Welty, and Harper Lee all reiterated these views in the aftermath of *Brown v. Board of Education*, a point that Bloom and Schlesinger missed. The "disuniting" of America, to borrow from the title of Schlesinger's book trashing diversity, had begun long before.[21]

CHAPTER SIXTEEN

Missouri v. Jenkins

By the close of the twentieth century, southerners themselves had begun to shovel dirt on the memory of the plural South. A new generation of liberals condemned Jim Crow and reconciled diversity not with the South's dual society but with integration and *Brown*. No figure loomed more prominently in this movement than William Jefferson Clinton, who during his presidency joined diversity with the project of desegregation, working hard to distance himself from Jim Crow. Clinton, who had been governor of Arkansas, supported a variety of efforts aimed at making race an issue of national discussion, including a specially appointed race relations panel, as well as policy measures aimed at reducing racial disparities, including federally sponsored empowerment zones that provided tax incentives and grants to low-income communities, increased enforcement of fair-housing laws, and generated uniform standards to measure proficiency in reading and math in public schools. Clinton also endorsed minority scholarships as a means of "fostering racial and ethnic diversity on America's college campuses," a point that seemed to coincide with Powell's reasoning in *Bakke* but was in fact a sharp turn away from the Virginian's views. Unlike Powell, Clinton endorsed minority scholarships that allowed schools to take race into account expressly in order to "remedy past discrimination," a clear violation of *Bakke*. The Fourth Circuit Court of Appeals received a challenge to the program and sided with Powell, but Clinton paid little notice. He authorized individual schools to assess students differently based on who had suffered past discrimination and to what extent they had suffered discrimination, "without any court order or administrative finding."[1]

Clinton confessed publicly that white southerners "knew that segregation was wrong" and argued that Jim Crow had deprived whites of "the opportunity to know people, to share their feelings, to share their life experiences, to share their music, [and] their culture." Of course, southern pluralists had made the opposite argument, namely that segregation had allowed the races to develop their own cultures, but Clinton demonstrated little interest in such nostalgia. Instead, he spoke movingly about his youth in the South, including memories of segregated buses and water fountains, while warning opponents of affirmative action not to "re-segregate" America.[2]

As Clinton worked to place diversity firmly within a liberal frame of ameliorating past discrimination and achieving integration, southern conservatives took the bait, also coming to view diversity through a liberal lens—and rejecting it. Such was the position of Georgia congressman Newt Gingrich, who attacked Clinton's affirmative action plans as "reverse discrimination" and diversity itself as a code word for racial favoritism and handouts. Others, like South Carolina senator Strom Thurmond, who had once praised Jim Crow for promoting black culture, gradually began focusing on local authority, states' rights, and religious freedom—old Agrarian points now divorced from race. Mississippi senator Trent Lott did likewise, adopting much of the same interest in critiquing "modern liberalism" as the Agrarians but without a concomitant interest in promoting black culture and art. To the extent that conservatives did discuss race, it was generally to stop affirmative action and charge liberals with reverse racism in a campaign that often seemed pitted against the concept of diversity, not for it. North Carolina senator Jesse Helms became a prominent leader in this brand of politics, as did—to some extent—the federal courts. In 1998, for example, the Fifth Circuit struck down a University of Texas admissions program that allowed the consideration of race for purposes of diversity, a decision that flew in the face of Powell's opinion in *Bakke*.[3]

Only one prominent federal official seemed to carry the torch for southern pluralism, a Supreme Court justice from coastal Georgia named Clarence Thomas. Born in 1948, Thomas had risen to prominence from humble beginnings—a poor African American family from a small black township outside Savannah named Pin Point, a place not entirely unlike Eatonville, Florida. Founded by freed slaves, Pin Point formed part of an elaborate network of black communities along the Georgia and South Carolina coast, places where large numbers of African Americans owned their own farms and, according to historian J. William Harris, "had no need of regular contact with whites." Such independence was further strengthened by a "strong tradition of black community activism" and a deep distrust of white authority. During the final days of the Civil War, Union Army general William Tecumseh Sherman promised African Americans from Charleston to Jacksonville that they were entitled to the plantations that they had worked as slaves, an initiative that won widespread black support. However, President Andrew Johnson reneged on Sherman's deal following Abraham Lincoln's assassination, ordering that the land be returned to its original white owners, a betrayal that engendered deep resentment but also a sense of regional self-reliance, a belief that government—North or South—could not be trusted.[4]

Clarence Thomas inherited his region's commitment to black self-reliance. His father abandoned him when he was young, and his mother placed him in the care of his maternal grandfather, a hard-driving, independent businessman who enrolled Clarence in a private Catholic school and kept a close eye on his grandson's comings and goings, encouraging him to stay off the streets and in his room, reading. By sixteen, Thomas had discovered Richard Wright, an author that so inspired him he began committing entire passages of *Native Son* to memory, imagining himself "slipping into a similar vortex of self-destructive behavior" as Bigger Thomas. By college, however, Thomas had turned to Ralph Ellison's *Invisible Man*, a book that inspired him to forge his own path, merging the discipline he learned from his grandfather, the Catholic teachings he had absorbed at school, and a commitment to black self-reliance that would guide his professional career, leading him from Pin Point to Holy Cross College in Worcester, Massachusetts, and finally to Yale Law School.[5]

After Thomas did stints at the Equal Employment Opportunity Commission and the D.C. Circuit Court of Appeals, President George Herbert Walker Bush nominated him to the Supreme Court in 1991, prompting a rocky confirmation after a former female colleague accused Thomas of sexual harassment. "After a lifetime of struggle and achievement," Thomas recalled later, "I'd been thrust back into Bigger Thomas's world, a dark, cramped hell devoid of hope." That the allegations against him were sexual in nature reminded Thomas of another literary character as well, Tom Robinson. "I knew exactly what Atticus Finch was talking about," confessed Thomas. "Nothing I could say, however eloquent or sincere, was capable of overcoming the evil assumptions in which my accusers had put their trust."[6]

Unlike his literary precursors, however, Thomas survived. He squeaked through his confirmation hearings and began, almost immediately, to express southern pluralist views on the Court. In a 1992 case styled *United States v. Fordice*, for example, he spoke out strongly in favor of historically black colleges and universities (HBCs), an issue that arose when the United States joined a suit against Mississippi for maintaining three predominantly black colleges that boasted lower entrance requirements but offered many of the same courses as the state's flagship universities, all of which boasted higher entrance requirements that, according to the plaintiffs, kept minorities out. A majority on the Court held that the state's black colleges were suspect and risked closure as vestiges of Jim Crow. Thomas, however, argued that black colleges and universities "exercised leadership in developing educational opportunities for young blacks" and collectively symbolized "the highest attainments of black culture," a nod to the role that segregated institutions had played in developing black identity. Thomas further held that states should be encouraged to "operate a diverse assortment of institutions—including historically black institutions," on the grounds that they promoted "diversity" in higher education generally, a position that resonated powerfully with Powell's argument that diversity could be served not simply by integrating classrooms but also by segregating them, thereby creating a disaggregated landscape that did not reflect a single approach to education but rather many approaches. In such a system, states could not bar students from entry to schools based on their race—per *Brown*—but could fund institutions that were majority black, not least because such institutions had traditionally benefited black students, like Warren's briar patch. "It would be ironic, to say the least," concluded Thomas, "if the institutions that sustained blacks during segregation were themselves destroyed in an effort to combat its vestiges."[7]

Thomas conveyed a similar sentiment in a 1995 case brought by the state of Missouri against a lower court order demanding the construction of magnet schools to attract suburban white students into black inner city schools in Kansas City. *Missouri v. Jenkins* resulted in a majority holding that the district court had exceeded its constitutional bounds, a point with which Thomas agreed. "It never ceases to amaze me," he declared in a concurring opinion, "that the courts are so willing to assume that anything that is predominantly black must be inferior," a jab at the district court's emphasis on attracting white students rather than addressing the educational needs of the black students already in the schools. The district's emphasis on luring white students back into the school district struck Thomas as racist, a move rooted in the false presumption that blacks suffered "unspecified psychological harm" simply because they did not rub shoulders with whites, a position that had undergirded the Supreme Court's argument in *Brown v. Board of Education* but with which black intellectuals like Zora Neale Hurston and Ralph Ellison had long taken issue. To them, and to Thomas, such notions rested on the false "assumption of black inferiority." Echoing Hurston's 1955 letter to the *Orlando Sentinel* criticizing *Brown*, Thomas maintained that it was simply not the case that "blacks cannot succeed without the benefit of the company of whites," even though this is what the district court had in fact held. Indignant, Thomas applied the same reasoning to primary and secondary schools that he had to HBCs, suggesting that "despite their origins in the 'shameful history of state-enforced segregation,' these institutions can be 'both a source of pride to blacks who have attended them and a source of hope to black families who want the benefits of . . . learning for their children.'"[8]

Precisely because of his faith in black schools, Thomas went even farther than Powell in endorsing racial pluralism, to the point of deriding Powell's arguments about diversity in *Bakke*. As Thomas saw it, Powell's invocation of diversity was little more than a ploy to benefit white students at the expense of blacks. Little pedagogical benefit would inure to black students, argued Thomas, who were accepted into majority white schools for "diversity" purposes rather than grades, for they would find themselves behind academically yet also on display so that white students and white institutions could feel better about themselves. Better, argued Thomas, to send black students to HBCs, where they would be free from white micro-aggressions, free from having to teach white students about black history, and statistically more likely to enjoy "higher academic achievement."[9]

Thomas made these points clear in a 2003 case styled *Grutter v. Bollinger*, a challenge to the admissions policy at the University of Michigan Law School, which allowed administrators to take race into account when admitting students with lower than average test scores. Tailored to fit Powell's opinion in *Bakke*, the policy allowed for the consideration of race as one of several "soft" variables that might be noted in deciding to admit a student with lower scores for the express purpose of achieving "that diversity which has the potential to enrich everyone's education." A white applicant named Barbara Grutter challenged the policy, leading the Court to reassess the role of racial preferences in university admissions. Writing for the majority, Justice Sandra Day O'Connor upheld Powell's designation of diversity as a compelling state interest but misinterpreted his reasoning in three key ways: first, by reading his invocation of diversity as a ruse for affirmative action; then by taking diversity to be important primarily as a means of enhancing academic quality; and finally, by making the tenuous claim that diverse law school classes contributed to a more diverse national leadership and therefore bolstered the compelling interest of national security.[10]

None comported with Powell's view of diversity as a defense to centralized rule, an omission that actually weakened the opinion. For example, Justice O'Connor argued that the invocation of diversity in university admissions should not be considered a permanent measure but rather a stopgap solution to the larger problem of racial inequality. "The requirement that all race-conscious admissions programs have a termination point," she reasoned, "'assure[s] all citizens that the deviation from the norm of equal treatment of all racial and ethnic groups is a temporary matter, a measure taken in the service of the goal of equality itself." This was a complete misreading of Powell, who did not link diversity to equality and, for precisely that reason, did not believe that diversity should be considered a "temporary matter." As Powell saw it, diversity was a permanent matter because it helped preserve liberty. Racial equality, to his mind, had already been achieved.[11]

To establish her second point, that diversity contributed to educational quality, O'Connor deferred to the University of Michigan, which claimed that diversity was "essential to its educational mission" because it promoted "cross-racial understanding," broke down "racial stereotypes," and "enable[d] [students] to better understand persons of different races." While this may well have been true, O'Connor confused diversity's pedagogical utility with its trans-institutional value. For example, she failed to mention the manner in which Powell tied diversity to a fear of "orthodoxy," and in so doing failed to recognize that the freedom to assemble interracial classes was only one way that institutions might decide to pursue diversity. Some might aim for classrooms that were homogenous—all Catholic, all Protestant, all female, and so on. As Powell made clear, same-sex schools contributed to diversity because they provided students with more options for college, not because they boasted diverse classrooms or promoted a "robust exchange of ideas." On the contrary, their very homogeneity guaranteed uniform ideas and/or identities, a point that went to the heart of Powell's belief in the value of institutional pluralism, or diversity across institutions rather than just within them. His was a case for institutional freedom, one that might incorporate diverse classrooms to be sure, but not one that recognized diverse classrooms as the only model for achieving legitimate pedagogical goals.[12]

O'Connor's third tenet was the flimsiest. To establish that diversity promoted national security by producing leaders who understood different perspectives, O'Connor discounted Powell's argument that some institutions might rightfully decide not to promote diversity and still produce excellent leaders. This was a point that Powell had made in 1967 by praising private schools for producing leaders precisely because they remained free from government indoctrination, forming the last "major remaining barrier to maximum integration" or state-imposed orthodoxy in the United States. This was also the case for the so-called Seven Sisters, the New England women's colleges that had graduated some of the most prominent female leaders in American business and politics.[13]

O'Connor's narrow reading of *Bakke* hewed closely to the multicultural notion of diversity as a vehicle for achieving racial equality, and in so doing weakened the concept. An Arizona native, she penned an opinion that placed diversity in a posture that aligned more with the racial justice/multicultural frame than Powell's southern-inflected opinion had been. For example, O'Connor put a time limit on diversity's viability, assuming that it would no longer be needed in twenty-five years, because by then African Americans would have presumably achieved equality. By missing the link between diversity and the prevention of centralized government power, however, she left out a justification for the concept that, although rooted in the history of the Jim Crow South, could have provided a permanent place for the principle. Certainly, it would not have included a twenty-five-year limit. Instead, she assumed that blacks would rise (provided they were given a helping hand), and America would converge.[14]

Thomas found this insulting. As he saw it, Michigan's plan patronized African Americans and threatened black institutions. Citing Frederick Douglass, Thomas rejected the majority opinion and argued that "blacks can achieve in every avenue of American life without the meddling of university administrators." Whether they went to Michigan or not, he argued, black students faced the same chances at future success, and may even have done better at black institutions. For example, Thomas cited "growing evidence" that racial "heterogeneity actually impairs learning among black students," and that many African American students "experience superior cognitive development at Historically Black Colleges." This raised a point similar to the one that Thomas had made in *Fordice*, namely that HBCs warranted public support and suffered when black students were siphoned away to majority white flagship schools.[15]

Thomas's defense of HBCs proved an even stronger endorsement of southern pluralism than Powell's nod to diversity in *Bakke*. Certainly, diverse classrooms could enhance the educational experience in some contexts, but this was not always the case, as Powell himself had argued in the context of same-sex schools, private schools, and parochial schools. Thomas extended this analysis to HBCs, identifying two in particular: Morehouse College in Atlanta, "one of the most distinguished HBCs in the Nation," boasting only .1 percent white students, and Mississippi Valley State, which boasted only 1.1 percent white students in its 2001 entering freshman class. Neither, argued Thomas, suffered from lack of a "critical mass" of white students. In fact, they probably benefited from it.[16]

Unable to sway a majority on the Court, Thomas remained a dissenting voice. However, his arguments in *Grutter*, like his arguments in *Jenkins* and *Fordice*, resonated strongly with arguments that southern intellectuals had made since the early days of the twentieth century. Certainly, white intellectuals had made these arguments, but African Americans did as well. Thomas was personally influenced by Ellison and Wright, but his views could have come from Zora Neale Hurston too. Her letter to the *Orlando Sentinel* decrying *Brown* in 1955 foreshadowed many of the same arguments that Thomas made in 2003.

Conclusion

If most Americans were asked to identify a legacy of Jim Crow, they would probably cite persistent racial inequality, overpolicing, or mass incarceration. However, Jim Crow also gave us diversity. Out of many, it made two: black and white. By segregating the races in the American South, Jim Crow created a dual society, one with parallel institutions, parallel traditions, and some would even say parallel cultures. The legacy of this society is complex but remains with us today, informing the way that we view race in the United States, and perhaps the United States itself.

For example, even though we now live in a nation of many races and many peoples, the legal frame through which we assess diversity remains rooted firmly in the Jim Crow South. The architect of this frame was a Supreme Court justice from Richmond, Virginia, named Lewis F. Powell, Jr., who decried Reconstruction and expressly prohibited reparations for either slavery or Jim Crow, holding instead that diversity could only be invoked for pedagogical reasons, because African Americans brought a unique perspective to the classroom. This notion, which the Court has misinterpreted as a nod to racial equality that will no longer be necessary in twenty-five years, and is therefore doomed to die, was tied to a complex set of southern ideas, a sense that defending segregation was also about defending pluralism, and that diversity was not about achieving equality so much as defending separate institutional spheres. This form of diversity, which legal scholar Heather Gerken has termed "second-order diversity," is generally not associated with racial segregation, but for Powell and southerners like him, the two were linked. Segregated institutions prevented the mass production of ideas, as Powell liked to say, and segregated institutions created zones of freedom, or a "briar patch," as Robert Penn Warren put it in 1929.[1]

Such concerns might sound like Confederate claptrap to us, but they remain oddly salient today. First, Powell's definition of diversity may provide us with a more enduring vision than the one currently held by the Supreme Court. Two, the visions of diversity articulated in this book might provide us with a new lens through which to understand race generally in the United States." As late as 2008, for example, many dreamed of a "postracial" America, a land that appeared within reach as a young black senator from Illinois ran for president and won. The son of a white mother from Kansas and a black father from Kenya, Barack Obama boasted little connection to the Jim Crow South, gained widespread support from white voters, and avoided speaking in "race-specific terms about the plight of the African American community," preferring instead to emphasize that which was "universal" about the black experience in the United States.[2]

Veterans of the civil rights movement like Jesse Jackson questioned Obama's credentials, wondering whether he was "black enough" to truly represent African Americans, while others like Newark, New Jersey, mayor Cory Booker endorsed Obama, declaring that he had given African Americans the "courage to be themselves," to defy stereotypes and embrace aspects of their personalities that were not traditionally associated with black culture or identity. Philadelphia mayor Michael Nutter became so convinced that America had entered a new, postracial phase that he refused to endorse Obama at all, siding instead with Hillary Clinton based on her policies, not her color, and declaring that anyone who criticized him for doing so was "presumptuous."[3]

However, signs that America had not transcended race emerged quietly in 2010, when a legal scholar named Michelle Alexander published a book calling attention to the high incarceration rate of African Americans in the United States, suggesting that "the American penal system" had become a "system of racialized social control" so all-encompassing it warranted consideration as a "new" Jim

Crow. Evidence that this might be the case exploded in 2013, when a majority-white jury acquitted a neighborhood watch volunteer named George Zimmerman for killing Trayvon Martin, an unarmed black teenager in Sanford, Florida. Three Martin supporters—Alicia Garza, Patrisse Cullors, and Opal Tometi—came up with the slogan #blacklivesmatter to focus attention on what they perceived to be a discounting of black life in America, particularly at the hands of the courts. One year later, Twitter posts featuring the #blacklivesmatter hashtag surged when news broke of an officer-involved shooting in Ferguson, Missouri. The victim, Michael Brown, proved to be an unarmed African American teenager, like Trayvon Martin.[4]

By 2016, the house burned again. Garza, Cullors, and Tometi's Black Lives Matter organization joined a larger coalition of groups christened The Movement for Black Lives, which indicted America for tolerating "constant exploitation and perpetual oppression," issuing a laundry list of policy recommendations aimed at addressing persistent racial inequality in the United States. Ironically, not one of the prescriptions mentioned integration. Instead, the platform called for reinvestment in black businesses, a recommitment to black institutions, and reparations, an agenda that substituted the assimilationist vision of *Brown* for an eerily southern emphasis on equalizing racial spheres, essentially compensating African Americans for past harm in a way that put them on the same economic plane, but not necessarily in the same classroom, as whites.[5]

If mass incarceration was a legacy of Jim Crow, so was this: a commitment to independent spheres capable of fostering an independent black critique of white America. Not only did Black Lives Matter endorse such a stand but so too did conservative Supreme Court justice Clarence Thomas, whose impassioned defense of historically black colleges in *Grutter v. Bollinger* indicated that southern pluralism may—at the end of the day—have been bipartisan, a perspective forged in the South that fostered diversity and fueled dissent, and for that very reason holds out hope for the future. After all, most experts agree that *Brown v. Board of Education* has run its course—perhaps for the best. Despite its good intentions, the decision rested on the unsupportable assumption that black history, black traditions, and black institutions were inferior and should be destroyed, erased in favor of assimilating blacks into mainstream white America. Black intellectuals, as this book shows, objected. They also challenged the Court's holding that racial segregation had instilled a feeling of inferiority in African Americans. It had not. As Zora Neale Hurston, Ralph Ellison, Richard Wright, and James Baldwin agreed, segregation had convinced African Americans that whites were inferior, not biologically but morally—racist, violent, and childlike in their claims to American innocence; warped by their obsession with racial status; and in need of guidance. Black leaders in the civil rights movement provided that guidance, as did black writers, who worked not simply to dismantle de jure segregation and attain racial parity but to awaken whites to their history of oppression and abuse while at the same time positioning themselves—blacks—as bearers of the nation's truth, moral arbiters of the nation's past, and rightful architects of its future.

Arguably no figure connected the dots between these two periods more successfully than Ta-Nehisi Coates, a Baltimore native and staff writer for *The Atlantic*, who met with Obama in 2013 and became disenchanted with the president's optimistic endorsement of American progress. Coates looked back to James Baldwin and Richard Wright for inspiration, drawing a title from a Wright poem and the idea of writing a public letter to a child from Baldwin, resulting in *Between the World and Me*, a scathing critique of the "dream" that Martin Luther King, Jr., once espoused of an integrated America. This "dream," lamented Coates, was an illusion, an artifice that "rests on our backs," its "bedding made from our bodies," a testament to the "heritage" of racial violence in the United States. By contrast, Coates praised black institutions, "scattered like forts in the great wilderness of the Old Confederacy," and also the black perspective, "a view of the American galaxy taken from a dark and essential planet." He concluded with a tribute to the black experience that would have made Zora Neale Hurston or Ralph Ellison proud. "We have made something down here," Coates announced. "We have taken the one-drop rules of Dreamers and flipped them. They made us into a race. We made ourselves into a people."[6]

Although some complained that Coates exaggerated black suffering and ignored clear gains made in the United States toward racial equality, his arguments evoked many of the same debates that southern writers conducted in the 1950s and 1960s, a conversation over what Ralph Ellison termed "the nature of reality." For some, that reality was a critique of the white South. For others, it was a critique of America generally: its emphasis on materialism, its focus on status-seeking, its single-minded endorsement of free-market economics and technology. To counter, southerners—white and black—endorsed authenticity, creative self-expression, spiritual communion, and a close tie to the land. They viewed America as a "burning house," a point worth recovering today, both for the legal legacy they left behind—the endorsements of diversity and pluralism in constitutional law—and for the intellectual legacy: the idea that a house divided might stand after all, accommodating rooms for dissent, maybe even fires of unrest, a beacon on a hill, a burning bush.[7]

Out of the American South, in other words, came a particular type of disunion, a dialectical approach to organizing society that was dual, if unequal, and therefore by its very nature conducive to heterogeneity, to placing limits on assimilation, centralization, and uniformity. Southern intellectuals, white and black, disputed claims about America's history, expressed anger at America's triumphant national myth, and shared a bizarre tendency to look to the rural South for examples of counter-realities and counter-values that might inspire a new national vision—whether rooted in agrarian communities, historically black institutions, or racially specific cultural practices like folklore and music, a culturally rich cacophony to which writers, precisely because they were also cultural producers, were specially qualified to speak. Their sensibility provides us with a unique window into the racial politics of their time, and maybe also ours, including an entirely new frame for viewing the South's role in shaping modern America.

As statues of Confederate generals fall across Dixie, perhaps new, more nuanced ways of remembering the South need to emerge: monuments not to the monolithic face of white supremacy but to the dissident voices who questioned that supremacy, who detailed white shortcomings and hailed black achievements, who embraced difference and raised rebel voices to the rise of a triumphalist American state. Jim Crow set fire to America, and the flames still burn.

Notes

Introduction

1. James Baldwin, "Letter from a Region in My Mind," *New Yorker*, Nov. 17, 1962, reprinted as "Down at the Cross: Letter from a Region in My Mind," in James Baldwin, *The Fire Next Time* (1963; New York: Vintage, 1993), 22, 23, 42, 93, 96.
2. Richard Kluger, *Simple Justice: The History of Brown v. Board of Education and Black America's Struggle for Equality* (New York: Vintage, 1977), 474; *Brown et al. v. Board of Education, Shawnee County, Kan., et al.*, 347 U.S. 483, 494, n. 11, citing Gunnar Myrdal, *An American Dilemma* (New York: Harper and Brothers, 1944).
3. Cleanth Brooks, *William Faulkner: The Yoknapatawpha Country* (New Haven, Conn.: Yale University Press, 1963), 439; Robert Penn Warren and James Baldwin, interview, tape 1, April 27, 1964, Robert Penn Warren Center for the Humanities, Vanderbilt University, Nashville, who speaks.library.vanderbilt.edu/interviews. Warren condensed the interview in his book *Who Speaks for the Negro?* (New York: Vintage, 1965), 284. For Warren's view of *Brown* as a threat to diversity, see *Talking with Robert Penn Warren*, ed. Floyd C. Watkins et al. (Athens: University of Georgia Press, 1990), 47.
4. Although Warren and Ellison were both born in border states, Kentucky and Missouri respectively, and Baldwin was born in New York, all three boasted family histories rooted firmly in the American South. Baldwin's mother and stepfather (he did not know his biological father) were both from the South, as were Warren's and Ellison's families.
5. Grace Elizabeth Hale argues in *Making Whiteness: The Culture of Segregation in the South, 1890–1940* (New York: Pantheon, 1998), that the culture of Jim Crow was one that enforced white supremacy in almost every aspect of southern life, including commercial life, a point confirmed by Stephen A. Berrey, who argues in *The Jim Crow Routine: Everyday Perfor-*

mances of Race, Civil Rights, and Segregation in Mississippi (Chapel Hill: University of North Carolina Press, 2015), that southern whites demanded elaborate shows of deference on sidewalks, in stores, and in other public places where the races encountered one another. Both are right but miss the extent to which white supremacy also coincided with a distinctly southern view of diversity, or what Robert Penn Warren called "pluralism." This faith in pluralism was aspirational but also unequal, and it undergirded Jim Crow. Most historians discount adherents to this view as quixotic, if not duplicitous, focusing instead on whites who demeaned, denigrated, and terrorized African Americans. See, e.g., Sarah Haley, *No Mercy Here: Gender, Punishment, and the Making of Jim Crow Modernity* (Chapel Hill: University of North Carolina Press, 2016); Danielle McGuire, *At the Dark End of the Street: Black Women, Rape, and Resistance: A New History of the Civil Rights Movement, from Rosa Parks to the Rise of Black Power* (New York: Knopf, 2010); Crystal Feimster, *Southern Horrors: Women and the Politics of Rape and Lynching* (Cambridge, Mass.: Harvard University Press, 2009); Glenda Elizabeth Gilmore, *Defying Dixie: The Radical Roots of Civil Rights, 1919–1950* (New York: Norton, 2008); Jane Dailey, *Before Jim Crow: The Politics of Race in Postemancipation Virginia* (Chapel Hill: University of North Carolina Press, 2000); Jane Dailey et al., eds., *Jumpin' Jim Crow: Southern Politics from Civil War to Civil Rights* (Princeton, N.J.: Princeton University Press, 2000); Leon F. Litwack, *Trouble in Mind: Black Southerners in the Age of Jim Crow* (New York: Knopf, 1998); Glenda Elizabeth Gilmore, *Gender and Jim Crow: Women and the Politics of White Supremacy in North Carolina, 1896–1920* (Chapel Hill: University of North Carolina Press, 1996); Neil R. McMillen, *Dark Journey: Black Mississippians in the Age of Jim Crow* (Champaign: University of Illinois Press, 1989); Joel Williamson, *The Crucible of Race: Black/White Relations in the American South Since Emancipation* (New York: Oxford University Press, 1986); and C. Vann Woodward, *The Strange Career of Jim Crow*, 3rd ed. (1955; New York: Oxford University Press, 1974). Although correct that violence and repression were hallmarks of Jim Crow, these works downplay the aspirational case for Jim Crow that was commonly made by southern intellectuals, in particular writers. Arguably the historian who has come closest to capturing the aspirational thinking of southern elites is David L. Chappell, who discusses efforts by educated white southerners to articulate reasonable, enlightened defenses of Jim Crow. However, Chappell focuses mainly on constitutional arguments, not cultural ones. As he puts it, segregationists found more hope in law than in culture for culture quickly became dominated by the "prophetic radicalism" of black leaders like Martin Luther King, Jr. David L. Chappell, *A Stone of Hope: Prophetic Religion and the Death of Jim Crow* (Chapel Hill: University of North Carolina Press, 2004), 47, 165–71. While King was certainly successful at framing black politics in biblical terms, another vector to the cultural debate emerged in the guise of pluralism, an argument that would culminate in the canonization of diversity as a constitutional principle in *Regents v. Bakke* in 1978. At the root of this debate was a particular notion of southern identity, rooted not in the idea of integration but pluralism, an idea that had emerged in the South long before *Brown*. This challenges James C. Cobb's argument that black allegiance to southern identity emerged only in the post–civil rights era, a point he makes in *The Brown Decision: Jim Crow and Southern Identity* (Athens: University of Georgia Press, 2005), 63.

Two scholars that discuss southern intellectuals and writers explicitly are Jonathan W. Gray and Carol Polsgrove, both of whom mention many of the same characters that appear in my book. See Jonathan W. Gray, *Civil Rights in the White Literary Imagination: Innocence by Association* (Jackson: University Press of Mississippi, 2013), and Carol Polsgrove, *Divided Minds: Intellectuals and the Civil Rights Movement* (New York: Norton, 2001). However, Polsgrove and Gray contend not that southern intellectuals aimed to subvert the civil rights movement, so much as that they suffered from a lack of courage and resolve when it came to standing up for racial equality, which all thoughtful, cosmopolitan individuals must naturally have presumed to be right. Missing from this argument is sufficient awareness that southern intellectuals did not, as a group, necessarily agree with the civil rights movement nor with the goals of integration set forth in *Brown*. My book argues that many southern intellectuals lobbied instead for a racial politics that focused on preserving, even respecting pluralism. Perhaps the literary scholar who has come the closest to capturing this sentiment is Michael Kreyling, who traces the legacy of Agrarianism in southern letters through the civil rights era. See Michael Kreyling, *The South That Wasn't There: Postsouthern Memory and History* (Baton Rouge: Louisiana State University Press, 2010), and *Inventing Southern Literature* (Jackson: University Press of Mississippi, 1998). Otherwise, literary scholars tend to side with Polsgrove and Gray, finding southern writers lacking in conviction, inhibited, or quietly siding with the movement by introducing subtle, racially progressive themes into their works. See, for example, Richard H. King, *A Southern Renaissance: The Cultural Awakening of the American South, 1930–1955* (New York: Oxford University Press, 1980); James A. Grimshaw, *Understanding Robert Penn Warren* (Columbia: University of South Carolina Press, 2001); Hugh M. Ruppersburg, *Robert Penn Warren and the American Imagination* (Athens: University of Georgia Press, 1990); John Burt, *Robert Penn Warren and American Idealism* (New Haven, Conn.: Yale University Press, 1988); Harriet Pollack, ed., *Eudora Welty, Whiteness, and Race* (Athens: University of Georgia Press, 2013); Suzanne Marrs, *One Writer's Imagination: The Fiction of Eudora Welty* (Baton Rouge: Louisiana State University Press, 2002); and Harriet Pollack and Suzanne Marrs, eds., *Eudora Welty and*

Politics: Did the Writer Crusade? (Baton Rouge: Louisiana State University Press, 2001).

6. For early justifications of Jim Crow as pluralism, see Robert Penn Warren, "The Briar Patch," in John Crow Ransom et al., *I'll Take My Stand: The South and the Agrarian Tradition by Twelve Southerners* (1930; New York: Harper and Row, 1962), 246–59; Donald Davidson, *The Attack on Leviathan: Regionalism and Nationalism in the United States* (1938; Gloucester, Mass.: Peter Smith, 1962). For works that canvas segregationist thought generally, see I. A. Newby, ed., *The Development of Segregationist Thought* (Homewood, Ill.: Dorsey Press, 1968), and I. A. Newby, *Jim Crow's Defense: Anti-Negro Thought in America, 1900–1930* (Baton Rouge: Louisiana State University Press, 1965). For interpretations of Jim Crow that discounted white defenses of the system as a mutually acceptable arrangement which promoted racial harmony, see Woodward, *Strange Career;* Williamson, *The Crucible of Race;* McMillen, *Dark Journey;* Gilmore, *Gender and Jim Crow;* Litwack, *Trouble in Mind;* Dailey, *Before Jim Crow;* Dailey et al., eds., *Jumpin' Jim Crow;* Gilmore, *Defying Dixie;* and Ward, *Defending White Democracy.*

   This discourse dovetailed with older traditions in southern thought, as captured by Eugene D. Genovese in, for example, *The Southern Front: History and Politics in the Cultural War* (Columbia: University of Missouri Press, 1995); *The Southern Tradition: The Achievement and Limitations of an American Conservatism* (Cambridge, Mass.: Harvard University Press, 1994); and Charles Eagles, ed., *Is There a Southern Political Tradition?* (Jackson: University Press of Mississippi, 1996). For more on southern conservatism and resistance to Jim Crow, see Richard H. King, "The Struggle Against Equality: Conservative Intellectuals in the Civil Rights Era, 1954–1975," in *The Role of Ideas in the Civil Rights South*, ed. Ted Ownby and Anthony Badger (Jackson: University Press of Mississippi, 2002), 113–36. The argument that Jim Crow was pluralist also coincides, to some extent, with the claims of historians who maintain that Jim Crow was a moderate, even progressive compromise that garnered some level of biracial support, a point made by Howard N. Rabinowitz, Michael McGerr, and John W. Cell. See, for example, Howard N. Rabinowitz, "More Than the Woodward Thesis: Assessing the Strange Career of Jim Crow," *Journal of American History* 75 (1988): 842–56; Howard N. Rabinowitz, "From Exclusion to Segregation: Southern Race Relations, 1865–1890," in *Race, Ethnicity and Urbanization*, ed. Howard N. Rabinowitz (Columbia: University of Missouri Press, 1994), 137–66; Howard N. Rabinowitz, *Race Relations in the Urban South, 1865–1890* (New York: Oxford University Press, 1978); John W. Cell, *The Highest Stage of White Supremacy: The Origins of Segregation in South Africa and the American South* (New York: Cambridge University Press, 1982); and Michael Mc-

Gerr, *A Fierce Discontent: The Rise and Fall of the Progressive Movement in America, 1870–1920* (New York: Free Press, 2003).

7. Kluger, *Simple Justice*, 474; *Brown et al. v. Board of Education*, 494, n. 11.

8. Zora Neale Hurston to Editor, *Orlando Sentinel*, Aug. 11, 1955, reprinted in *Zora Neale Hurston: A Life in Letters*, ed. Carla Kaplan (New York: Doubleday, 2002), 738–39.

9. Ralph Ellison, "An American Dilemma: A Review" (1944), reprinted in *Shadow and Act* (1964; New York: Vintage, 1995), 316.

10. Ta-Nehisi Coates, *Between the World and Me* (New York: Spiegel and Grau, 2015), 103, 106, 107, 12. Mark Brilliant locates the origins of diversity in California—in part due to the Supreme Court's opinion in *Regents v. Bakke* in 1978—but misses the fact that even though Justice Powell's opinion in *Bakke* focused on UC Davis, Powell himself drew inspiration from southern sources. See Mark Brilliant, *The Color of America Has Changed: How Racial Diversity Shaped Civil Rights Reform in California, 1941–1978* (New York: Oxford University Press, 2010). A similar problem emerges in Matthew Frye Jacobson's reading of *Bakke* in *Roots Too: White Ethnic Revival in Post-Civil Rights America* (Cambridge, Mass.: Harvard University Press, 2006), which describes a surge of interest in white ethnicity in the North following the civil rights movement but fails to account for an earlier interest in white ethnicity, and pluralism, in the Jim Crow South. Arguably the best exponent of the northern variant of diversity that animated *Brown* is Daryl Michael Scott, who argues that proponents of integration believed only "a strong state dedicated to pluralism" could "rid the society of authoritarian personalities along with hate and prejudice." Daryl Michael Scott, "Postwar Pluralism, *Brown*, and Multicultural Education," *Journal of American History* 91 (June 2004): 74. Southerners rejected this view, adopting the opposite position that an expansive "power state," as Robert Penn Warren termed it, actually threatened individual identity and cultural particularity, risking instead a homogenized mass society. Robert Penn Warren, *Segregation: The Inner Conflict* (New York: Random House, 1956), 31. Of course, this anticipated literary scholar Walter Benn Michaels's argument that the invocation of culture as a way of preserving identity can actually serve to mask racism, something that became particularly problematic in the post-*Brown* South as white southerners began to jettison overtly racialist language for references to cultural preservation as part of their larger struggle against the Supreme Court. This book maintains—with Walter Benn Michaels—that a system can be both racially repressive and also racially diverse; indeed, repression can itself, at times, engender diversity, which is precisely what happened under Jim Crow. Walter Benn Michaels, *Our America: Nativism, Modernism, and Pluralism* (Durham, N.C.: Duke University Press, 1995), 13.

11. See *Regents of the University of California v. Bakke*, 438 U.S. 265 (1978). Most scholars misread *Bakke* as a compromise to save civil rights. See, e.g., John C. Jeffries, Jr., *Justice Lewis F. Powell, Jr.* (New York: Charles Scribner's Sons, 1994), 469–70, and Joel Dreyfuss and Charles Lawrence III, *The Bakke Case: The Politics of Inequality* (New York: Harcourt Brace Jovanovich, 1979), 211. Others, however, have noted *Bakke*'s adverse implications for racial justice. For example, legal scholar Richard Thompson Ford argues that Powell stressed the "cultural identity of racial minority groups . . . at the expense of the history of racism," a move that was harmful precisely because it encouraged institutions and minority groups to "emphasize cultural difference," essentially requiring that universities "incorporate a substantive theory of racial difference into their admission processes" and ultimately creating a situation where minority students could only "justify their presence in the universities that had admitted or might admit them" by stressing "their own distinctiveness." Richard Thompson Ford, *Racial Culture: A Critique* (Princeton, N.J.: Princeton University Press, 2005), 45–46. *Bakke*'s declaration that race could not be considered for the purpose of addressing past harm also gave it a southern cast. It did not have to be so—it is not the case for gender—yet it coincided with a larger, southern tendency not to see discrimination against African Americans as particularly severe, and certainly no different from discrimination suffered by other groups, including southern whites during the Civil War. This means—as a practical matter—that the manner in which Powell invoked diversity precluded the possibility that state or federal legislatures will ever be able to enact programs aimed expressly at helping African Americans to gain compensation for past or present harm, a point that proponents of reparations like Ta-Nehisi Coates tend to miss. Ta-Nehisi Coates, "The Case for Reparations," *The Atlantic*, June 2014), www.theatlantic.com/magazine/archive/2014/06/the-case-for-reparations/361631/. It would have been better, argues Ford, if Powell had acknowledged that "racial minorities are likely to have suffered from a distinctive type of discrimination that often will affect detrimentally their grades." Pursuant to such a rationale, diversity could be restored to its original place in the larger project of affirmative action, of helping African Americans overcome past discrimination. "It's not too late," argues Ford. "We should refine the 'diversity' rationale for university affirmative action" and fight against "*Bakke's* rejection of the societal discrimination rationale." As Ford sees it, the "days" of the diversity rationale are "numbered" anyway, particularly after the Supreme Court held in *Grutter v. Bollinger* in 2003 that "we expect that 25 years from now, the use of racial preferences will no longer be necessary." Ford, *Racial Culture*, 52, 57.

12. James T. Patterson, *Brown v. Board of Education: A Civil Rights Milestone and Its Troubled Legacy* (New York: Oxford University Press, 2002);

Charles J. Ogletree, Jr., *All Deliberate Speed: Reflections on the First Half-Century of Brown v. Board of Education* (New York: Norton, 2005); Charles T. Clotfelter, *After Brown: The Rise and Retreat of School Desegregation* (Princeton, N.J.: Princeton University Press, 2004).

13. Robert Penn Warren, *Segregation: The Inner Conflict* (New York: Random House, 1956).

Chapter One. The Briar Patch

1. Thomas J. Schaeper and Kathleen Schaeper, *Rhodes Scholars, Oxford, and the Creation of an American Elite* (New York: Berghahn Books, 2010), 82–84.
2. For Warren's travels during his time at Oxford, see ibid., 107.
3. Ibid., 106. For Warren's take on his time at Oxford, see ibid., 106–8. See also Joseph Blotner, *Robert Penn Warren: A Biography* (New York: Random House, 1997), 91–92.
4. John Crow Ransom et al., *I'll Take My Stand: The South and the Agrarian Tradition by Twelve Southerners* (1930; New York: Harper and Brothers, 1962), vii, xxiii–xiv; Donald Davidson, "A Mirror for Artists," in ibid., 55; Donald Davidson, "Some Day, in Old Charleston," in *Still Rebels, Still Yankees and Other Essays* (Baton Rouge: Louisiana State University Press, 1957), 223.
5. Robert Penn Warren to Allen Tate, May 19, 1930, in *Selected Letters of Robert Penn Warren*, vol. 1, *The Apprentice Years*, ed. William Bedford Clark (Baton Rouge: Louisiana State University Press, 2000), 185; Joel Chandler Harris, "How Mr. Rabbit Was Too Sharp for Mr. Fox," in *Uncle Remus: His Songs and Sayings* (New York: D. Appleton, 1881), 29–31.
6. Robert Penn Warren, "The Briar Patch," in Ransom et al., *I'll Take My Stand*, 251, 256–57.
7. Ibid., 254, quoting Booker T. Washington, Atlanta Exposition Address, 1895, reprinted in *The Booker T. Washington Papers*, ed. Louis R. Harlan (Urbana: University of Illinois Press, 1974), 3:583–87. The notion that segregation encouraged "separate development" dated at least as far back as the 1890s. John W. Cell, *The Highest Stage of White Supremacy: The Origins of Segregation in South Africa and the American South (New York: Cambridge University Press, 1982)*, 177; Charles Brantley Aycock, "A Message to the Negro" (1901), reprinted in *Life and Speeches of Charles B. Aycock*, ed. R. D. W. Connor and Clarence Poe (Garden City, N.Y.: Doubleday, 1912), 250. Glenda Elizabeth Gilmore demonstrates that even as Aycock espoused progressive rhetoric, he also colluded with a cadre of whites in North Carolina to seize power from blacks. Glenda Elizabeth Gilmore, *Gender and Jim Crow: Women and the Politics of White Supremacy in North Carolina, 1896–1920* (Chapel Hill: University of North Carolina Press, 1996); Eric R. Wolf, "Perilous Ideas: Race, Culture, People," *Current Anthropology* 35 (Feb. 1994): 6. For the distinction

between "high" and "low," or "popular," culture, see Raymond Williams, "On High and Popular Culture," *New Republic*, Nov. 22, 1974, 5. For an example of the antebellum argument that slavery improved slaves by exposing them to Christianity, see William Harper et al., *The Pro-Slavery Argument: As Maintained by the Most Distinguished Writers of the Southern States* (Philadelphia: Lippincott, Grambo, 1853), 60. For a general overview of this argument, see Alfred L. Brophy, *University, Court, and Slave: Pro-Slavery Thought in Southern Colleges and Courts and the Coming of Civil War* (New York: Oxford University Press, 2016), 37–42. For the prevalence of interracial relationships during slavery, see Thomas D. Morris, *Southern Slavery and the Law, 1619–1860* (Chapel Hill: University of North Carolina Press, 1996), 24–25; Yvonne Pitts, *Family, Law, and Inheritance in America: A Social and Legal History of Nineteenth Century Kentucky* (New York: Cambridge University Press, 2013), 72; and Annette Gordon-Reed, *The Hemingses of Monticello: An American Family* (New York: Norton, 2009), 81. Nicholas Guyatt demonstrates that even as southern slave owners disregarded prohibitions against interracial sex, so too did northern abolitionists promise that emancipation would not lead to miscegenation, for freed slaves would be returned to Africa. See Nicholas Guyatt, *Bind Us Apart: How Enlightened Americans Invented Racial Segregation* (New York: Basic Books, 2016). For the postbellum panic over miscegenation, see Peggy Pascoe, *What Comes Naturally: Miscegenation Law and the Making of Race in America* (New York: Oxford University Press, 2009), 24–25; Julie Novkov, *Racial Union: Law, Intimacy, and the White State in Alabama, 1865–1954* (Ann Arbor: University of Michigan Press, 2008), 11; and Peter W. Bardaglio, *Reconstructing the Household: Families, Sex, and the Law in the Nineteenth Century South* (Chapel Hill: University of North Carolina Press, 1995), 289n19 (noting that Arkansas, Florida, Louisiana, and Mississippi dispensed with bans on interracial marriage during Reconstruction only to reinstate them at the end of the nineteenth century).

8. Jane Dailey demonstrates that concerns over interracial sex even led proponents of interracial coalitions to lobby for separate, private social spheres. Jane Dailey, *Before Jim Crow: The Politics of Race in Postemancipation Virginia* (Chapel Hill: University of North Carolina Press, 2000), 12, 88, 98. See also Bardaglio, *Reconstructing the Household*, 177–79; Novkov, *Racial Union*, 37–40; Pascoe, *What Comes Naturally*, 28; Gilmore, *Gender and Jim Crow*, 82–89, 91; Lawrence Goodwyn, *The Populist Moment: A Short History of the Agrarian Revolt in America* (New York: Oxford University Press, 1978), 118–23; C. Vann Woodward, *The Strange Career of Jim Crow*, 3rd ed. (New York: Oxford University Press, 1974), 79–80; and Henry W. Grady, "In Plain Black and White," *XXIX Century Illustrated Magazine*, April 1885, 909–17.
9. Grady, "In Plain Black and White," 911.

10. Woodward, *Strange Career*, 22; Howard N. Rabinowitz, "More Than the Woodward Thesis: Assessing the Strange Career of Jim Crow," *Journal of American History* 75 (1988): 847. Glenda Gilmore stresses the work required to forge a politics of white supremacy in the South, work that would not have been necessary had segregation been a foregone conclusion. Gilmore, *Gender and Jim Crow*, 73. While integration persisted on trolley cars and in public assemblies, in other words, white southerners stressed the notion that blacks did not necessarily want to commune with their white counterparts. Blaire L. M. Kelley, *Right to Ride: Streetcar Boycotts and African American Citizenship in the Era of Plessy v. Ferguson* (Chapel Hill: University of North Carolina Press, 2010); Grady, "In Plain Black and White," 910.
11. For white violence, see Gilmore, *Gender and Jim Crow*, 91–118, and LeeAnna Keith, *The Colfax Massacre: The Untold Story of Black Power, White Terror, and the Death of Reconstruction* (New York: Oxford University Press, 2009). For segregation and the promise of peace, see Edward L. Ayers, *The Promise of the New South: Life After Reconstruction* (New York: Oxford University Press, 1992), 322.
12. Grady, "In Plain Black and White," 912, 914.
13. Ayers, *The Promise of the New South*, 427–28; Tomiko Brown-Nagin, *Courage to Dissent: Atlanta and the Long History of the Civil Rights Movement* (New York: Oxford University Press, 2011), 27, 29; Grady, "In Plain Black and White," 912.
14. For black resistance to Jim Crow, see Paul Ortiz, *Emancipation Betrayed: The Hidden History of Black Organizing and White Violence in Florida from Reconstruction to the Bloody Election of 1920* (Berkeley: University of California Press, 2005); Osha Davidson Gray, *The Best of Enemies: Race and Redemption in the New South* (Chapel Hill: University of North Carolina Press, 1996); Gilmore, *Gender and Jim Crow;* and Aldon D. Morris, *Origins of the Civil Rights Movement: Black Communities Organizing for Change* (New York: Free Press, 1984). For blacks who endorsed the continuation of black institutions, see David Cecelski, *Along Freedom Road: Hyde County, North Carolina, and the Fate of Black Schools in the South* (Chapel Hill: University of North Carolina Press, 1994); Washington, Atlanta Exposition Address; Robert J. Norrell, *Up from History: The Life of Booker T. Washington* (Cambridge, Mass.: Harvard University Press, 2009); Michael B. Boston, *The Business Strategy of Booker T. Washington: Its Development and Implementation* (Gainesville: University Press of Florida, 2010); W. E. B. Du Bois, "Conservation of the Races," (1897) reprinted in *Du Bois: Writings*, ed. Nathan I. Huggins (New York: Library of America, 1986), 820; and Brown-Nagin, *Courage to Dissent*, 33. David Levering Lewis captures the outrage that Du Bois fostered by hinting at the advantages of segregation in 1934, a shift in his original position. David Levering Lewis, *When Harlem Was in Vogue* (1979; New York: Knopf, 1981), 298; Louis R. Har-

lan, *Booker T. Washington: The Wizard of Tuskegee* (New York: Oxford University Press, 1983); Louis R. Harlan, "The Southern Education Board and the Race Issue in Public Education," *Journal of Southern History* 23 (May 1957): 189–202; C. Vann Woodward, *Origins of the New South, 1877–1913* (1951; Baton Rouge: Louisiana State University Press, 1971), 353–57; Gary M. Pomerantz, *Where Peachtree Meets Sweet Auburn: A Saga of Race and Family* (New York: Penguin, 1996), 92. Of course, proponents of Jim Crow downplayed the extent to which violence and humiliation infused segregation. See generally, Gilmore, *Gender and Jim Crow.*

15. Robert Francis Engs, *Freedom's First Generation: Black Hampton, Virginia, 1861–1890* (1979; New York: Fordham University Press, 2004), 62, 65.
16. Leon Litwack, *Been in the Storm So Long: The Aftermath of Slavery* (New York: Knopf, 1979), 477; James M. McPherson, *The Abolitionist Legacy: From Reconstruction to the NAACP* (Princeton, N.J.: Princeton University Press, 1975), 201; Jacqueline Jones, *Soldiers of Light and Love: Northern Teachers and Georgia Blacks, 1865–1873* (Chapel Hill: University of North Carolina Press, 1980); David Wallace Adams, "Philanthropists, Progressives, and Southern Black Education," *History of Education Quarterly* 23 (1983): 99, 100; Henry Lee Swint, *The Northern Teacher in the South, 1862–1870* (Nashville: Vanderbilt University Press, 1941), 77; "President Resents Negro's Criticism," *New York Times*, Nov. 13, 1914, 1.
17. Robert Penn Warren, *John Brown: The Making of a Martyr* (1929; Nashville: J. S. Sanders, 1993), 62–63. For a discussion of Warren's dismissal of W. E. B. Du Bois's work on Brown, see Michael Kreyling, "Robert Penn Warren: The Real Southerner and the 'Hypothetical Negro,'" *American Literary History* 21 (Summer 2009): 276.
18. Warren, *John Brown: The Making of a Martyr*, 61, 62–63, 277. For a more critical reading of Warren's views of race, see R. Blakeslee Gilpin, *John Brown Still Lives! America's Long Reckoning with Violence, Equality, and Change* (Chapel Hill: University of North Carolina Press, 2011), 120–43.
19. W. E. B. Du Bois, "The Talented Tenth," (1903), reprinted in Huggins, ed., *Du Bois: Writings*, 842; Warren, "The Briar Patch," 250–51.
20. Warren, "The Briar Patch," 251.
21. James R. Grossman, *Land of Hope: Chicago, Black Southerners, and the Great Migration* (Chicago: University of Chicago Press, 1989); Isabel Wilkerson, *The Warmth of Other Suns: The Epic Story of America's Great Migration* (New York: Random House, 2010); Warren, "The Briar Patch," 255.
22. James C. Cobb, *Away Down South: A History of Southern Identity* (New York: Oxford University Press, 2005). Zora Neale Hurston and James Weldon Johnson both hailed from Florida. Countee Cullen, like Robert Penn Warren, was born in Kentucky. See Lewis, *When Harlem Was in Vogue*, 76–77.
23. Warren, "The Briar Patch," 261, 263.
24. Ibid., 252, 254–55; Robert Penn Warren, *Segregation: The Inner Conflict*

(New York: Random House, 1956), 264. Popularized by white author Joel Chandler Harris in the 1880s, the briar patch metaphor itself boasted an older history in African folklore, underscoring Warren's claim that the races possessed their own unique cultural traditions. Joel Chandler Harris, *Nights with Uncle Remus: Myths and Legends of the Old Plantation* (New York: McKinlay, Stone, and McKenzie, 1911). That Warren knew the African origins of Harris's tales is likely. As early as 1913, John A. Lomax reported on the African origins of Brer Rabbit in the *Journal of American Folklore*. See John A. Lomax, "Stories of an African Prince: Yoruba Tales," *Journal of American Folklore* 26 (1913): 5. Warren's interest in improving conditions for African Americans without ending segregation was shared by whites across the South who identified with interracialism, as George Brown Tindall shows in *The Emergence of the New South, 1913–1945* (Baton Rouge: Louisiana State University Press, 1967), 177.

25. For the relationship between *Culture in the South* and *I'll Take My Stand*, see Amanda Adams, "'Painfully Southern': 'Gone with the Wind,' the Agrarians, and the Battle for the New South," *Southern Literary Journal* 40 (Fall 2007): 62.
26. Daniel Joseph Singal, *The War Within: From Victorian to Modernist Thought in the South, 1919–1945* (Chapel Hill: University of North Carolina Press, 1982), 136, 282–83.
27. Howard W. Odum, "Standards of Measurement for Race Development," *Journal of Race Development* 5 (1915): 364–67; Howard W. Odum, *Negro Workaday Songs* (Chapel Hill: University of North Carolina Press, 1926); Singal, *The War Within*, 143; Howard W. Odum, "Fundamental Principles Underlying Inter-Racial Co-operation," *Journal of Social Forces* 1 (March 1923): 283–84.
28. Odum, "Fundamental Principles Underlying Inter-Racial Co-operation," 284; Howard W. Odum, "Lynchings, Fears, and Folkways," *Nation*, Dec. 30, 1931, 720; Howard W. Odum, "Notes on the Study of Regional and Folk Society," *Social Forces* 10 (Dec. 1931): 171. For a critical view of Odum's take on folkways, see Glenda Elizabeth Gilmore, *Defying Dixie: The Radical Roots of Civil Rights, 1919–1950* (New York: Norton, 2008), 227–28. For a less critical view, see Morton Sosna, *In Search of the Silent South: Southern Liberals and the Race Issue* (New York: Columbia University Press, 1977).
29. Gilmore, *Defying Dixie*, 15; Stephen A. Berrey, *The Jim Crow Routine: Everyday Performances of Race, Civil Rights, and Segregation in Mississippi* (Chapel Hill: University of North Carolina Press, 2015); Crystal Feimster, *Southern Horrors: Women and the Politics of Rape and Lynching* (Cambridge, Mass.: Harvard University Press, 2009); McGuire, *At the Dark End of the Street*; McMillen, *Dark Journey*.
30. Odum, "Notes on the Study of Regional and Folk Society," 171. Glenda Elizabeth Gilmore criticizes Odum for not challenging segregation, sug-

gesting that his arguments about folkways amounted to little more than a "tautological" justification for racial repression. Gilmore, *Defying Dixie*, 22 (arguing that Odum "disdained" challenges to Jim Crow), 228. For a slightly less critical view of Odum, see Singal, *The War Within*, 147 (noting that Odum doubted the feasibility of changing southern "folkways" overnight). Morton Sosna takes a less critical view as well, showing that Odum was willing to challenge folkways when it came to lynching, just not segregation. Sosna, *In Search of the Silent South*, 53; Odum, "Lynchings, Fears, and Folkways," 720; Gilmore, *Gender and Jim Crow*, 138.

31. Melville J. Herskovits, *Life in a Haitian Valley* (New York: Knopf, 1937), 303–4, cited in Sidney W. Mintz and Richard Price, *The Birth of African-American Culture: An Anthropological Perspective* (Boston: Beacon Press, 1976), xiii.

32. Lewis, *When Harlem Was in Vogue*, 143, 147–49; Lawrence J. Oliver and Terri L. Walker, "James Weldon Johnson's 'New York Age' Essays on 'The Birth of a Nation' and the 'Southern Oligarchy,'" *South Central Review* 10 (Winter 1993): 5; James Weldon Johnson, "Preface," in *The Book of American Negro Poetry*, ed. James Weldon Johnson (New York: Harcourt, Brace, 1922), vii.

33. James Weldon Johnson to Guy B. Johnson, Jan. 29, 1926; Guy B. Johnson to James Weldon Johnson, Feb. 9, 1926, both Guy B. Johnson Papers, Southern Historical Collection, University of North Carolina, Chapel Hill.

34. Lewis, *When Harlem Was in Vogue*, 148; Guy B. Johnson, "Negro Folk Songs," in *Culture in the South*, ed. W. T. Couch (Chapel Hill: University of North Carolina Press, 1935), 547, 548, 551, 553.

35. Christina L. Ruotolo, "James Weldon Johnson and the Autobiography of an Ex-Colored Musician," *American Literature* 72 (June 2000): 252, 257–58, 261; Lewis, *When Harlem Was in Vogue*, 145, 116.

36. Florida native James Weldon Johnson became a critical organizer for the Harlem Renaissance, one of six African Americans who distinguished "the Harlem cultural scene" from smaller scenes in Philadelphia and Washington. Lewis, *When Harlem Was in Vogue*, 48, 120–21, 125.

37. Ibid., 87, 117, 120–21, 144–45; Alain Locke, *The New Negro: An Interpretation of Negro Life* (1925; New York: Touchstone, 1997); Carme Manuel, "Mule Bone: Langston Hughes and Zora Neale Hurston's Dream Deferred of an African-American Theatre of the Black Word," *African American Review* 35 (Spring 2001): 77; Alain Locke to Guy B. Johnson, Oct. 10, 1928, Guy B. Johnson Papers.

38. Gunnar Myrdal to Guy B. Johnson, May 2, 1939, Guy B. Johnson Papers; Walter A. Jackson, *Gunnar Myrdal and America's Conscience: Social Engineering and Racial Liberalism, 1938–1987* (Chapel Hill: University of North Carolina Press, 1990), 16–17, 20–21, 109.

39. Gunnar Myrdal, *An American Dilemma: The Negro Problem and Modern*

Democracy (1944; New Brunswick: Transaction, 2003), 2:863, 877; Jackson, *Gunnar Myrdal and America's Conscience*, 33, 131, 227. To support his conclusions on black culture, Myrdal referenced black sociologist E. Franklin Frazier, who cited high rates of illegitimacy in black families as evidence of pathology. Yet Frazier did not argue that black culture was the cause, focusing instead on "urban ecology." Daryl Michael Scott, *Contempt and Pity: Social Policy and the Image of the Damaged Black Psyche* (Chapel Hill: University of North Carolina Press, 1997), 44. Myrdal's work did have precedent in the United States. Frazier had also studied the black family but did not see "the matriarchal family as inherently disorganized." Alice O'Connor, *Poverty Knowledge: Social Science, Social Policy, and the Poor in Twentieth-Century U.S. History* (Princeton, N.J.: Princeton University Press, 2001), 83.

40. Jackson, *Gunnar Myrdal and America's Conscience*, 109; Guy B. Johnson to Gunnar Myrdal, May 8, 1939; Gunnar Myrdal to Guy B. Johnson, Feb. 10, 1939, both Guy B. Johnson Papers; Myrdal, *An American Dilemma*, 2:863, 877.
41. Myrdal, *An American Dilemma*, 2:927–29, 933; Scott, *Contempt and Pity*, 44.
42. Jackson, *Gunnar Myrdal and America's Conscience*, 170–71, 225; Warren, "The Briar Patch," 251.
43. New York *Herald Tribune*, Jan. 26, 1944, cited in Jackson, *Gunnar Myrdal and America's Conscience*, 241–42. Even E. Franklin Frazier praised the work for its assault on segregation, endorsing its view that "the Negro community" amounted to little more than a "pathological phenomenon in American life." E. Franklin Frazier, "Race: An American Dilemma," *Crisis*, April 1944, 106.
44. Howard W. Odum, "Problem and Methodology in an American Dilemma," *Social Forces* 23 (Oct. 1944): 98; Richard Kluger, *Simple Justice: The History of Brown v. Board of Education and Black America's Struggle for Equality* (New York: Vintage, 1977), 259; Brief of Petitioner at 34, 51, 52, *Sipuel v. Board of Regents of University of Oklahoma*, 332 U.S. 631 (1948); Brief for Appellant at 34, 35, 36, *McLaurin v. Oklahoma State Regents*, 339 U.S. 637 (1950); "The Effects of Segregation and the Consequences of Desegregation: A Social Science Statement," appendix to Appellant's Brief at 3, *Brown v. Board of Education of Topeka*, 347 U.S. 483 (1954).
45. Brief for Appellee at 26, 28, 58, *Davis v. County School Board of Prince Edward County*, 103 F. Supp. 337 (E.D. Va. 1952).
46. Daryl Michael Scott argues that *Brown* "marked the acceptance of the therapeutic perspective on race relations in American institutional life," but that "therapeutic pluralism did not find its way into the opinion because the Court was steeped in psychology." Here, Scott's emphasis on therapeutic pluralism is significant. Contrary to the pluralism advanced by Robert Penn Warren and segregationists after him, therapeutic plu-

ralists lobbied for integration as a way of achieving cultural diversity. See Daryl Michael Scott, "Postwar Pluralism, *Brown*, and Multicultural Education," *Journal of American History* 91 (June 2004): 79.

47. Ibid., 76, 78; Kluger, *Simple Justice*, 705–6. While Scott is right that the battle over integration eventually resulted in the notion that the public school curriculum "had to include the study of blacks," this occludes the more sinister role that pluralism played in white resistance to integration generally, extolling segregation itself as a regime that preserved racial difference. If *Brown* "opened the door for the struggle for pluralism in the schools," as Scott argues, it opened a much larger door for the discussion of pluralism as a defense of the segregated South. Contrary to Scott's "therapeutic pluralism," in other words, southern pluralism maintained that the very institution blamed for harming the black psyche in *Brown*, namely racial segregation, actually bolstered black traditions, black culture, and black pride.

Chapter Two. The White Mare

1. Zora Neale Hurston to Editor, *Orlando Sentinel*, Aug. 11, 1955, reprinted in *Zora Neale Hurston: A Life in Letters*, ed. Carla Kaplan (New York: Doubleday, 2002), 740. Newspapers across the South reprinted Hurston's letter. William W. Taylor, special counsel to North Carolina's Advisory Committee on Education, wrote Hurston on August 25, 1955, requesting permission to "reprint" the letter in "pamphlet form" for distribution around the state. "We believe that it might be of great help in our efforts to find a reasonable solution to the problem now facing the public schools," wrote Taylor, "and that it is an excellent implementation of the recent policy address of the Governor of this State." William W. Taylor, Jr., to Zora Neale Hurston, Aug. 25, 1955, Zora Neale Hurston Correspondence, box 1, Zora Neale Hurston Papers, Special Collections, University of Florida, Gainesville. See also Virginius Dabney to Martin Andersen, Aug. 15, 1955 (discussion of the decision to reprint Hurston's letter in the *Richmond Times-Dispatch*) and Burke, Kuipers & Mahoney to Martin Andersen, Oct. 19, 1955 (discussing Hurston's letter in the *Dallas News*), both Zora Neale Hurston Correspondence, box 1, Zora Neale Hurston Papers. Werner Sollers notes that aspects of Hurston's argument "come troublingly close to those invoked by southern white conservatives." Werner Sollers, "Of Mules and Mares in a Land of Difference; or, Quadrupeds All?" *American Quarterly* 42 (June 1990): 172.
2. Robert E. Hemenway, *Zora Neale Hurston: A Literary Biography* (Urbana: University of Illinois Press, 1977), 16–17, 21, 31; Zora Neale Hurston, "Drenched in Light," *Opportunity*, Dec. 1924, 371.
3. Lori Jirousek, "'That Commonality of Feeling': Hurston, Hybridity, and Ethnography," *African American Review* 38 (Autumn 2004): 417; Hemen-

way, *Hurston*, 100; Alain Locke, "The Negro's Contribution to American Culture," *Journal of Negro Education* 8 (July 1939): 525.

4. Hemenway, *Hurston*, 43, 128. See also Zora Neale Hurston to Alain Locke, May 10, 1928, and June 14, 1928, reprinted in Kaplan, ed., *Zora Neale Hurston*, 118–21. Hurston also came into conflict with Locke, joining Wallace Thurman and Langston Hughes in the founding of a literary magazine dedicated to capturing a more accurate depiction of black folklife than Locke's *New Negro* anthology. Zora Neale Hurston, *Mules and Men* (1935; New York: Perennial, 1990).
5. Zora Neale Hurston to Editor, *Orlando Sentinel*, Aug. 11, 1955, 738–39.
6. Ibid. Hurston had long insinuated that communists used sex to sway African Americans, noting in 1935 that "Communists [were] making a play of being the friend of the Negro at present and stopping at nothing, absolutely nothing to accomplish their ends." Zora Neale Hurston to John Lomax, Sept. 16, 1935, reprinted in Kaplan, ed., *Zora Neale Hurston*, 359.
7. Zora Neale Hurston to Katherine Tracy L'Engle, Nov. 4, 1945, reprinted in Kaplan, ed., *Zora Neale Hurston*, 535. Hurston claimed that her first brush with communism came through Langston Hughes. See Zora Neale Hurston to *Saturday Evening Post*, Sept. 2, 1954, and Zora Neale Hurston to Katherine Tracy L'Engle, Dec. 11, 1945, both reprinted in ibid., 718, 538.
8. Glenda Elizabeth Gilmore, *Defying Dixie: The Radical Roots of Civil Rights, 1919–1950* (New York: Norton, 2008), 29, 64, 70, 80–84, 96–97.
9. Herbert Hill, "The Communist Party—Enemy of Negro Equality," *Crisis*, June–July 1951, 365–71. Zora Neale Hurston to Editor, *Orlando Sentinel*, Aug. 11, 1955, 738–39.
10. Zora Neale Hurston, *Dust Tracks on a Road* (1942), reprinted in *Zora Neale Hurston: Folklore, Memoirs, and Other Writings*, ed. Cheryl A. Wall (New York: Literary Classics, 1995), 793; Zora Neale Hurston, *Dust Tracks on a Road* (1942), reprinted in Wall, ed., *Zora Neale Hurston*, 790–91. For Hurston's account of the Ocoee massacre, see Zora Neale Hurston, "The Ocoee Riot" (1942), reprinted in *Wall, ed., Zora Neale Hurston*, 897–901. For another account of the Ocoee riot, see Paul Ortiz, *Emancipation Betrayed: The Hidden History of Black Organizing and White Violence in Florida from Reconstruction to the Bloody Election of 1920* (Berkeley: University of California Press, 2005), 221–22.
11. Zora Neale Hurston, "The Sanctified Church" (1938), reprinted in Wall, ed., *Zora Neale Hurston*, 901–5; Zora Neale Hurston, "How It Feels to Be Colored Me," *The World Tomorrow*, May 1928, reprinted in Wall, ed., *Zora Neale Hurston*, 827; Zora Neale Hurston, "Characteristics of Negro Expression," in *Negro: An Anthology*, ed. Nancy Cunard (1934), reprinted in Wall, ed., *Zora Neale Hurston*, 841; Zora Neale Hurston, "Folklore and Music," (1938), reprinted in Wall, ed., *Zora Neale Hurston*, 876.
12. Robert Penn Warren, "The Briar Patch," in John Crow Ransom et al., *I'll*

Take My Stand: The South and the Agrarian Tradition by Twelve Southerners (1930; New York: Harper and Brothers, 1962), 255; Hurston, "Folklore and Music," 876.

13. Zora Neale Hurston, *Seraph on the Suwanee* (1948; New York: HarperCollins, 2008), 3–4, 6, 7. Scholars have alternately dismissed *Seraph on the Suwanee* as a failure or they have tried to read it as a continuation of themes in Hurston's other works, including for example the damaging effects of "racist ideology" and/or gender violence. While there may be some truth to this, the book strikes me first and foremost as a satirical rebuttal to white supremacy. See, e.g., Laura Dubek, "The Social Geography of Race in Hurston's Seraph on the Suwanee," *African American Review* 30 (Autumn 1996): 341, 344, 347, and Ann duCille, *The Coupling Convention: Sex, Text, and Tradition in Black Women's Fiction* (New York: Oxford University Press, 1994), 115, 132.
14. Hurston, *Seraph*, 29, 57.
15. Ibid., 68, 120, 126.
16. Ibid., 44, 125, 139. Hurston came to recognize the close relationship between white and black in the South, noting for example that whites were not simply "copying" black cultural forms but that many black forms had in fact originated with whites. See Zora Neale Hurston to Marjorie Kinnan Rawlings and Norton Baskin, Dec. 22, 1948, reprinted in Kaplan, ed., *Zora Neale Hurston*, 577.
17. Zora Neale Hurston to Margrit De Sablonière, Dec. 3, 1955, reprinted in Kaplan, ed., *Zora Neale Hurston*, 743.
18. *Brown v. Board of Education*, 347 U.S. 483, 493, 494 n. 11 (1954).
19. Zora Neale Hurston to Mary Holland, June 13, 1955; Zora Neale Hurston to Max Eastman, Aug. 2, 1955, reprinted in Kaplan, ed., *Zora Neale Hurston*, 730, 732, 737.
20. Zora Neale Hurston to Max Eastman, Aug. 2, 1955, reprinted in ibid., 736–37.
21. Zora Neale Hurston, Herod the Great, Typescript 1–87, pp. 3, 6, 24, 31, 32, 60, binder 3, Zora Neale Hurston Papers.
22. Hemenway, *Hurston*, 345; Hurston, Herod the Great, Typescript 1–87, p. 37.
23. Michael Lackey provides insight into Hurston's rejection of Moses as a black ideal in "Moses, Man of Oppression: A Twentieth-Century African American Critique of Western Theocracy," *African American Review* 43 (Winter 2009): 577.

Chapter Three. Inner Conflict

1. Joseph Blotner, *Robert Penn Warren: A Biography* (New York: Random House, 1997), 295; Robert Thomas Jr., "Eleanor Clark Is Dead at 82; A

Ruminative Travel Essayist," *New York Times*, Feb. 19, 1996, B5; Stacey Stowe, "Live Where a Writer Lived, but Don't Dwell on the Past," *New York Times*, March 21, 2005, B5.

2. Robert Penn Warren, "Introduction to the Modern Library Edition of *All the King's Men*," in *A Robert Penn Warren Reader*, ed. Albert Erskine (New York: Random House, 1987), 225.
3. Robert Penn Warren, *Band of Angels* (New York: Random House, 1955), 31, 33. Warren began work on *Band of Angels* before Brown was decided, completing the galleys by the end of April 1955. Blotner, *Warren*, 290, 297.
4. Manty's husband, Tobias Sears, abandons her on the night that she confesses her racial identity, only to reappear later in the novel injured by southerners intent on denying blacks the vote. Manty and Sears remain married, though he subsequently cheats on her with a white woman, a sign that "New England idealism failed in the debacle of the Civil War." William Bedford Clark, *The American Vision of Robert Penn Warren* (Lexington: University Press of Kentucky, 1991), 27. Hugh Ruppersburg downplays the extent to which Warren portrayed slavery in a benevolent light, arguing simply that the novel "explores the mystery of self-knowledge and identity" and that "the racial issues which grow out of her [Starr's] discovery seem of only secondary importance." Hugh Ruppersburg, *Robert Penn Warren and the American Imagination* (Athens: University of Georgia Press, 1990), 151.
5. William Bedford Clark reads *Band of Angels* as a commentary on the disillusionment of the post-*Brown* moment. See Clark, *The American Vision of Robert Penn Warren*, 111. Hugh Ruppersburg views *Band of Angels* as a commentary on the fallacies of Yankee idealism. Ruppersburg, *Robert Penn Warren and the American Imagination*, 5.
6. Edward E. Baptist, "'Cuffy,' 'Fancy Maids,' and 'One-Eyed Men': Rape, Commodification, and the Domestic Slave Trade in the United States," *American Historical Review* 106 (Dec. 2001): 1626, 1631, 1639.
7. Warren, *Band of Angels*, 164–65.
8. The African kingdom of Dahomey received considerable attention in British journals in the nineteenth century, all likely sources for Warren's research in *Band of Angels*. See Richard F. Burton, "The Present State of Dahome," *Transactions of the Ethnological Society of London* 3 (1865): 401, 402, and J. Duncan, "Notice of a Journey from Whyddah on the W. Coast of Africa to Adofoodia in the Interior," *Journal of the Royal Geographical Society of London* 16 (1846): 154–62, 155. For a recent assessment of Duncan's travels, see Robin Law, "Further Light on John Duncan's Account of the 'Fellatah Country' (1845)," *History in Africa* 28 (2001): 129, 131. The last of the "grand customs," according to Burton, "were performed in November 1860 by Gelele, the present sovereign, to honour the manes

of his sire Gezo," the name of the king in *Band of Angels*. Burton, "The Present State of Dahome," 403–4; Warren, *Band of Angels*, 162.

9. Melville J. Herskovits, *Dahomey: An Ancient West African Kingdom* (New York: J. J. Augustin, 1938). See also Ralph J. Bunche, "Review of *Dahomey*, by Melville J. Herskovits," *Journal of Negro Education* 8 (April 1939): 209–12.
10. Warren, *Band of Angels*, 88; Robert Penn Warren, interviewed by Ralph Ellison and Eugene Walter, "The Art of Fiction No. 18," *Paris Review*, Spring–Summer 1957, reprinted in *Talking with Robert Penn Warren*, ed. Floyd C. Watkins et al. (Athens: University of Georgia Press, 1990), 43–44.
11. Robert Penn Warren and John Baker, interview, spring 1977, reprinted in Watkins et al., eds., *Talking with Robert Penn Warren*, 262.
12. Not long after *Life* contacted him, Warren flew to Memphis, rented a car, and drove to Mississippi to visit Hodding Carter, a Pulitzer Prize–winning journalist who lived in the Delta town of Greenville, and Eudora Welty, an accomplished writer from Jackson whose career Warren had helped launch while working at Louisiana State University in the 1930s. Warren discussed his time with Carter and Welty in a letter to Arnold Stein. Robert Penn Warren to Arnold Stein, Dec. 18, 1955, in Hendricks and Perkins, eds., *Selected Letters of Robert Penn Warren*, 4:111–13.
13. Robert Penn Warren, *Segregation: The Inner Conflict* (New York: Random House, 1956), 16.
14. For background on Milam and Bryant, see William Bradford Huie, "The Shocking Story of Approved Killing in Mississippi," *Look*, Jan. 24, 1956, 47, and John H. Popham, "Trial Under Way in Youth's Killing," *New York Times*, Sept. 20, 1955, 32. See also Timothy B. Tyson, *The Blood of Emmett Till* (New York: Simon and Schuster, 2017), 46–50. For Bryant's version of events, see Tyson, *Blood of Emmett Till*, 4–5; Huie, "The Shocking Story of Approved Killing in Mississippi," 47; and "Nation Horrified by Murder of Kidnapped Chicago Youth," *Jet*, Sept. 15, 1955, 6–9.
15. Stephen J. Whitfield, *A Death in the Delta: The Story of Emmett Till* (Baltimore: Johns Hopkins University Press, 1988), 91; Popham, "Trial Under Way in Youth's Killing," 32; Huie, "The Shocking Story of Approved Killing in Mississippi," 47; "Mississippi Jury Acquits 2 Accused in Youth's Killing," *New York Times*, Sept. 24, 1955, 1; "Kidnapping Case Revived in the South," *New York Times*, Oct. 30, 1955, 87.
16. "Boycott Is Urged in Youth's Killing," *New York Times*, Oct. 12, 1955, 62; "North Asked to Aid Southern Negroes," *New York Times*, Oct. 16, 1955, 42; National Association for the Advancement of Colored People, *M is for Mississippi and Murder* (New York: NAACP, 1955).
17. Robert Penn Warren to Arnold Stein, Dec. 18, 1955, in Hendricks and Perkins, eds., *Selected Letters of Robert Penn Warren*, 4:111–13.
18. Peter Kihss, "Negro Co-ed Is Suspended to Curb Alabama Clashes," *New York Times*, Feb. 7, 1956, 1.

19. Warren, *Segregation: The Inner Conflict*, 6, 7–8.
20. Ibid., 15.
21. "Emmett Till's Day in Court: Mississippians Refuse to Convict White Men of Killing a Negro Boy," *Life*, Oct. 3, 1955, 37–38; "Kidnapping Case Revived in the South," 87. John Edgar Wideman casts doubt on Louis Till's guilt in *Writing to Save a Life: The Louis Till File* (New York: Scriber, 2016).
22. Robert Penn Warren, Manuscript Fragment for *Segregation: The Inner Conflict*, box 188, folder 3325, Robert Penn Warren Papers, YCAL 51, Beinecke Library, Yale University, New Haven, Conn.
23. Ibid.
24. Warren, *Segregation: The Inner Conflict*, 43; "Four Youths Face Rape Charges," *Chicago Defender*, Oct. 1, 1955, 5.
25. Warren, *Segregation: The Inner Conflict*, 52.
26. Ibid., 41, 53.
27. Although not mentioned in the book, the organizer's affiliation with the Citizens' Councils was mentioned in the abbreviated *Life* magazine article. Robert Penn Warren, "Divided South Searches Its Soul," *Life*, July 9, 1956, 98, 101; Warren, *Segregation: The Inner Conflict*, 25.
28. Warren, *Segregation: The Inner Conflict*, 31; Donald Davidson, *The Attack on Leviathan: Regionalism and Nationalism in the United States* (1938; Gloucester, Mass.: Peter Smith, 1962).
29. Warren, *Segregation: The Inner Conflict*, 64, 65.
30. Ibid., 63.
31. Warren, "Divided South Searches Its Soul," 108.
32. Ibid.; Warren, *Segregation: The Inner Conflict*, 42.
33. Warren, *Segregation: The Inner Conflict*, 63, 65.
34. "Buses Boycotted over Race Issue: Montgomery, Ala., Negroes Protest Woman's Arrest for Defying Segregation," *New York Times*, Dec. 6, 1955, 31; "Shots Strike Negro Homes," *New York Times*, Dec. 9, 1955, 23; "Bus Boycott Continues: Alabama Line Rejects Negro Demands on Seating," *New York Times*, Dec. 10, 1955, 13. Warren completed his first draft of *Segregation: The Inner Conflict* in March 1956. See Robert Penn Warren to Brainard Cheney, March 5, 1956, in Hendricks and Perkins, eds., *Selected Letters of Robert Penn Warren*, 4:117, and "A Bold Boycott Goes On: Montgomery Negroes Keep up Bus Protest as Leaders Are Arrested," *Life*, March 6, 1956, 40.

Chapter Four. Invisible Man

1. Ralph Ellison to Albert Murray, Oct. 22, 1955, reprinted in *Trading Twelves: The Selected Letters of Ralph Ellison and Albert Murray*, ed. Albert Murray and John F. Callahan (New York: Modern Library, 2000), 97–100.
2. For Ellison's background, see Arnold Rampersad, *Ralph Ellison: A Biography* (New York: Alfred Knopf, 2007). For works that have shaped my

views on Ellison's writing, see M. Cooper Harris, *Ralph Ellison's Invisible Theology* (New York: New York University Press, 2017); Timothy Parrish, *Ralph Ellison and the Genius of America* (Amherst: University of Massachusetts Press, 2012); Adam Bradley, *Ralph Ellison in Progress: From Invisible Man to Three Days Before the Shooting* (New Haven, Conn.: Yale University Press, 2010); Lucas E. Morel, "Ralph Ellison's American Democratic Individualism," in *Ralph Ellison and the Raft of Hope: A Political Companion to Invisible Man*, ed. Lucas E. Morel (Lexington: University Press of Kentucky, 2004), 58–90; and Lawrence Patrick Jackson, *Ralph Ellison: Emergence of Genius* (New York: John Wiley, 2002).

3. Ralph Ellison, "An American Dilemma: A Review" (1944), reprinted in *Shadow and Act* (1964; New York: Vintage, 1995), 303, 316.
4. Ibid., 315; Ralph Ellison, *Invisible Man* (1952; New York: Vintage, 1980), 6.
5. Ellison, "An American Dilemma: A Review," 316.
6. Ibid., 317; Ralph Ellison, interviewed by Alfred Chester and Vilma Howard, "The Art of Fiction No. 8," *Paris Review*, Spring 1955, reprinted in *Shadow and Act*, 172; Aldon D. Morris, *The Origins of the Civil Rights Movement: Black Communities Organizing for Change* (New York: Free Press, 1984), 51–56.
7. King, by contrast, failed to see how his leadership defied the vision of America set forth by Myrdal. In his memoir of the Montgomery bus boycott, for example, King actually cited the Swedish sociologist for the point that "the problem of race is America's greatest moral dilemma," meanwhile ignoring Myrdal's indictment of black culture, including the black church. Martin Luther King, Jr., *Stride Toward Freedom: The Montgomery Story* (1958; San Francisco: Harper and Row, 1986), 205.
8. Ellison, "The Art of Fiction," 171. As Timothy Parrish notes, "Ellison did not understand his role as a black intellectual to be to nourish his 'blackness' but to work to integrate black experience with American experience." Parrish, *Ralph Ellison and the Genius of America*, 131.
9. Ellison, "The Art of Fiction," 171–72.
10. Ibid., 177; Ralph Ellison, "Brave Words for a Startling Occasion," National Book Award address, January 27, 1953, reprinted in *Shadow and Act*, 104. While some early reviewers charged that *Invisible Man* did not take a sufficiently aggressive stance against racism in the United States, later critics began to interpret the work in a more radical light. For a discussion of the scholarly literature and a radical reading of the work, see Christopher Z. Hobson, "'Invisible Man' and African American Radicalism in World War II," *African American Review* 39 (Fall 2005): 355–56. See also Bradley, *Ralph Ellison in Progress*, 60–61.
11. Ellison, *Invisible Man*, 5.
12. Ellison, "Brave Words for a Startling Occasion," 105, 104, 106.
13. Irving Howe, "Black Boys and Native Sons," *Dissent*, Autumn 1963, 363, 64.

14. Ellison, "The Art of Fiction," 174, 176–77.
15. Ralph Ellison, "Richard Wright's Blues," *Antioch Review* (Summer 1945), reprinted in *Shadow and Act*, 80, 81.
16. Ralph Ellison, "Twentieth-Century Fiction and the Black Mask of Humanity," *Confluence* (December 1953), reprinted in *Shadow and Act*, 26.
17. Ralph Ellison to Albert Murray, Jan. 30 1956, reprinted in Murray and Callahan, eds., *Trading Twelves*, 104, 110.
18. Robert Penn Warren to John Palmer, July 15, 1956, in *Selected Letters of Robert Penn Warren*, vol. 4, *New Beginnings and New Directions, 1953–1968*, ed. Randy Hendricks and James A. Perkins (Baton Rouge: Louisiana State University Press, 2008), 125. For an excellent discussion of Ellison and Warren's relationship, see Parrish, *Ralph Ellison and the Genius of America*, 128–73.
19. Robert Penn Warren, interviewed by Ralph Ellison and Eugene Walter, "Art of Fiction No. 18," *Paris Review* (Spring–Summer 1957), reprinted in *Talking with Robert Penn Warren*, ed. Floyd C. Watkins et al. (Athens: University of Georgia Press, 1990), 28, 29–30.
20. Ibid., 32–33, 44.
21. Ibid., 34.
22. Ibid., 47.
23. Ralph Ellison to Albert Murray, March 16, 1956; Ralph Ellison to Albert Murray, Feb. 4, 1952, both reprinted in Murray and Callahan, eds., *Trading Twelves*, 117, 29; "Warren, "Art of Fiction," 47.

Chapter Five. The Color Curtain

1. Richard Wright, *Uncle Tom's Children* (1938), reprinted in Richard Wright, *Early Works*, ed. Arnold Rampersad (New York: Library of America, 1991), 225–37.
2. Lawrence P. Jackson, "The Birth of the Critic: The Literary Friendship of Ralph Ellison and Richard Wright," *American Literature* 72 (June 2000): 324–35.
3. Richard Wright, *Black Boy* (1945), reprinted in *Early Works*, 246. For Wright on Myrdal, see Michel Fabre, *The Unfinished Quest of Richard Wright* (Urbana: University of Illinois Press, 1993), 270.
4. Richard Wright, "Review of Their Eyes Were Watching God," *New Masses*, Oct. 5, 1937, 22–23. For Wright's views on Wheatley, see Richard Wright, *White Man Listen!* (1957; New York: Anchor, 1964), 76.
5. Zora Neale Hurston, "Uncle Tom's Children" (1938), reprinted in *Richard Wright: Critical Perspectives Past and Present*, ed. Henry Louis Gates, Jr., and K. A. Appiah (New York: Amistad Press, 1993), 3–4; Fabre, *The Unfinished Quest of Richard Wright*, 281.
6. Richard Wright, "Blueprint for Negro Writing" (1937), reprinted in *Within the Circle: An Anthology of African American Literary Criticism from*

the Harlem Renaissance to the Present, ed. Angelyn Mitchell (Durham, N.C.: Duke University Press, 1994), 99–101.

7. Richard Wright, *Native Son* (New York: Harper, 1940). For Wright's critique of American culture, see Fabre, *The Unfinished Quest of Richard Wright*, 258.
8. Charles Poore, "Books of the Times," *New York Times*, March 1, 1940, 25. For insight into the inspiration behind *Native Son*, see Keneth Kinnamon, "How Native Son Was Born," in Gates and Appiah, eds., *Richard Wright*, 110–27, and Virginia Whatley Smith, "Down South/Up North: Bigger Thomas's Carceral Societies in Native Son," in *Richard Wright: Writing America at Home and from Abroad*, ed. Virginia Whatley Smith (Jackson: University Press of Mississippi, 2016), 31–51.
9. Fabre, *The Unfinished Quest of Richard Wright*, 275–76, 297.
10. Ibid., 312; Richard Wright, *The Color Curtain* (1956; Jackson: University Press of Mississippi, 1994),199–203; Wright, *White Man Listen!* 106–37.
11. Richard Wright, *Black Power* (London: Dennis Dobson, 1954), 55, 60, 104. Scholars have proven critical of Wright's comments on Africa, seeing in them what Anthony Appiah calls "condescension and paranoia." Kwame Anthony Appiah, "A Long Way from Home: Wright in the Gold Coast," in *Richard Wright*, ed. Harold Bloom (New York: Chelsea House, 1987), 181. I am primarily interested in Wright's positive reactions to developments in Africa, independent of whether he actually understood what he was seeing. See, e.g., John M. Reilly, "Richard Wright's Discovery of the Third World," *Minority Voices* 2 (1978): 47–53, and S. Shankar, "Richard Wright's Black Power: Colonial Politics and the Travel Narrative," in *Richard Wright's Travel Narratives*, ed. Virginia Whatley Smith (Jackson: University Press of Mississippi, 2001), 3–19.
12. Wright, *The Color Curtain*, 73, 78. Scholars have seen a tendency on Wright's part to view Bandung through the lens of "biased Western patriarchal discourse," a perspective similar to the one he adopts in Black Power. I am primarily interested in how his observations about Bandung fit into his larger vision of cultural pluralism and racial reform. Virginia Whatley Smith, "Richard Wright's Passage to Indonesia: The Travel Writer/Narrator as Participant/Observer of Anti-Colonial Imperatives in The Color Curtain," in Smith, ed., *Richard Wright's Travel Writings*, 96.
13. Wright, *The Color Curtain*, 140, 175, 187.
14. Ibid., 219, 220.
15. Ibid., 217, 218. For a discussion of Wright's continued interest in American racial politics following his departure for Europe, see Eve Dunbar, "Black Is a Region: Segregation and American Literary Regionalism in Richard Wright's 'The Color Curtain,'" *African American Review* 42 (Spring 2008): 109–19.
16. Richard Wright, *Pagan Spain* (1957; New York: HarperCollins, 1995), 229; Wright, *The Color Curtain*, 15.

17. Wright, *The Color Curtain*, 220.
18. Ibid., 220–21.
19. Ibid., 217.
20. Wright, *White Man Listen!* 127, 135. For a discussion of Wright's thoughts on Africa and its future, see John M. Reilly, "Richard Wright and the Art of Non-Fiction: Stepping Out on the Stage of the World," *Callaloo* 28 (Summer 1986): 507, 514.

Chapter Six. Intruder in the Dust

1. Joseph Blotner, *Faulkner: A Biography* (1974; New York: Vintage, 1991), 628; Allen Tate, "William Faulkner, 1897–1962," *Sewanee Review* 71 (Winter 1963): 160–61.
2. Blotner, *Faulkner*, 628.
3. Robert Penn Warren, "The Snopes World," *Kenyon Review* 3 (Spring 1941): 253, 254–55.
4. William Faulkner, "Mississippi," *Holiday*, April 1954, reprinted in *Essays, Speeches, and Public Letters by William Faulkner*, ed. James B. Meriwether (New York: Random House, 1965), 13.
5. Tate, "William Faulkner," 163; Cleanth Brooks, *William Faulkner: The Yoknapatawpha Country* (New Haven, Conn.: Yale University Press, 1963), 102.
6. William Faulkner, *Absalom, Absalom!* (1936; New York: Random House, 1964), 20.
7. Brooks, *Yoknapatawpha Country*, 306.
8. Ibid., 317.
9. Ibid., 317–18; Edward Baptist, *The Half Has Never Been Told: Slavery and the Making of American Capitalism* (New York: Basic Books, 2014), 235, 238. For the invisible line analogy, see Daniel Sharfstein, *The Invisible Line: Three American Families and the Secret Journey from Black to White* (New York: Penguin, 2011).
10. Baptist, *The Half Has Never Been Told*, 235; Faulkner, *Absalom, Absalom!* 194, 240, 356.
11. Peggy Pascoe, *What Comes Naturally: Miscegenation Law and the Making of Race in America* (New York: Oxford University Press, 2009), 1–2.
12. Thadious Davis notes that Faulkner's description of Dilsey was itself a stereotype, albeit one that contrasted positively to the Compsons. "In working his way out of the quandary and despair of the Compson world," Davis observes, "Faulkner turns to his preconceived notions of the black world." Thadious Davis, *Faulkner's Negro: Art and the Southern Context* (Baton Rouge: Louisiana State University Press, 1983), 109. Of course, this does not contradict the claim made here, which was that Faulkner's romantic view of blacks helped him to rationalize segregation. Blotner, *Faulkner*, 352; William Faulkner, *The Sound and the Fury* (1929; New York:

Norton, 2014), 190, 194. Cleanth Brooks noted that Faulkner referred to Sutpen's Hundred as a burning house in an early version of the manuscript. See Brooks, *Yoknapatawpha Country*, 439.

13. Thadious Davis makes the important observation that Faulkner's rendering of blacks as undefeated was itself a stereotype, as was his notion that blacks constituted a "coherent social group." Davis, *Faulkner's Negro*, 109, 242; William Faulkner, *Intruder in the Dust* (New York: Vintage, 1948), 7, 149, 153, 154–56.
14. Faulkner, *Intruder in the Dust*, 156.
15. William Faulkner to Richard Wright, [probably Sept. 11, 1945], reprinted in *Selected Letters of William Faulkner*, ed. Joseph Blotner (New York: Vintage, 1978), 201; Michel Fabre, *The Unfinished Quest of Richard Wright* (Urbana: University of Illinois Press, 1993), 282.
16. William Faulkner to Richard Wright, [probably Sept. 11, 1945], 201.
17. Blotner, *Faulkner*, 199–200; Fabre, *The Unfinished Quest of Richard Wright*, 280–83.
18. Faulkner, *Intruder in the Dust*, 154, 155.
19. Ibid., 154, 156.
20. William Faulkner, "Address upon Receiving the Nobel Prize for Literature," Dec. 10, 1950, reprinted in Meriwether, ed., *Essays, Speeches, and Public Letters*, 119–20; Blotner, *Faulkner*, 523.
21. William Faulkner, "Address to the Graduating Class University High School, Oxford Mississippi," May 28, 1951, reprinted in Meriwether, ed., *Essays, Speeches, and Public Letters*, 123; William Faulkner, "Address to the Delta Council," May 15, 1952, reprinted in ibid., 130, 133. Some critics have questioned Faulkner's affinity for the Nashville Agrarians, a point that is worth noting. My interpretation focuses on a few shared themes but shies away from maintaining a too close connection. See, e.g. Thadious Davis, *Games of Property: Law, Race, Gender, and Faulkner's Go Down, Moses* (Durham, N.C.: Duke University Press, 1987), 3. Cleanth Brooks noted that any similarities between the Agrarians and Faulkner amounted to a fairly vague "generalization," a point that my reading concedes. See Cleanth Brooks, *On the Prejudices, Predilections, and Firm Beliefs of William Faulkner* (Baton Rouge: Louisiana State University Press, 1987), 11. For a fascinating discussion of Faulkner and the Fugitives, see Daniel Spoth, "Totalitarian Faulkner: The Nazi Interpretation of 'Light in August,' and 'Absalom, Absalom!'" *ELH* 78 (Spring 2011): 239, 246.
22. Numan V. Bartley, *The Rise of Massive Resistance: Race and Politics in the South During the 1950s* (1969; Baton Rouge: Louisiana State University Press, 1999), 85.
23. William Faulkner, "Address to the Southern Historical Association," Nov. 10, 1955, reprinted in Meriwether, ed., *Essays, Speeches, and Public Letters*, 146–47, 150.
24. Ibid., 150. Retaining segregated schools was not something that Faulkner

was particularly interested in, a point he made in a letter to the Memphis *Commercial Appeal* in March 1955, where he complained that segregation had depleted Mississippi's coffers by forcing the state to build two parallel systems, neither of which excelled. If allowed to continue, he joked, "we will have two identical systems neither of which are good enough for anybody." William Faulkner to Editor of the Memphis *Commercial Appeal*, March 20, 1955, reprinted in Meriwether, ed., *Essays, Speeches, and Public Letters*, 216.

25. William Faulkner, "Letter to the North," *Life*, March 5, 1956, 51–52.

Chapter Seven. Fire Next Time

1. James Baldwin, "Nobody Knows My Name: A Letter from the South," *Partisan Review*, Winter 1959, reprinted in James Baldwin, *The Price of the Ticket: Collected Nonfiction, 1948–1985* (New York: St. Martin's, 1985), 187; James Baldwin, *Go Tell It on the Mountain* (New York: Knopf, 1952); James Baldwin, *Notes of a Native Son* (1955; Boston: Beacon Press, 1987).
2. James Baldwin, "Faulkner and Desegregation," *Partisan Review*, Fall 1956, 568, 570; William Faulkner, "Letter to the North," *Life*, March 5, 1956, 52.
3. Baldwin, "Nobody Knows My Name," 183. Baldwin discussed his fear of the South in a 1958 essay for *Harper's*, "A Fly in the Buttermilk," *Harper's Magazine*, Oct. 1958, reprinted in *The Price of the Ticket*, 161.
4. Baldwin, "Nobody Knows My Name," 183.
5. Ibid., 72, 74; Luther Hodges, "Address by Governor Luther H. Hodges of North Carolina on State-wide Radio-Television Network," August 8, 1955, box 39, folder "Segregation Advisory Committee on Integration," Luther Hodges Papers, North Carolina State Archives, Raleigh.
6. Baldwin, "Nobody Knows My Name," 74.
7. Baldwin, "A Fly in the Buttermilk," 162. See also W. J. Weatherby, *James Baldwin: Artist on Fire* (New York: Donald I. Fine, 1989), 137, and Martha Biondi, *The Black Revolution on Campus* (Berkeley: University of California Press, 2000).
8. Weatherby, *James Baldwin*, 137; Tomiko Brown-Nagin, *Courage to Dissent: Atlanta and the Long History of the Civil Rights Movement* (New York: Oxford University Press, 2011), 2.
9. David Bird, "Marvin Griffin, 74 Former Governor," *New York Times*, June 14, 1982, D11; David J. Garrow, *Bearing the Cross: Martin Luther King, Jr., and the Southern Christian Leadership Conference* (1986; New York: Vintage, 1988), 60.
10. James Baldwin, "The Dangerous Road Before Martin Luther King," *Harper's Magazine*, Feb. 1961, reprinted in *The Price of the Ticket*, 248; Martin Luther King, Jr., *Stride Toward Freedom: The Montgomery Story (1958; San Francisco: Harper and Row, 1986)*, 190. For Baldwin's initial

impressions of King, see David Leeming, *James Baldwin: A Biography* (New York: Henry Holt, 1994), 142–43.

11. Baldwin, "The Dangerous Road Before Martin Luther King," 249–50.
12. Ibid., 247. I argue that even Baldwin's novel *Another Country*, published in 1962, conveys a relatively stock portrait of whites, in particular the "southern jezebel," Leona. This coincides with Vaughn Rasberry's interpretation of the work, which as he describes it, "furnishes concrete imagery for the famous question Baldwin posed in The Fire Next Time: 'Do I really want to be integrated into a burning house?'" Vaughn Rasberry, "'Now Describing You': James Baldwin and Cold War Liberalism," in *James Baldwin: America and Beyond*, ed. Cora Kaplan and Bill Schwarz (Ann Arbor: University of Michigan Press, 2011), 95. Douglas Field raises the interesting possibility that *Another Country* is a response to Richard Wright's *Native Son*, a book that focuses not on the ubiquity of interracial violence but on the absence of interracial love. This coincides with Baldwin's charge to his nephew in *The Fire Next Time* that "if the word integration means anything, this is what it means: that we, with love, shall force our brothers to see themselves as they are." Looked at in this way, African Americans occupy a special place in America as moral arbiters and also moral teachers. See, e.g. Douglas Field, *All Those Strangers: The Art and Lives of James Baldwin* (New York: Oxford University Press, 2015), 5, and James Baldwin, *The Fire Next Time* (1963; New York: Vintage, 1993), 9–10.
13. James Baldwin, "Notes for a Hypothetical Novel," Address at Esquire Symposium, San Francisco State College, Oct. 22, 1960, reprinted in *The Price of the Ticket*, 241, 244; Erik Erikson, *Childhood and Society* (New York: Norton, 1950); James Baldwin, "In Search of a Majority," Address at Kalamazoo College, 1960, reprinted in *The Price of the Ticket*, 231–32.
14. Baldwin, "Notes for a Hypothetical Novel," 241–42; James Baldwin, "A Letter to My Nephew," *The Progressive*, December 1962, reprinted as "My Dungeon Shook: Letter to My Nephew on the One Hundredth Anniversary of Emancipation," in Baldwin, *The Fire Next Time*, 9. For an excellent discussion of Baldwin's critique of "the American Dream," including the "heightened consumerism, retreat into the domestic sphere, suburbanization, and alienation" that characterized the post–World War II period, see Leah Mirakhor, "Resisting the Temptation to Give Up: James Baldwin, Robert Adams, and the Disavowal of the American Way of Life," *African American Review* 46 (Winter 2013): 653, 654.
15. Baldwin, "Notes for a Hypothetical Novel," 243–44. As Cheryl Wall puts it, "Baldwin makes a purposeful and strategic use of American exceptionalism to advance the scrupulously visible political interest of African Americans, indeed, Americans in general." Rather than reject the United States, in other words, Baldwin came to believe that "what is unique about the United States," as Wall explains it, "is the presence of black

people and the challenge that their presence poses to Americans' sense of the nation and of themselves." Cheryl A. Wall, "Stranger at Home: James Baldwin on What It Means to Be an American," in Kaplan and Schwarz, eds., *James Baldwin: America and Beyond*, 37.

16. Baldwin, "A Letter to My Nephew," 4, 5, 6.
17. Ibid., 4, 5, 8–10. By 1964, Baldwin's critique of whites had come to include both conservatives and liberals. See Rebecca Aanerud, "Now More Than Ever: James Baldwin and the Critique of White Liberalism," in *James Baldwin Now*, ed. Dwight A. McBride (New York: New York University Press, 1999), 61.
18. King, *Stride Toward Freedom*, 217; Baldwin, "A Letter to My Nephew," 10.
19. James Baldwin, "Letter from a Region in My Mind," *New Yorker*, Nov. 17, 1962, reprinted as "Down at the Cross: Letter from a Region in My Mind," in James Baldwin, *The Fire Next Time* (1963; New York: Vintage, 1993), 13, 22–23, 94.
20. Ibid., 96.
21. Ibid., 42, 93, 95, 98.
22. Ibid., 101–2. As Darryl Pinckney put it, Baldwin retained a sense that America was "salvageable," even as black intellectuals like Richard Wright looked abroad. Darryl Pinckney, "The Magic of James Baldwin," *New York Review of Books*, Nov. 19, 1998, www.nybooks.com/articles/1998/11/19/the-magic-of-james-baldwin/.
23. James Baldwin, "The Fire Next Time" (1963), in Clayborne Carson et al., eds., *Reporting Civil Rights, Part One: American Journalism, 1941–1963* (New York: Literary Classics of the United States, 2003), 760.
24. James Baldwin, "From Nationalism, Colonialism, and the United States: One Minute to Twelve—A Forum" (1961), reprinted in James Baldwin, *The Cross of Redemption: Uncollected Writings*, ed. Randall Kenan (New York: Pantheon, 2010), 11–12, 27.

Chapter Eight. Everything That Rises Must Converge

1. Flannery O'Connor to Maryat Lee, May 24, 1964, reprinted in Flannery O'Connor, *The Habit of Being* (New York: Farrar, Straus, Giroux, 1979), 580.
2. Flannery O'Connor to Maryat Lee, April 25, 1959, reprinted in *The Habit of Being*, 329; James Baldwin, "My Dungeon Shook," reprinted in James Baldwin, *The Fire Next Time* (1963; New York: Vintage, 1993), 8; Flannery O'Connor to Maryat Lee, May 24, 1964; Flannery O'Connor to Betty Hester, Oct. 28, 1961, box 2, folder 5, Flannery O'Connor Papers, Manuscript, Archives, and Rare Book Library, Emory University, Atlanta; Flannery O'Connor to Betty Hester, Aug. 24, 1962, box 2, folder 7, Flannery O'Connor Papers; Flannery O'Connor to Betty Hester ("A"), Sept. 1, 1963, reprinted in *The Habit of Being*, 537.

3. Flannery O'Connor, "Revelation," *Sewanee Review* 72 (Spring 1964), reprinted in *The Complete Stories of Flannery O'Connor*, ed. Robert Giroux (New York: Farrar, Straus, and Giroux, 1971), 490–91, 96; *Naim v. Naim*, 87 S.E.2d 749 (1955); 350 U.S. 891 (1955); 350 U.S. 985 (1956). For an excellent analysis of Turpin's character in "Revelation," see Jacky Dumas and Jessica Hooten Wilson, "The Unrevealed in Flannery O'Connor's 'Revelation,'" *Southern Literary Journal* 45 (Spring 2013): 75–77. See also Barbara Wilkie Tedford, "Flannery O'Connor and the Social Classes," *Southern Literary Journal* 13 (Spring, 1981), 27, 29–31. Others have commented on O'Connor's tendency to elevate black characters above white or, as Frederick Crews puts it, "the black characters in her [O'Connor's] fiction generally do come off better than the whites—more humane, more intuitively sensible, and of course markedly less susceptible to the status anxiety and self-aggrandizement that she loved to pillory." Frederick Crews, *The Critics Bear It Away: American Fiction and the Academy* (New York: Random House, 1992), 157–58; Thomas F. Haddox, "On Belief, Conflict, and Universality: Flannery O'Connor, Walter Benn Michaels, Slavoj Zizek," in *Flannery O'Connor and the Age of Terrorism: Essays on Violence and Grace*, ed. Avis Hewitt and Robert Donahoo (Knoxville: University of Tennessee Press, 2010), 233.
4. O'Connor, "Revelation," 502, 508.
5. Chappell, *Stone of Hope*, 105–30.
6. Millennialism has two iterations, postmillennialism, which holds that Christ will return once justice has been achieved on Earth, and premillennialism, which holds that Christ will return and impose peace and justice. O'Connor took umbrage at the first iteration, a historically popular view in the United States. Daniel Walker Howe, *What Hath God Wrought: The Transformation of America, 1815–1848* (New York: Oxford University Press, 2007), 285.
7. Normand J. Paulhus, "Uses and Misuses of the Term 'Social Justice' in the Roman Catholic Tradition," *Journal of Religious Ethics* 15 (Fall 1987): 262.
8. Martin Luther King, Jr., "Letter from Birmingham Jail" (April 16, 1963), reprinted in Martin Luther King, Jr., *Why We Can't Wait* (1964; New York: Signet, 2000), 79.
9. Ralph C. Wood, *Flannery O'Connor and the Christ-Haunted South* (Grand Rapids, Mich.: Eerdmans, 2004), 59.
10. *Conversations with Flannery O'Connor*, ed. Rosemary M. Magee (Oxford: University Press of Mississippi, 1987), 109; "An Interview with Flannery O'Connor and Robert Penn Warren," in *Talking with Robert Penn Warren*, ed. Floyd C. Watkins et al. (Athens: University of Georgia Press, 1990), 61–62.
11. Flannery O'Connor, "Everything That Rises Must Converge," *New World Writing* 19 (1961), reprinted in *The Complete Stories of Flannery O'Connor*, 405, 406, 407, 408, 409, 412, 419.

12. Ibid., 420.
13. Gerard E. Sherry, "An Interview with Flannery O'Connor," *The Critic* 21 (Spring 1963), reprinted in Magee, ed., *Conversations with Flannery O'Connor*, 102, 103, 109.
14. Flannery O'Connor, "Judgement Day," reprinted in *The Complete Stories of Flannery O'Connor*, 531, 534, 542, 544, 545, 549. For an insightful discussion of "Judgement Day," see Bryan N. Watt, "The Domestic Dynamics of Flannery O'Connor: Everything That Rises Must Converge," *Twentieth Century Literature* 38 (Spring 1992): 66, 85–88.

Chapter Nine. Who Speaks for the Negro?

1. Robert Penn Warren to John Lewis Longley, July 26, 1963, in *Selected Letters of Robert Penn Warren*, vol. 4, *New Beginnings and New Directions, 1953–1968*, ed. Randy Hendricks and James A. Perkins (Baton Rouge: Louisiana State University Press, 2008), 385. Warren revealed to Peter Taylor that he was contemplating a "piece of journalism" on "Negro leaders" on July 6, 1963. Robert Penn Warren to Peter Taylor, July 6, 1963, in ibid., 378.

   The *New York Times* first invoked the term "civil rights movement" in 1953 but repeated it only sporadically for the next ten years, until 1963, when uses of the term spiked dramatically. Luther A. Huston first mentioned the term in the *Times* in 1953 in an article entitled "Segregation Arguments Put Before High Court," *New York Times*, Nov. 22, 1953, E4. The second reference did not occur until three years later, in 1956, in an article styled "Reds Act to Join Civil Rights Push," *New York Times*, Feb. 22, 1956, 14. Next came "City May Ban Bias in Private Rental," *New York Times*, May 21, 1957, 1 (the only article to mention the term "civil rights movement" in 1957); "Communists Linked to Little Rock Rift," *New York Times*, Dec. 19, 1958, H2 (the only use in 1958); "Humphrey Backs N.A.A.C.P. Anew," *New York Times*, July 16, 1959, 15 (the first of two articles mentioning the phrase in 1959); "Senate Unit Ends Rights Deadlock," *New York Times*, Aug. 4, 1959, 1; "Students Impatient with Old Efforts: Rights Strategy Young Negro Groups Press for Stronger Action," *New York Times*, April 24, 1960, E4 (the only article mentioning "civil rights movement" in 1960); "A.F.L.–C.I.O. Chiefs Score Randolph," *New York Times*, Oct. 13, 1961, 1 (the only use in 1961). In 1962, the *Times* mentioned "civil rights movement" 10 times. In 1963, the *Times* mentioned "civil rights movement" 119 times; in 1964, 283 times; and in 1965, 327 times.

   For civil rights sources cited in this paragraph, see Aldon D. Morris, *The Origins of the Civil Rights Movement: Black Communities Organizing for Change* (New York: Free Press, 1984), 21, 40–76; David J. Garrow, *Bearing the Cross: Martin Luther King, Jr., and the Southern Christian Leadership*

Conference (1986; New York: Vintage, 1988), 85, 90, 133–34; and Charles Payne, *I've Got the Light of Freedom: The Organizing Tradition and the Mississippi Freedom Struggle* (Berkeley: University of California Press, 1995), 78–79, 81–90. The Freedom Rides were initially sponsored by CORE but quickly attracted the support of other civil rights groups, including the SCLC, SNCC, and the Nashville Christian Leadership Council, all of whose efforts were coordinated by an umbrella organization christened the Freedom Ride Coordinating Committee. Raymond Arsenault, *Freedom Riders: 1961 and the Struggle for Racial Justice* (New York: Oxford University Press, 2006), 24, 94, 282; Clayborne Carson, *In Struggle: SNCC and the Black Awakening of the 1960s* (1981; Cambridge, Mass.: Harvard University Press, 1995), 19–20; Payne, *I've Got the Light of Freedom*, 62, 130.

2. *Why We Can't Wait* hit book stores on June 8, 1964. "Books—Authors," *New York Times*, May 22, 1964, 32; Martin Luther King, Jr., *Why We Can't Wait* (1964; New York: Signet, 2000), 1–12.
3. Rayford Logan, ed., *What The Negro Wants* (Chapel Hill: University of North Carolina Press, 1944). Warren began in earnest to arrange for interviews with prominent black leaders in January 1964, even asking individuals like civil rights attorney Louis H. Pollak for advice on who to contact. On January 19, 1964, Warren wrote Donald E. Stanford announcing that he was "doing a piece of journalism on the integration question, and while I'm in Baton Rouge I should like to meet and talk with some of the Negro students at LSU." Robert Penn Warren to Donald E. Stanford, Jan. 19, 1964, in Hendricks and Perkins, eds., *Selected Letters of Robert Penn Warren*, 4:399. Louis Pollak noted that "there were a handful of national Negro leaders whom you will want to talk to, if for no other reason than because they carry primary institutional responsibilities." L. H. Pollak to Robert Penn Warren, Oct. 30, 1963, Robert Penn Warren Papers, box 213, folder 3720, Special Collections, Beinecke Library, Yale University, New Haven, Conn.
4. Robert Penn Warren, *Who Speaks for the Negro?* (New York: Vintage, 1965), 362. Most black students, posited Warren, lacked "personal involvement" with the movement, exhibiting instead "considerable apathy, indifference, or selfishness." Ibid., 366. Of course, the same observation could be applied to white youth, but black apathy introduced the kind of nuanced read that Warren would provide throughout the book.
5. Ibid., 282; Robert Penn Warren and James Baldwin, interview, April 27, 1964, tape 1, at 5, Robert Penn Warren Center for the Humanities, Vanderbilt University, Nashville, Tenn., whospeaks.library.vanderbilt.edu/interviews.
6. Warren, *Who Speaks for the Negro?* 282, 292, 294.
7. Robert Penn Warren and James Baldwin, interview, April 27, 1964, tape 1, at 6, 7–8.

8. Ibid., tape 2, at 6; E. Franklin Frazier, *The Negro Family in the United States* (Chicago: University of Chicago Press, 1939). See also E. Franklin Frazier, *The Negro Family in Chicago* (Chicago: University of Chicago Press, 1932); Daryl Michael Scott discusses Frazier, Powdermaker, and Dollard in *Contempt and Pity: Social Policy and the Image of the Damaged Black Psyche, 1880–1996* (Chapel Hill: University of North Carolina Press, 1997), 43–44, 45, 47, 52–53; Charles S. Johnson, *In the Shadow of the Plantation* (Chicago: University of Chicago Press, 1934), 1–5, 80–89; and Allison Davis and John Dollard, *Children of Bondage: The Personality Development of Negro Youth in the Urban South* (Washington, D.C.: American Council on Education, 1940).
9. Warren, *Who Speaks for the Negro?* 288.
10. Ibid., 190.
11. Ibid., 191.
12. Ibid., 191–93.
13. Ibid., 206–8.
14. Ibid., 209.
15. Ibid., 209, 215.
16. Ibid., 216.
17. Martin Luther King, Jr., "I Have a Dream," reprinted in *A Call to Conscience: The Landmark Speeches of Dr. Martin Luther King, Jr.*, ed. Clayborne Carson and Kris Shepard (New York: Warner, 2001), 85.
18. Warren, *Who Speaks for the Negro?* 244, 249, 251. For the date of the interview, see Robert Penn Warren and Malcolm X, interview, June 2, 1964, tape 1, Special Collections, Vanderbilt University, Nashville, Tenn.
19. Warren, *Who Speaks for the Negro?* 246, 253.
20. Ibid., 246, 256, 257, 264.
21. Ibid., 327, 328, 329.
22. Ibid., 345–46.
23. Ibid., 349–50, 351. In a 1964 essay entitled "Shadow and Act," Ellison had attacked Myrdal for presenting a damaged image of black America. "Ellison served as a bridge between the New Negro intellectuals of the interwar years and the Black Powerites of the 1960s and 1970s. While he celebrated black culture more than many New Negroes, he shared their group pride and distaste for posing as psychologically damaged to manipulate the therapeutic sensibilities of whites." Scott, *Contempt and Pity*, 167.
24. Warren described the apartment in *Who Speaks for the Negro?* 358. However, he did not mention that Carmichael, Thornton, and Wheeler were present nor did he mention the date. For that information, see "Transcript of Taped Conversation with Stokely Carmichael, Izell Blair, Lucy Thornton and Jean Wheeler," Howard University, March 4, 1964, YCAL 51, series II, box 208, folder 3630.
25. Warren, *Who Speaks for the Negro?* 358.
26. "Transcript of Taped Conversation with Stokely Carmichael, Izell Blair,

Lucy Thornton and Jean Wheeler"; Warren, *Who Speaks for the Negro?* 374–75. For weapons of the weak, see James C. Scott, *Domination and the Arts of Resistance* (New Haven, Conn.: Yale University Press, 1990), 162–66.

27. Warren, *Who Speaks for the Negro?* 398.

28. Ibid., 254, 369, 386–87. Warren's conversations with students led to several revelations. For one, his conversations prompted him to conclude that "the image which Martin Luther King afforded the young" effectively "converted the inferior outsider—the Negro stranded in the shallows beyond the mainstream of American life—into the superior insider; for the Negro, by appealing to the fundamental premises of American society, to the Declaration of Independence and the subsequent muniments, puts the white community in the position of the betrayers of the dream. The Negro becomes the defender of the faith for the salvation of all. He not only affirms his right to join society; he affirms his mission to redeem society by affirming the premises of society. He is not only an 'old American' in the cultural sense; he becomes, as Stokely Carmichael has said of Negroes, 'more American than the Americans.'" Ibid., 372–73.

Chapter Ten. The Demonstrators

1. Eudora Welty to Robert Penn Warren, Aug. 22, 1965, box 77, folder 1519, Robert Penn Warren Papers, Special Collections, Beinecke Library, Yale University, New Haven, Conn.; Charles Poore, "Books of the Times: Who Speaks for the Negro Speaks for Mankind," *New York Times*, June 1, 1965, 37; "Faces of Change," *Newsweek*, June 7, 1965, clipping found in box 213, folder 3720, Robert Penn Warren Papers. *Newsweek* captured Warren's subtle efforts at impugning civil rights activists, meanwhile praising black leaders who were more conservative in their views. Noting that "it is the more conservative leaders that Warren feels most comfortable with," *Newsweek* went on to note that "Warren sees the younger negro leaders as troubled, agonized, uncertain—even somewhat neurotic."

2. Warren stopped at Welty's house, spending an evening with her and her friend Charlotte Capers, an employee of the Mississippi Department of Archives and History, who "revealed all about major political figures" in the state, including Governor Ross Barnett. Charlotte Capers to Robert Penn Warren, June 21, 1976, box 77, folder 1519, Robert Penn Warren Papers; Lewis P. Simpson, "Foreword," to *Cleanth Brooks and Robert Penn Warren: A Literary Correspondence*, ed. James A. Grimshaw, Jr. (Columbia: University of Missouri Press, 1998), xii; Eudora Welty, "Preface," in *The Collected Stories of Eudora Welty* (New York: Harcourt, 1980), ix; Eudora Welty, "Preface," in *One Time One Place: Mississippi in the Depression: A Snapshot Album* (1971; Jackson: University of Mississippi Press, 1996), 7,

9. As Barbara Ladd notes, Welty's photograph "A Pageant of Birds" was "an assertion of native [black] talent and resourcefulness where many readers of the New Republic would least expect to find it." Barbara Ladd, "'Writing Against Death': Totalitarianism and the Nonfiction of Eudora Welty at Midcentury," in *Eudora Welty and Politics: Did the Writer Crusade?* ed. Harriet Pollack and Suzanne Marrs (Baton Rouge: Louisiana State University Press, 2001), 166.

3. Welty, *One Time One Place*, 95, 9, 10; Hunter Cole and Seetha Srinivasan, "Eudora Welty and Photography: An Interview," in *More Conversations with Eudora Welty*, ed. Peggy Whitman Prenshaw (Jackson: University Press of Mississippi, 1996), 209–10. As Barbara Ladd notes, Thompson's pageant "draws a good deal of its significance from the religious and political traditions of the African American church, linking political and commercial symbols subversively with religious discourse and community (rather than State) activism." Ladd, "'Writing Against Death,'" 170.

4. Eudora Welty to Robert Penn Warren, Aug. 22, 1965. For Welty's talk at Millsaps, see Suzanne Marrs, *Eudora Welty: A Biography* (New York: Mariner, 2006), 299–300. In discussing the murder of Medgar Evers, Welty noted that she "had been having a feeling of uneasiness over the things being written about the South at that time because most of them were done in other parts of the country, and I thought most were synthetic. They were perfectly well-intentioned stories but generalities written from a distance to illustrate generalities. When that murder was committed, it suddenly crossed my consciousness that I knew what was in that man's mind because I'd lived all my life where it happened." Eudora Welty, interview with Linda Kuehl, "The Art of Fiction No. 47," *Paris Review*, Fall 1972, 72.

5. Eudora Welty, "Where Is the Voice Coming From?" *New Yorker*, July 6, 1963, 24; Eudora Welty, "Must the Novelist Crusade?" *Atlantic Monthly*, Oct. 1965, 104.

6. Eudora Welty, "The Demonstrators," *New Yorker*, Nov. 26, 1966, 56–61.

7. Ibid. Suzan Harrison argues that Welty's portrayal of the black South was charged with "sexuality, violence and exotic chaos," a point that does not necessarily conflict with the argument made here, which is that Welty boasted an appreciation for the African American experience—even if that appreciation was itself based on racial stereotypes. Suzan Harrison, "'Racial Content Espied': Modernist Politics, Textuality, and Race in Eudora Welty's 'The Demonstrators,'" in Pollack and Marrs, eds., *Eudora Welty and Politics*, 94. A fascinating take on "The Demonstrators" is provided by Rebecca Mark, who reads the story as an "elaborately choreographed political drama" by Holden's black population, who hope to "educate the doctor and save their own people." Mark's reading coincides with the interpretation presented here insofar as she underscores the

contrast between Holden's black community, who "are engaged in living —going to church, [and] working as productive members of the community," versus Holden's white population, who "are in bad shape." Echoing the theme of white decline that emerges in Zora Neale Hurston's *Seraph on the Suwannee* and William Faulkner's *Absalom, Absalom!* and *The Sound and the Fury*, Mark notes that in Welty's telling, "examples of feeblemindedness, degeneracy, and stupidity are everywhere in this white community and nowhere in the black community." Rebecca Mark, "Ice Picks, Guinea Pigs, and Dead Birds: Dramatic Weltian Possibilities in 'The Demonstrators,'" in *Eudora Welty, Whiteness, and Race*, ed. Harriet Pollack (Athens: University of Georgia Press, 2013), 205, 206.

8. Welty, "The Demonstrators," 61.
9. Ibid. Suzanne Marrs notes that a similar story had a run in the *Jackson Daily News*. Suzanne Marrs, *One Writer's Imagination: The Fiction of Eudora Welty* (Baton Rouge: Louisiana State University Press, 2002), 187; Martin Luther King, Jr., *Why We Can't Wait* (1964; New York: Signet, 2000), 89; Robert Penn Warren, *Who Speaks for the Negro?* (New York: Vintage, 1965), 91.
10. Suzanne Marrs reads Welty's account as a critique of the "slanted and ungrammatical newspaper reporting" in the South at the time. This it was, to be sure, but it was also a jab at the northern press's single-minded interest in publicizing racially motivated crimes, not crimes of violence generally. Marrs, *One Writer's Imagination*, 185; Welty, "The Demonstrators," 62–63.
11. Welty's first story, "Where Is the Voice Coming From?" addressed the assassination of Medgar Evers, shot outside his house in the dark on June 12, 1963. Welty published the story in the *New Yorker* on July 6, 1963. Welty, "Must the Novelist Crusade?" 105. For evidence that the piece began as a speech at Millsaps College in December 1964, see William Maxwell to Eudora Welty, Oct. 27, 1965, reprinted in Marrs, ed., *What There Is to Say We Have Said*, 183n64.
12. Welty, "Must the Novelist Crusade?" 105; William Maxwell to Eudora Welty, Nov. 22, 1965, reprinted in Marrs, ed., *What There Is to Say We Have Said*, 183–84; see also William Maxwell to Eudora Welty, Dec. 1, 1965, reprinted in Marrs, ed., *What There Is to Say We Have Said*, 184–86. Later that fall, Welty sent a second short story to William Maxwell, her editor at the *New Yorker*. In a letter to Maxwell, she confessed to struggling with the word "Mississippi," precisely because "just the sight of the word 'Mississippi' written out tends to signal a certain kind of story these days," pressing her to use the abbreviation "Miss." instead. Eudora Welty to William Maxwell, Dec. 7, 1965, reprinted in Marrs, ed., *What There Is to Say We Have Said*, 190, 202.
13. Welty, "Must the Novelist Crusade," 107.
14. Ibid., 107–8.

Chapter Eleven. Mockingbirds

1. "Harper Lee Twits School Board in Virginia for Ban on Her Novel," *New York Times*, Jan. 16, 1966, 82. *Mockingbird* had sold over 3 million copies by May 1962.
2. Ibid. See "'Bird' in Hand: Producers Accent Authentic Southern Ways in Adapting Novel to Screen," *New York Times*, May 6, 1962, 149.
3. Harper Lee, *Go Set a Watchman* (New York: HarperCollins, 2015), 149, 150; Murray Schumach, "Prize for Novel Elates Film Pair: Mulligan and Pakula Had Rights to 'Mockingbird,'" *New York Times*, May 19, 1961, 26; Jonathan Mahler, "The Invisible Hand Behind Harper Lee's 'To Kill a Mockingbird,'" *New York Times*, July 12, 2015, http://nyti.ms/1LougnQ.
4. Lee, *Watchman*, 159, 160.
5. Robert Penn Warren, *The Legacy of the Civil War: Meditations on the Centennial* (New York: Random House, 1961), 26; Robert Penn Warren, *Segregation: The Inner Conflict* (New York: Random House, 1956), 25, 31; Lee, *Watchman*, 110, 159–61, 239–40.
6. Warren, *Segregation: The Inner Conflict*, 57; Lee, *Watchman*, 159–161, 166. The notion that *Brown* hardened race relations in the South helps explain Atticus Finch's decision to join the Citizens' Councils, a point made by his brother Jack when Jean Louise confronts him about her father's transformation. "When a man's looking down the double barrel of a shotgun," explains Jack Finch, "he picks up the first weapon he can find to defend himself, be it a stone or a stick of stovewood or a citizens' council." Ibid., 200, 161, 166.
7. Warren, *Segregation: The Inner Conflict*, 53, 55; Lee, *Watchman*, 195–96, 272.
8. Warren's memoir, also about a southerner returning home to engage local racists, had not generated particularly positive reviews, especially not among African Americans interested in civil rights, like James Baldwin. Baldwin's attack on Warren (and Faulkner), as we have seen, may have convinced Hohoff that Lee's manuscript was not worth pursuing, either because it lacked sufficient quality and originality or because it would simply be viewed by critics like Baldwin as an apology for segregation, neither promising outcomes. Mahler, "The Invisible Hand Behind Harper Lee's 'To Kill a Mockingbird'"; Lee, *Watchman*, 148–49.
9. Harper Lee, *To Kill a Mockingbird* (Philadelphia: J. B. Lippincott, 1960), 11, 12; Monroe E. Deutsch, "The Women of Caesar's Family," *Classical Journal* 13 (1918): 510. Jennifer Murray also comments on the quasi-spousal role played by Calpurnia. Jennifer Murray, "More Than One Way to (Mis)Read a 'Mockingbird,'" *Southern Literary Journal* 43 (2010): 85.
10. Lee, *Mockingbird*, 27, 33, 37, 82, 108.
11. Ibid., 83, 85, 96.
12. Ibid., 98–99, 254; Martin Luther King, Jr., *Stride Toward Freedom: The Montgomery Story* (1958; San Francisco: Harper and Row, 1986), 32.

13. Lee, *Mockingbird*, 105, 106, 107.
14. Ibid., 109, 117, 118.
15. Ibid., 42, 129, 130–34, 136, 247. For Adler's development of ethical culture, see Benny Kraut, *From Reform Judaism to Ethical Culture: The Religious Evolution of Felix Adler* (Cincinnati: Hebrew Union College Press, 1979).
16. Lee, *Mockingbird*, 27.
17. Ibid., 172.
18. Ibid., 131, 155–56, 157, 176, 259.
19. Ibid., 37, 129, 135, 181.
20. Ibid., 25, 165.
21. Ibid., 168.
22. Ibid., 166, 167, 216.
23. Ibid., 218, 224, 226, 228, 232, 234, 239.
24. Ibid., 218, 224, 226, 228, 232, 234, 239; *Taylor v. Louisiana*, 419 U.S. 522 (1975).
25. Lee, *Mockingbird*, 239, 240, 249–50.
26. Ibid., 284, 296; Robert Franc Schulkers, *The Gray Ghost* (Cincinnati: Robert F. Schulkers, 1926).
27. James A. Ramage, *Gray Ghost: The Life of Col. John Singleton Mosby* (Lexington: University Press of Kentucky, 1999).
28. Ibid., 342.
29. Robert F. Schulkers, *The Gray Ghost: A Seckatary Hawkins Mystery* (1921; Lexington: University Press of Kentucky, 2016); James A. Ramage, *Gray Ghost: The Life of Col. John Singleton Mosby* (Lexington: University Press of Kentucky, 1999), 342.
30. Lee, *Mockingbird*, 283, 285.
31. Ibid., 290, 291.
32. Frank H. Lyell, "One-Taxi Town: To Kill a Mockingbird," *New York Times*, July 10, 1960, BR5; Herbert Mitgang, "Books of the Times," *New York Times*, July 13, 1960, 33; Phoebe Adams, "'To Kill a Mockingbird,' by Harper Lee," *Atlantic Monthly*, Aug. 1, 1960, 98.
33. Yale law professor Reva Siegel claims that *To Kill a Mockingbird* constituted nothing less than "a legitimation of *Brown*." Reva Siegel, "Equality Talk: Antisubordination and Anti-Classification Values in Constitutional Struggles over *Brown*," *Harvard Law Review* 117 (2004): 1501.

Chapter Twelve. The Cantos

1. James Jackson Kilpatrick, *The Southern Case for School Segregation* (Springfield, Ohio: Crowell-Collier, 1962), 22–23, 24.
2. "Harper Lee Twits School Board in Virginia for Ban on Her Novel," *New York Times*, Jan. 16, 1966, 82.
3. Ezra Pound, "In a Station of the Metro," *Poetry*, April 1913, 12.

4. Burton Hatlen, "Pound and Fascism," in Marianne Korn, ed., *Ezra Pound and History* (Orono, Maine: National Poetry Foundation, 1985), 146–52.
5. Thomas A. Underwood, "A Bard Among Bibliographers: Allen Tate's Washington Year," *Southern Literary Journal* 23 (Spring 1992): 41.
6. Allen Tate, "Ezra Pound's Golden Ass," *The Nation*, June 10, 1931, 633.
7. Cleanth Brooks, Jr., and Robert Penn Warren, *Understanding Poetry: An Anthology for College Students* (New York: Holt, 1938); Cleanth Brooks, Jr., and Robert Penn Warren, *Understanding Fiction* (New York: Appleton-Century-Crofts, 1959); Karen Leick, "Ezra Pound v. 'The Saturday Review of Literature,'" *Journal of Modern Literature* 25 (Winter 2001–2): 19, 21; Allen Tate, "Ode to the Confederate Dead," reprinted in Allen Tate, *Collected Poems, 1919–1976* (New York: Farrar Straus Giroux, 1977). For evidence that the Agrarians saw themselves as writing against fascism, see Robert H. Brinkmeyer, Jr., *The Fourth Ghost: White Southern Writers and European Fascism, 1930–1950* (Baton Rouge: Louisiana State University Press, 2009).
8. Robert Penn Warren and David Farrell, "Poetry as a Way of Life: An Interview with Robert Penn Warren," in *Talking with Robert Penn Warren*, ed. Floyd C. Watkins et al. (Athens: University of Georgia Press, 1990), 366; Robert Penn Warren, *The Wilderness: A Tale of the Civil War* (New York: Random House, 1961).
9. Leick, "Ezra Pound v. 'The Saturday Review of Literature,'" 20.
10. James Jackson Kilpatrick, "A Conversation with Ezra Pound," *National Review*, May 24, 1958, 491–92.
11. Ezra Pound, "French Elections," Nov. 25, 1958; "The Mind of Europe," March 8, 1959; James Jackson Kilpatrick to Ezra Pound, July 6, 1959, all in Papers Relating to Ezra Pound, accession #6272, Special Collections, University of Virginia Library, Charlottesville.
12. For a discussion of how interposition coincided with an effort to raise the level of discourse about *Brown* in the South, see Chappell, *Stone of Hope*, 168–69.
13. Numan V. Bartley, *The Rise of Massive Resistance: Race and Politics in the South During the 1950s* (1969; Baton Rouge: Louisiana State University Press, 1999), 116, 131.
14. Powell recognized the argument that segregation promoted black development early on, in a term paper written while a law student at Washington and Lee in 1930. See Lewis F. Powell, Jr., "Recognition of Validity and Incidents of Marriages Between Whites and Blacks," April 28, 1931, Lewis F. Powell, Jr., Papers, Washington and Lee University Law School, Lexington, Va. For Powell's early life and reaction to *Brown*, see John C. Jeffries, Jr., *Justice Lewis F. Powell, Jr.* (New York: Charles Scribner's Sons, 1994), 139.
15. Lewis F. Powell, Jr., to Edward R. Murrow, Jan. 9, 1959, box 15, folder 27, Lewis F. Powell, Jr., Papers; Bartley, *The Rise of Massive Resistance*,

113; Jeffries, *Justice Lewis F. Powell, Jr.*, 140, 141, 169–70; Anders Walker, "A Lawyer Looks at Civil Disobedience: Why Lewis F. Powell, Jr., Divorced Diversity from Affirmative Action," *Colorado Law Review* 86 (2015): 1229; Anders Walker, "Diversity's Strange Career: Recovering the Racial Pluralism of Lewis F. Powell, Jr.," *Santa Clara Law Review* 50 (2010): 647.

16. Jeffries, *Justice Lewis E. Powell, Jr.*, 146–48.

17. Ibid., 137; Lewis F. Powell, Jr., to James Jackson Kilpatrick, Feb. 3, 1956; Lewis F. Powell, Jr., to Thomas B. Stanley, Jan. 19, 1956, box 25, folder 5, both Lewis F. Powell, Jr., Papers.

18. Jeffries, *Justice Lewis F. Powell, Jr.*, 151–52; *Cooper v. Aaron*, 358 U.S. 1 (1958).

19. James Jackson Kilpatrick to Edward E. Lane, Jan. 7, 1960, box 31, folder L-1960, James Jackson Kilpatrick Papers, Special Collections, University of Virginia, Charlottesville.

20. James Jackson Kilpatrick, "View from a Southern Exposure," in *100 Years of Emancipation*, ed. Robert A. Goldwin (Chicago: Rand McNally, 1964), 117, 123, 124, 126.

21. James Jackson Kilpatrick, "Blunders on the Left," *Richmond News Leader*, March 30, 1965, 8. Kilpatrick's take was not completely inaccurate; the Birmingham demonstrations at the heart of the book had struggled through the early spring of 1963 as King found "tremendous resistance" to protest, even among the city's black population. This led King to encourage fellow black strategists like Wyatt T. Walker to find ways of provoking "brutal tactics" from local police in order to gain "national coverage" for the movement, an objective that was achieved when a black marcher "lunged" at a police dog with a knife. When law enforcement responded with force, through the use of police dogs and clubs, Walker and King rejoiced, even as black activists like James Forman confessed to being "disgusted" at the movement's manipulation of violence to advance its agenda. David J. Garrow, *Bearing the Cross: Martin Luther King, Jr., and the Southern Christian Leadership Conference* (1986; New York: Vintage, 1988), 239; Glenn T. Eskew, *But for Birmingham: The Local and National Movements in the Civil Rights Struggle* (Chapel Hill: University of North Carolina Press, 1997), 228. Kilpatrick found similar Machiavellian tactics on display in Selma in 1965, as demonstrators traveled from the North to "create conditions of deliberately contrived disorder." "The sincerity of this whole affair," lamented Kilpatrick, "viewed as an effort to register Lowndes County Negroes, stands gravely in doubt. In January, when it was possible for Negroes to come and register, as ordinary citizens following ordinary procedures, they did not come. Then, on signal, they came in unmanageable droves," including "children, non-residents, [and] out-of-state sympathizers." While African Americans had long struggled

to vote in Lowndes County, Kilpatrick remained fixated on the movement's efforts to draw northern volunteers and northern media to the region, in the hopes of exploiting white-on-black violence. Precisely such violence exploded in March, when black protesters led a march across Lowndes County's Edmund Pettus Bridge, only to be met by police on horseback firing teargas and wielding whips. Kilpatrick was unsympathetic. "The Negroes' provocative 'dramatizations,'" he lambasted, "are a violation of the rights of others. The highways of Alabama were not meant to be a sound-set for Martin Luther King." James Jackson Kilpatrick, "A Conservative View" (manuscript), March 16, 1965, James Jackson Kilpatrick Papers, accession #6626-I, University of Virginia Library; James Jackson Kilpatrick, "Tramping on Rights," *Richmond News Leader*, March 10, 1965, 10; Clayborne Carson, *In Struggle: SNCC and the Black Awakening of the 1960s* (1981; Cambridge, Mass.: Harvard University Press, 1995), 162, 165; Garrow, *Bearing the Cross*, 413.

22. Lewis F. Powell, Jr., "A Lawyer Looks at Civil Disobedience," *Washington and Lee Law Review* 23 (1966): 210 (quoting Burke Marshall, "The Protest Movement and the Law," *Virginia Law Review* 51 [1965], 785), 216; "Rain Soaks Crowd: Sit-Ins Mar Festivities at Some Pavilions—Attendance Cut; World's Fair Is Opened by Johnson Despite Rain and Racial Demonstrations," *New York Times*, April 23, 1964, 1.
23. Powell, "A Lawyer Looks at Civil Disobedience," 216, 225.
24. Ibid., 226.
25. Lewis F. Powell, Jr., "Civil Disobedience: Prelude to Revolution?" *New York State Bar Journal* 40 (1968): 172, 173. For the disagreement between Carmichael and King, see Aram Goudsouzian, *Down to the Crossroads: Civil Rights, Black Power, and the Meredith March Against Fear* (New York: Farrar, Straus, and Giroux, 2014), 7, 38, 57; Carson, *In Struggle*, 209; "Black Militant: Focus on Rap Brown," *New York Times*, Aug. 13, 1967, 153; Gene Roberts, "The New S.N.C.C.: Weaker, Fierier," *New York Times*, Aug. 20, 1967, 45; and "Rap Brown Calls Nation on 'Eve' of a Negro Revolt," *New York Times*, Sept. 11, 1967, 76. A shadow of its former self, SNCC had lost most of its members by the time Powell addressed the New York Bar. Some estimated that the group was down from three hundred permanent staff to eighty and running out of money. Brown had joined Carmichael in taking the group down a radically different path from its initial commitment to nonviolence and political process (voter registration), turning instead to calls like Brown's and stunning crowds with demands for an armed uprising against whites. Roberts, "The New S.N.C.C.," 45.
26. Powell, "Civil Disobedience: Prelude to Revolution?" 172, 175.
27. Martin Luther King, Jr., *Why We Can't Wait* (1964; New York: Signet, 2000), 124, 128–30.

28. James Jackson Kilpatrick, "A Look at Lewis Powell: 'A Conservative View,'" *Washington Star*, Nov. 23, 1971, 18; Lewis F. Powell, Jr., to James Jackson Kilpatrick, Nov. 30, 1971, Lewis F. Powell, Jr., Papers.

Chapter Thirteen. *Regents v. Bakke*

1. Matthew D. Lassiter, *The Silent Majority: Suburban Politics in the Sunbelt South* (Princeton, N.J.: Princeton University Press, 2006), 15–16, 101. Joseph Crespino agrees with Lassiter that Nixon's so-called southern strategy was not a top-down campaign imposed on the South so much as a savvy response to a groundswell of anger at "liberal social reforms," including racial integration, "rampant secularism," and "elitism." Crespino goes on to argue that Nixon made overtures to rural conservatives in the South, not just educated suburbanites, a move that helped him win 78 percent of the popular vote in Mississippi in 1972. Mississippi proved a nexus for the intersection between segregation and southern pluralism as resistance to *Brown* prompted the establishment of private, Christian schools. Joseph Crespino, *In Search of Another Country: Mississippi and the Conservative Counterrevolution* (Princeton, N.J.: Princeton University Press, 2007), 236.
2. H. L. Mencken, "The Sahara of the Bozart," *Evening Mail* (New York), Nov. 13, 1917, reprinted in H. L. Mencken, *The American Scene: A Reader*, ed. Huntington Cairns (New York: Knopf, 1977), 157; Conrad Black, *Richard M. Nixon: A Life in Full* (New York: Public Affairs, 2007), 34–36.
3. Christopher Strain, "Soul City, North Carolina: Black Power, Utopia, and the African American Dream," *Journal of African American History* 89 (Winter 2004): 57. Carswell's reputation as a racist surged when a reporter discovered a speech that he had delivered in 1948 extolling segregation and affirming white supremacy. Although Carswell tried to distance himself from the speech, its tone sounded reptilian in 1969. Jack Bass, *Unlikely Heroes: The Dramatic Story of the Southern Judges Who Translated the Supreme Court's Brown Decision into a Revolution for Equality* (New York: Touchstone, 1981), 319. If Nixon had wanted a Republican judge from the South who supported civil rights, a cadre of accomplished candidates sat in the wings, including prominent jurists like Georgia's Elbert Tuttle, Louisiana's John Minor Wisdom, and Alabama's Frank Johnson, all of whom had ruled favorably on behalf of civil rights demonstrators. Yet Nixon left these names alone, in part out of fear that they would never gain southern support in the Senate. As Jack Bass notes, for example, "Frank Johnson had been mentioned as a possible Supreme Court nominee when the Nixon administration began looking for a southerner, but southern Republicans blocked serious consideration because they objected to Johnson's progressive record on racial cases." Bass, *Unlikely Heroes*, 318–19.

4. Lewis F. Powell, Jr., "Political Warfare," June 30, 1970, 2, 7, box 117, folder 31; Lewis F. Powell, Jr., to Richard M. Nixon, June 26, 1970, box 117, folder 31, both Lewis F. Powell, Jr., Papers, Washington and Lee University School of Law, Lexington, Va.
5. Nixon wrote Powell a letter complimenting him on his political warfare missive on October 26, 1970. See Richard M. Nixon to Lewis F. Powell, Jr., Oct. 26, 1970, box 117, folder 31; Lewis F. Powell, Jr., "The Attack on American Institutions," Southern Industrial Relations Conference, Blue Mountain, N.C., July 15, 1970, 21, box 118, folder 1, both Lewis F. sPowell, Jr., Papers.
6. Powell, "The Attack on American Institutions."
7. Ibid., 15, 21, 24; Martin Luther King, Jr., *Why We Can't Wait* (1964; New York: Signet, 2000), 124; Robert Penn Warren, interviewed by Ralph Ellison and Eugene Walter, "The Art of Fiction No. 18," *Paris Review*, Spring–Summer 1957, reprinted in *Talking with Robert Penn Warren*, ed. Floyd C. Watkins et al. (Athens: University of Georgia Press, 1990), 47.
8. *San Antonio Independent School District v. Rodriguez*, 411 U.S. 1 (1973); Brief for Appellees at 3–4, *San Antonio Independent School District v. Rodriguez*, 411 U.S. 1 (1973) (No. 71–1332); Covert E. Parnell III to Lewis F. Powell, Jr., June 2, 1972, 2–4, box 382, folder 1, Lewis F. Powell, Jr., Papers.
9. Lewis F. Powell, Jr., to Larry A. Hammond, Oct. 9, 1972, 3–4, box 382, folder 7, Lewis F. Powell, Jr., Papers.
10. *San Antonio Independent School District v. Rodriguez*, 411 U.S. 1, 50.
11. Eugene D. Genovese, "The Voice of Southern Conservatism," in Eugene D. Genovese, *The Southern Front: History and Politics in the Cultural War* (Columbia: University of Missouri Press, 1995), 252.
12. *Keyes v. School District No. 1, Denver Colorado*, 412 U.S. 189, 192 (1973).
13. Ibid., 189, 208.
14. Ibid., 189, 224.
15. Ibid., 189, 218, 220, 241, 242. As Powell saw it, "An integrated school system does not mean—and indeed could not mean in view of the residential patterns of most of our major metropolitan areas—that every school must in fact be an integrated unit." In fact, integrating all units struck Powell as at best naive and at worst dangerous. After all, whites could, and probably would, simply abandon onerous school districts, as they had done in Richmond, leaving cities across the country segregated, bankrupt, and worse off than they had been under Jim Crow. The Constitution provided no remedy for black students in such situations, since federal causes of action only arose when segregation was alleged "within" school districts. Ibid., 189, 226–27, 228 (Powell, J. concurring).
16. Ibid., 189, 218–19, 227, 230 (Powell, J. concurring); Robert Penn Warren, *Legacy of the Civil War: Meditations on the Centennial* (New York: Random House, 1961), 59–66.

17. As James Jackson Kilpatrick put it, "The South itself has been wronged—cruelly and maliciously wronged, by men in high places whose hypocrisy is exceeded only by their ignorance, men whose trade is to damn the bigotry of the segregated South by day and to sleep in lily-white Westchester County by night." James Jackson Kilpatrick, *The Southern Case for School Segregation* (Springfield, Ohio: Crowell-Collier, 1962), 21.
18. *Milliken v. Bradley*, 418 U.S. 717, 729–30, 735, 741–42 (1974).
19. Relying on the majority opinion in *Keyes*, Burger held that federal judges could not simply discount district lines to achieve integration unless plaintiffs could prove that the districts in question had taken deliberate measures to segregate blacks. Ibid., 717, 745–46, 748–49, 761; Joseph Coates and Arnold Sagalyn, "Crime, Violence, and Social Disorder," *Science*, Dec. 4, 1970, 1120–21.
20. *Milliken v. Bradley*, 418 U.S. 717, 759, 760–61 (Douglas, J. dissenting).
21. Jesse T. Moore, Jr., "Seeking a New Life: Blacks in Post–Civil War Colorado," *Journal of Negro History* 78 (1993): 166–87.
22. See *Regents of the University of California v. Bakke*, 438 U.S. 265, 276–77 (1978), and John C. Jeffries, Jr., *Justice Lewis F. Powell, Jr.* (New York: Charles Scribner's Sons, 1994), 456.
23. *Bakke*, 438 U.S. 325, 412 (Brennan, J., concurring in the judgment); Jeffries, *Justice Lewis F. Powell, Jr.*, 486.
24. *Bakke*, 438 U.S. 325–26, 328, 336, 370, 374, 395 (Marshall J. concurring in part and dissenting in part).
25. Lewis F. Powell, Jr., "Bakke—Pre-Conference Notes," Oct. 13, 1977, 1978 Bakke76-811, folder 4, Lewis F. Powell, Jr., Papers, Washington and Lee University School of Law, Lexington, Va.
26. *Bakke*, 438 U.S. 292–93, citing *Yick Wo v. Hopkins*, 118 U.S. 356 (1886) (Chinese Americans); *Korematsu v. United States*, 323 U.S. 214 (1944) (Japanese Americans); *Hernandez v. Texas*, 347 U.S. 475 (1954) (Mexican Americans); *Strauder v. West Virginia*, 100 U.S. 303, 308 (1880) (Celtic Irishmen); *Truax v. Raich*, 239 U.S. 33, 41 (1915) (Austrian resident aliens); Powell, "Bakke—Pre-Conference Notes," Oct. 13, 1977.
27. Matthew Frye Jacobson, *Roots Too: White Ethnic Revival in Post–Civil Rights America* (Cambridge, Mass.: Harvard University Press, 2008); Brief for American Jewish Committee, American Jewish Congress, Hellenic Bar Association of Illinois, Italian-American Foundation, Polish American Affairs Council, Polish American Educators Association, Ukrainian Congress Committee of America (Chicago Division), and Unico National as Amici Curiae Supporting Respondents, *Bakke*, 438 U.S. 265; Brief for the Polish American Congress et al. as Amici Curiae Supporting Respondents, *Bakke*, 438 U.S. 265.
28. *Bakke*, 438 U.S. 295, 296. Powell's notion of whites as minorities echoed the views of Jewish intellectual Morris Cohen. Father of legal pluralist Felix Cohen, Morris believed that ultimately every "group of human

being" was "a minority in one situation or another." Dalia Tsuk Mitchell, *Architect of Justice: Felix S. Cohen and the Founding of American Legal Pluralism* (Ithaca, N.Y.: Cornell University Press, 2007), 15.

29. *Bakke*, 438 U.S. 295; Eric Foner, "The Supreme Court and the History of Reconstruction—and Vice Versa," *Columbia Law Review* 112 (Nov. 2012): 1585, 1605; Eric Foner, *Reconstruction: America's Unfinished Revolution, 1863–1877* (New York: Harper and Row, 1988), 446; J. Michael Martinez, *Coming for to Carry Me Home: Race in America from Abolition to Jim Crow* (Lanham, Md.: Rowman and Littlefield, 2012), 161.

30. Foner, "The Supreme Court and the History of Reconstruction—and Vice Versa," 1585, 1605; Foner, *Reconstruction*, 446; Martinez, *Coming for to Carry Me Home*, 161; *Bakke*, 438 U.S. 307.

31. *Bakke*, 438 U.S. 400, 401 (Marshall J. concurring in part and dissenting in part); William J. Brennan, Jr., "Narrative of Justice William J. Brennan," box 464, Papers of Justice William J. Brennan, Jr., Library of Congress, Washington, D.C. For a reprinted version, see Lee Epstein and Jack Knight, "Piercing the Veil: William J. Brennan's Account of Regents of the University of California v. Bakke," *Yale Law and Policy Review* 19 (2001): 341, 359.

32. As Powell saw it, race was simply a personal characteristic, like national origin or athletic ability, and nothing more. Powell, "Bakke—Pre-Conference Notes," Oct. 13, 1977.

    Powell disliked quota systems because they were noncompetitive, setting slots aside for applicants who then did not have to compete with the rest of the pool. "We all compete throughout life on an individual basis," wrote Powell. "A quota system—by whatever name—that accords non-competitive preferred status is contrary to basic traditions of this country." Ibid.; *Bakke*, 438 U.S. 311–12, 314–15, 323. To many, this rationale was confusing. "For reasons that were not—and could not be—satisfactorily explained," complained Powell biographer John Jeffries, "Powell insisted that fixed quotas 'would hinder rather than further attainment of genuine diversity.'" Jeffries, *Justice Lewis F. Powell, Jr.*, 477. Yet Jeffries missed the manner in which Powell felt that quotas eliminated competition, elevating race above other criteria that might also contribute to diversity, like cultural background or religion. *Bakke*, 438 U.S. 314–15.

33. Davidson, *The Attack on Leviathan*, 110, 113, 126.

34. Powell, "Bakke—Pre-Conference Notes," Oct. 13, 1977.

35. See Oliver B. Pollak, "Antisemitism, the Harvard Plan, and the Roots of Reverse Discrimination," *Jewish Social Studies* 45, no. 2 (1983): 113, 117,119; Jerome Karabel, *The Chosen: The Hidden History of Admission and Exclusion at Harvard, Yale, and Princeton* (New York: Houghton Mifflin, 2005), 86–89, 120.

36. *Bakke*, 438 U.S. 265, 316–17; Nathan Glazer, "University Autonomy and the *Bakke* Case," *New York Times*, July 30, 1977, 14, cited in Brief for

American Jewish Committee et al. as Amici Curiae Supporting Respondents, *Bakke*, 438 U.S. 265.

37. *Committee for Public Education and Religious Liberty v. Nyquist*, 413 U.S. 756, 773 (1973) (Powell, J., writing for the Court); *Wolman v. Walter*, 433 U.S. 229, 262 (1977) (Powell, J., concurring in part, dissenting in part).
38. Lewis F. Powell, Jr., "The Challenge to the Private Preparatory School," Jan. 31, 1967, 2–4, box 254, folder 3, Lewis F. Powell, Jr., Papers.
39. Powell took issue with state efforts to silence institutions promoting unpopular views, including moves by the IRS to deny certain nonprofit organizations tax-exempt status. *Bob Jones University v. United States*, 461 U.S. 574, 609 (1983) (Powell, J., concurring). In footnote 4 of his concurring opinion, Powell cited his dissent in *Mississippi University for Women v. Hogan*, 458 U.S. 718, 735, 738, 745 (1982), that diversity was "a distinctive feature of America's tradition." Same-sex education, continued Powell in *Hogan*, comprised "a small aspect of this diversity." "Coeducation," argued Powell, "is a novel educational theory," given that for "much of our history," most children were educated in "sexually segregated classrooms." He also cited his concurrence in *Wolman v. Walter*, 433 U.S. 262, that parochial schools provided "wholesome competition" to public schools. *Bob Jones University v. United States*, 461 U.S. 574, 610–11.
40. Powell, "Bakke—Pre-Conference Notes," Oct. 13, 1977.
41. Ibid.; Jeffries, *Justice Lewis F. Powell, Jr.*, 498; Edwin M. Yoder, Jr., *Telling Others What to Think: Recollections of a Pundit* (Baton Rouge: Louisiana State University Press, 2004), 180; See also Edward B. Fiske, "Educators Welcome *Bakke* Ruling as Signal to Retain Current Policy," *New York Times*, June 29, 1978, A23; Anthony Lewis, "A Solomonic Decision: Abroad at Home," *New York Times*, June 29, 1978, A25.
42. According to Jeffries, for example, Powell's decision reflected a clear break from his past, evidence that he suddenly felt "personal responsibility for racial justice." Jeffries, *Justice Lewis F. Powell, Jr.*, 499; John Herbers, "A Plateau for Minorities," *New York Times*, June 29, 1978, A1; "Civil Rights Unit Lauds Decision in *Bakke* Case," *New York Times*, July 2, 1978, 18; Roger Wilkins, "U.S. Officials Praise Bakke Ruling," *New York Times*, June 30, 1978, A10.
43. Guido Calabresi, "*Bakke:* Lost Candor," *New York Times*, July 6, 1978, A19.
44. *Bakke*, 438 U.S. 265, 292. See also Calabresi, "*Bakke*."
45. Alan Dershowitz and Laura Hanft, "Affirmative Action and the Harvard College Diversity-Discretion Model: Paradigm or Pretext," *Cardozo Law Review* 1 (1979): 379, 385, 387–88; *Bakke*, 438 U.S. 315.
46. Lewis F. Powell, Jr., "America's Values: Whither Tending," *New York State Bar Journal* 44 (1972): 513.
47. Dershowitz and Hanft, "Affirmative Action and the Harvard College Diversity-Discretion Model," 385; Davidson, *The Attack on Leviathan*, 33.

See also Russell Kirk, "Donald Davidson and the South's Conservatism," in *The Politics of Prudence* (Wilmington, Del.: Intercollegiate Studies Institute, 1993), 67.

Chapter Fourteen. The Last Lynching

1. Jimmy Carter, "Restoration of Citizenship Rights to Jefferson F. Davis Statement on Signing S. J. Res. 16 into Law," October 17, 1978, in *Jimmy Carter: Public Papers of the Presidents of the United States, 1978, Book II—June 30 to December 31, 1978* (Washington, D.C.: Government Printing Office, 1979), 1786; Tom Wicker, "Jimmy Carter's Appeal," *New York Times*, April 25, 1976, 161.
2. According to Michael Kreyling, southern literary critic Louis D. Rubin captured this sentiment in *The American South: Portrait of a Culture*, an anthology of essays "commemorating the admission of the south to the American mainstream." Michael Kreyling, *Inventing Southern Literature* (Jackson: University Press of Mississippi, 1998), 52, 53; Robert Penn Warren, *Jefferson Davis Gets His Citizenship Back* (Lexington: University of Kentucky Press, 1980), 47, 49, 56, 61–62, 68. Only one year before, Warren had lamented the inevitable "amalgamation of the country," expressing surprise that "the country has kept as many of its differences as it has over the last 35 years." Benjamin DeMott, "Talk with Robert Penn Warren," *New York Times*, Jan. 9, 1977, 238.
3. Christopher Lydon, "Carter Defends All-White Areas," *New York Times*, April 7, 1976, 1.
4. Christopher Lydon, "Carter Issues Apology on 'Ethnic Purity' Phrase," *New York Times*, April 9, 1976, 1; Robert Reinhold, "Carter Elaborates on His 'Ethnic' View," *New York Times*, April 10, 1976, 10.
5. Lydon, "Carter Issues Apology on 'Ethnic Purity' Phrase," 1; Tom Wicker, "The Burden on Carter," *New York Times*, April 9, 1976, 37; Lydon, "Carter Defends All-White Areas," 1.
6. Robert Penn Warren, "The Negro Movement in Upheaval," review of James Farmer, *Freedom When?* (New York: Random House, 1966), in *New York Review of Books*, Aug. 18, 1966, 22–25.
7. Ibid.
8. Robert Penn Warren, "Ballad of Mister Dutcher and the Last Lynching in Gupton," *New York Review of Books*, Jan. 24, 1974, reprinted in Robert Penn Warren, *The Collected Poems of Robert Penn Warren*, ed. John Burt (Baton Rouge: Louisiana State University Press, 1998), 282.
9. Robert Penn Warren, *Who Speaks for the Negro?* (New York: Vintage, 1965), 11.
10. Warren, "Ballad of Mr. Dutcher and the Last Lynching in Gupton."
11. Warren, *Who Speaks for the Negro?* 11, 12.
12. Robert Penn Warren, "Old Nigger on One-Mule Cart Encountered

Late at Night When Driving Home from Party in the Back Country," *New Yorker*, Dec. 8, 1975, 46, reprinted in Robert Penn Warren, *New and Selected Poems, 1923–1985* (New York: Random House, 1985), 173.

13. Cleanth Brooks to Robert Penn Warren, April 3, 1975, reprinted in *Cleanth Brooks and Robert Penn Warren: A Literary Correspondence*, ed. James A. Grimshaw, Jr. (Columbia: University of Missouri Press, 1998). See, e.g., John Stauffer, "Literary Neo-Confederates and Civil Rights," *Modern Language Studies* 39 (Summer 2009): 42–53. Stauffer demonstrates that Brooks and Warren retained decidedly Agrarian ideas through the 1970s, though he misses Warren's support for Black Power and black separatism as evinced in Warren's 1966 review of James Farmer's memoir. Stauffer also does not discuss Brooks's and Warren's inclusion of African American writers in their anthology *The Makers and the Making*.

14. Robert Penn Warren to Cleanth Brooks, August 29, 1970, reprinted in Grimshaw, ed., *Cleanth Brooks and Robert Penn Warren*, 316. For mention of the textbook's avant garde inclusion of minority voices, see Michael Anderson, "R. W. B. Lewis, Biographer and Critic, Is Dead at 84," *New York Times*, June 15, 2002, B18. Paul Lauter alludes to the anthology as "counter-hegemonic," in Lauter, "Taking Anthologies Seriously," *MELUS* 29 (Autumn–Winter 2004): 26. *American Literature: The Makers and the Making*, ed. Cleanth Brooks, R. W. B. Lewis, and Robert Penn Warren (New York: St. Martin's Press, 1973), 1:1175–77, 1166, 1167–69, 1172.

15. Brooks et al., eds., *American Literature*, 2:2711–21; Alice Walker, "Looking for Zora," *Ms.*, March 1975, reprinted in Alice Walker, *In Search of Our Mothers' Gardens* (San Diego: Harcourt Brace Jovanovich, 1983), 93–116. For Walker's role in resurrecting Hurston, see Henry Louis Gates, Jr., "Soul of a Black Woman: Zora Neale Hurston," *New York Times*, Feb. 19, 1978, BR4, and Evelyn C. White, *Alice Walker: A Life* (New York: Norton, 2004), 256–57.

16. See, e.g., Paul Lauter, "History and the Canon," *Social Text* 12 (Autumn 1985): 94–101; Stauffer, "Literary Neo-Confederates and Civil Rights," 42–53; and Brooks et al., eds., *American Literature*, 1:1173.

17. Robert Hemenway, *Zora Neale Hurston: A Literary Biography* (Urbana: University of Illinois Press, 1977), 323, 328; Henry Louis Gates, Jr., "'A Negro Way of Saying': *Dust Tracks on A Road* an Autobiography. By Zora Neale Hurston," *New York Times*, April 21, 1985, 43; Walker, "Looking for Zora," 93–116. Many leaders in BAM ignored Hurston, whose stories of black life in the Jim Crow South struck more militant artists as insufficiently critical of white oppression. Gates, "Soul of a Black Woman," BR4, 30. Consequently, Hurston and her work descended into almost complete obscurity following her death in 1960. Hemenway, *Hurston*, 323, 328.

Chapter Fifteen. Beyond the Peacock

1. Alice Walker, *The Third Life of Grange Copeland* (1970; New York: Mariner, 2003); Evelyn C. White, *Alice Walker: A Life* (New York: Norton, 2004), 11, 184–90; Alice Walker, "Zora Neale Hurston: A Cautionary Tale and a Partisan View" (1977), reprinted in Alice Walker, *In Search of Our Mothers' Gardens* (San Diego: Harcourt Brace Jovanovich, 1983), 83.
2. Walker, "Zora Neale Hurston," 83, 84, 85.
3. Ibid., 86, 87; Alice Walker, "Looking for Zora," *Ms.*, March 1975, reprinted in Walker, *In Search of Our Mothers' Gardens*, 93.
4. Henry Louis Gates, Jr., "Soul of a Black Woman: Zora Neale Hurston," *New York Times*, Feb. 19, 1978, BR4, 30; Henry Louis Gates, Jr., "'A Negro Way of Saying': *Dust Tracks on A Road* an Autobiography. By Zora Neale Hurston," *New York Times*, April 21, 1985, 43.
5. Henry Louis Gates, Jr., "The 'Blackness of Blackness': A Critique of the Sign and the Signifying Monkey," *Critical Inquiry* 9 (June 1983): 685, 686, 690, 692. Building in part on the black folklore that Hurston had captured in her novels and books, Gates shows how she and others had developed a "rhetorical practice" that involves the subtle use of metaphors, allusions, and double-meanings, a "language of trickery" to live together and also to survive the hostile conditions of the Jim Crow South. See also Henry Louis Gates, Jr., *The Signifying Monkey: A Theory of African American Literary Criticism* (New York: Oxford University Press, 1988), and Richard Wright, "Review of Their Eyes Were Watching God," *New Masses*, Oct. 5, 1937, 22–23.
6. Sidney W. Mintz and Richard Price, *The Birth of African-American Culture: An Anthropological Perspective* (Boston: Beacon Press, 1976), 62; Office of Policy Planning and Research, U.S. Department of Labor, *The Negro Family: The Case for National Action* (1965), reprinted in Lee Rainwater and William L. Yancey, *The Moynihan Report and the Politics of Controversy* (Cambridge, Mass.: MIT Press, 1967), 410.
7. *Moore v. City of East Cleveland*, 431 U.S. 494 (1977).
8. Lewis F. Powell, Jr., Preliminary Memorandum, no. 75–6289, *Moore v. City of East Cleveland*, Lewis F. Powell, Jr., Papers, Washington and Lee University School of Law, Lexington, Va.; *Moore v. City of East Cleveland*, 431 U.S. 494.
9. Alice Walker, "Beyond the Peacock: The Reconstruction of Flannery O'Connor," *Ms.*, Dec. 1975, reprinted in Walker, *In Search of Our Mothers' Gardens*, 58; Alice Walker "The Black Writer and the Southern Experience," reprinted in *In Search of Our Mothers' Gardens*, 21.
10. Walker, "Beyond the Peacock," 43, 44, 57, 58.
11. Alice Walker, "Only Justice Can Stop a Curse," *Mother Jones* (Sept.–Oct. 1982), reprinted in *In Search of Our Mothers' Gardens*, 340–41.

12. Alice Walker, "Zora Neale Hurston," reprinted in *In Search of Our Mothers' Gardens*, 85.
13. Ernest J. Gaines, *Conversations with Ernest Gaines*, ed. John Lowe (Jackson: University Press of Mississippi, 1995), 85; Gloria Naylor, *Conversations with Gloria Naylor*, ed. Maxine Lavon Montgomery (Jackson: University Press of Mississippi, 2004), 62; Toni Morrison, *Toni Morrison: Conversations*, ed. Carolyn C. Denard (Jackson: University Press of Mississippi, 2008), 114; Linda Wagner-Martin, *Maya Angelou: Adventurous Spirit* (New York: Bloomsbury Academic, 2016), 104.
14. Walker's anger at persistent inequality even led her to voice a profound desire for retribution against whites, a sentiment that resonated with black calls for reparations. Walker, "Only Justice Can Stop a Curse," 338–42.
15. Walker, "Beyond the Peacock," 50.
16. William A. Bake and James Jackson Kilpatrick, *The American South: Four Seasons of the Land* (Birmingham, U.K.: Oxmoor House, 1980), xxiv.
17. Paul D. Carrington, "Diversity!" *Utah Law Review* (1992): 1105, 1109, citing John Searle, "The Storm over the University," *New York Review of Books*, Dec. 6, 1990, 34–36. See also Martin E. Spencer, "Multiculturalism, 'Political Correctness,' and the Politics of Identity," *Sociological Forum* 9 (Dec. 1994): 556; Benjamin Baez, "Diversity and Its Contradictions: How Support for Diversity in Higher Education Can Undermine Social Justice," *Academe* 86 (Sept.–Oct. 2000): 43; Paul Lauter, "History and the Canon," *Social Text* 12 (Autumn 1985): 94–101; and Matthew Frye Jacobson, *Roots Too: White Ethnic Revival in Post–Civil Rights America* (Cambridge, Mass.: Harvard University Press, 2006), 207.

For Canadian debates on multiculturalism in the 1960s, see Royal Commission on Bilingualism and Biculturalism, *A Preliminary Report* (Ottawa: Queen's Printer, 1965); Royal Commission on Bilingualism and Biculturalism, *Report: General Introduction* (Ottawa: Queen's Printer, 1967); Second Canadian Conference on Multiculturalism, *Multiculturalism as State Policy* (Ottawa: Canadian Consultative Council on Multiculturalism, 1976), 81–118; Jean Burnet, "Myths and Multiculturalism," *Canadian Journal of Education* 4, no. 4 (1979): 45–46; and Nancy Baker Jones, "Confronting the PC 'Debate': The Politics of Identity and the American Image," *National Women's Studies Association Journal* 6 (Autumn 1994): 386. Multiculturalism did not truly enter common parlance in the United States until the 1990s. See Jacobson, *Roots Too*, 226. For Hayden's support of multiculturalism, see ibid., 236.

For the complex history of multiculturalism as a facet of civil rights and ethnic revival, see ibid., 208–45; Gwendolyn C. Baker, "Development of the Multicultural Program: School of Education, University of Michigan," in *Pluralism and the American Teacher: Issues and Case Studies*, ed. Frank H. Klassen and Donna M. Gollnick (Washington, D.C.: American Association for Colleges of Teacher Education, 1977), 163–69; Gwendolyn C. Baker, "Policy Issues in Multicultural Education in the United States," *Journal of Negro Education* 48 (Summer 1979): 253, 259; Faustine C. Jones, "Editorial Comment: Implementing Multiculturalism —The Challenge to Educators in the International Year of the Child," *Journal of Negro Education* 48 (Summer 1979): 233, 234 (linking multicultural education to an "affirmation of cultural and racial diversity"); and Spencer, "Multiculturalism, 'Political Correctness,' and the Politics of Identity," 557, 559. The movement borrowed its name from a concept that had been actively promoted by French speakers in Canada called "multiculturalism" and quickly boasted a profound impact on national debates over the teaching of American history, literature, and law, as well as the engineering of general curricula in American schools. Royal Commission on Bilingualism and Biculturalism, *A Preliminary Report;* Royal Commission on Bilingualism and Biculturalism, *Report: General Introduction;* Second Canadian Conference on Multiculturalism, *Multiculturalism as State Policy*, 81–118; Burnet, "Myths and Multiculturalism," 45–46; Jones, "Confronting the PC 'Debate,'" 386.

18. Calvin Sims, "World Views: Separatists and Pluralists Lay Claim to Multicultural Mantle," *New York Times*, Nov. 4, 1990, EDUC23. Diane Ravitch divided multiculturalists into pluralists and "particularists," simply another term for separatist. Diane Ravitch, "Multiculturalism: E Pluribus Plures," *American Scholar* 59 (1990): 340. See also Jones, "Confronting the PC 'Debate,'" 394; Molefi Kete Asanti, *The Afrocentric Idea* (Philadelphia: Temple University Press, 1987); Sims, "World Views," EDUC23; Arthur M. Schlesinger, Jr., *The Disuniting of America: Reflections on a Multicultural Society* (1991; New York: Norton, 1992), 69–70; Ben L. Martin, "From Negro to Black to African American," *Political Science Quarterly* 106 (1991): 83; Spencer, "Multiculturalism, 'Political Correctness,' and the Politics of Identity," 102–3.

19. Henry Louis Gates, Jr., "Pluralism and Its Discontents," *Contention: Debates in Society, Culture, and Science* 2 (Fall 1992): 69; Sims, "World Views," EDUC23; Schlesinger, *The Disuniting of America*, 66.

20. That ethnic groups were no longer assimilating into mainstream American society was something that critics had observed as early as the 1960s. Prominent social scientists Daniel Patrick Moynihan and Nathan Glazer published a popular book on precisely this topic in 1963, arguing that New York ethnics were departing from the melting-pot ideal. Nathan Glazer and Daniel Patrick Moynihan, *Beyond the Melting Pot: The Negroes, Puerto Ricans, Jews, Italians, and Irish of New York City* (1963; Cambridge, Mass.: MIT Press, 1971); Allan Bloom, *The Closing of the American Mind: How Higher Education Has Failed Democracy and Impoverished the Souls of Today's Students* (New York: Simon and Schuster, 1987), 27; Schlesinger, *The Disuniting of America*, 133. For the conservative assault on multicul-

turalism generally, see Jones, "Confronting the PC 'Debate,'" 386. See also Dinesh D'Sousa, *Illiberal Education: The Politics of Race and Sex on Campus* (New York: Free Press, 1998), and Richard Bernstein, *Dictatorship of Virtue: How the Battle over Multiculturalism Is Reshaping Our Schools, Our Country, and Our Lives* (New York: Vintage, 1995).

21. Davidson, *The Attack on Leviathan*, 10–11; Lewis F. Powell, Jr., "Bakke—Pre-Conference Notes," Oct. 13, 1977, Bakke 76-811, folder 4, Lewis F. Powell, Jr., Papers, Washington and Lee University School of Law, Lexington, Va.

Chapter Sixteen. *Missouri v. Jenkins*

1. "Excerpts from the Victory Speech by President-Elect Clinton," *New York Times*, Nov. 4, 1992, B3; David Stout, "Clinton Names 7 to Race Relations Panel," *New York Times*, June 13, 1997, A22; Gwen Ifill, "Clinton, Marking King Holiday, Pushes Domestic Policy Programs," *New York Times*, Jan. 18, 1994, B10; "Clinton, in 2 Speeches, Urges Racial Healing," *New York Times*, July 18, 1997, A20; Catherine S. Manegold, "U.S. Study Bolsters Case for Minority Scholarships," *New York Times*, Jan. 15, 1994, 8, A13; *Podberesky v. Kirwan*, 38 F.3d 147 (4th Cir. 1994); "Educators Scrambling to Assess Ruling That Struck Down a Scholarship Program for Blacks," *New York Times*, Oct. 29, 1994, 7. The Supreme Court allowed the Fourth Circuit ruling to stand, a move that left uncertain the status of race-based scholarships generally. For more on the Fourth Circuit's decision and its implications for race, see Terry H. Anderson, *The Pursuit of Fairness: A History of Affirmative Action* (New York: Oxford University Press, 2004), 241, and Catherine S. Manegold, "U.S. Officially Backs Race-Based Scholarships," *New York Times*, Feb. 18, 1994, A13.
2. Gwen Ifill, "Fight New Segregationism, President Urges Students: Stresses Role of '54 Ruling in World Change," *New York Times*, May 18, 1994, A20; Alison Mitchell, "Calls Diversity Essential and Issues Warning on Resegregation: Clinton Backs Affirmative Action, Urging Debate on Race," *New York Times*, June 15, 1997, 1; Todd S. Purdum, "Defending Affirmative Action, Clinton Details Plan to Review It," *New York Times*, March 24, 1995, A23; "Excerpts from President's Comments on School Desegregation," *New York Times*, Sept. 26, 1997, A20.
3. "Clinton Panel on Race Relations Is Itself Biased, Gingrich Says," *New York Times*, Nov. 21, 1997, A30; Joseph Crespino, *Strom's America* (New York: Hill and Wang, 2012), 286–87, 295–97. Crespino demonstrates the manner in which Thurmond initially defended Jim Crow as a "humane and realistic way of organizing a multiracial society, one that recognized cultural differences and racial preferences." See Crespino, *Strom's America*, 310; Joseph Crespino, *In Search of Another Country: Mississippi and the*

Conservative Counterrevolution (Princeton, N.J.: Princeton University Press, 2007), 236; Peter Applebome "Racial Politics in South's Contests: Hot Wind of Hate or a Last Gasp?" *New York Times*, Nov. 5, 1990, A1; and *Hopwood v. Texas*, 78 F.3d 932 (5th Cir. 1996).

4. J. William Harris, *Deep Souths: Delta, Piedmont, and Sea Island Society in the Age of Segregation* (Baltimore: Johns Hopkins University Press, 2001), 14, 49–50, 72, 78.
5. Clarence Thomas, *My Grandfather's Son* (New York: HarperCollins, 2007), 63–64; Andrew Peyton Thomas, *Clarence Thomas: A Biography* (San Francisco: Encounter, 2001), 70.
6. Thomas, *My Grandfather's Son*, 245, 251, 269.
7. *United States v. Fordice*, 505 U.S. 717, 748 (1992) (Thomas J. concurring).
8. *Missouri v. Jenkins*, 515 U.S. 70, 114, 118 (1995); *United States v. Fordice*, 505 U.S. 748.
9. *Grutter v. Bollinger*, 539 U.S. 306, 349 (2003) (Thomas J., dissenting).
10. Ibid., 306, 315, 337, 332–34, 342–43. O'Connor was not alone in mistaking Powell for being a supporter of affirmative action. See, for example, Kathleen Sullivan, "Sins of Discrimination: Last Term's Affirmative Action Cases," *Harvard Law Review* 100 (1986): 78, 80, arguing that the Supreme Court has tended to view diversity programs as "penance for the specific sins of racism a government, union, or employer has committed in the past."
11. *Grutter v. Bollinger*, 539 U.S. 306, 342.
12. Ibid., 306, 328, 330.
13. Lewis F. Powell, Jr., "The Challenge to the Private Preparatory School," Jan. 31, 1967, box 254, folder 3, Lewis F. Powell, Jr., Papers, Washington and Lee University School of Law, Lexington, Va.
14. See, e.g., *Fisher v. University of Texas at Austin*, 133 S.Ct. 2411 (2013), and *Schuette v. Coalition to Defend Affirmative Action, Integration and Immigrant Rights and Fight for Equality by Any Means Necessary (BAMN)*, 134 S.Ct. 1623 (2014). For the narrow reading of diversity as a compelling interest primarily due to its classroom benefits, see the majority opinions in *Fisher v. University of Texas at Austin*, 133 S.Ct. 2411, and *Schuette v. BAMN*, 134 S.Ct. 1623. For the interpretation of diversity as a form of affirmative action, see Justice Ruth Bader Ginsburg's dissent in *Fisher v. Texas*, 133 S.Ct. 2411, 2433 (Ginsburg J. dissenting), and Justice Sonia Sotomayor's dissent in *Schuette v. BAMN*, 134 S.Ct. 1623 (Sotomayor J. dissenting).
15. *Grutter v. Bollinger*, 539 U.S. 306, 349–50, 364.
16. Ibid., 349, 364, 372.

Conclusion

1. Heather K. Gerken, "Second-Order Diversity," *Harvard Law Review* 118 (2005): 1099, 1102.

2. Anne Bernard, "Gauging Reality That Grew from a Dream," *New York Times*, Jan. 21, 2008, B1; Juan Williams, "Obama's Color Line," *New York Times*, Nov. 30, 2007, A23; "Barack Obama's Speech on Race," reprinted in *New York Times*, March 18, 2008, nytimes.com/2008/03/18/us/politics/18text-obama.html.
3. Matt Bai, "What Would a Black President Mean for Black Politics: Post-Race," *New York Times*, Aug. 10, 2008, A34, A50; Williams, "Obama's Color Line," A23.
4. Elizabeth Day, "#BlackLivesMatter: The Birth of a New Civil Rights Movement," *The Guardian*, July 19, 2015, http://www.theguardian.com/world/2015/jul/19/blacklivesmatter-birth-civil-rights-movement; John Eligon, "Anger, Hurt, and Moments of Hope in Ferguson," *New York Times*, Aug. 21, 2014, 1; Michelle Alexander, *The New Jim Crow: Mass Incarceration in the Age of Color-Blindness* (2010; New York: New Press, 2012), 8, 11.
5. Movement for Black Lives, "A Vision for Black Lives: Policy Demands for Black Power, Freedom, and Justice," 2016, https://policy.m4bl.org/wp-content/uploads/2016/07/20160726-m4bl-Vision-Booklet-V3.pdf; Ta-Nehisi Coates, "The Case for Reparations," *The Atlantic*, June 2014, 54.
6. Ta-Nehisi Coates, *Between the World and Me* (New York: Spiegel and Grau, 2015), 11, 39–40, 103, 149; Benjamin Wallace-Wells, "The Hard Truths of Ta-Nehisi Coates," *New York*, July 12, 2015, 24, 29.
7. Ralph Ellison, "Twentieth-Century Fiction," reprinted in *Shadow and Act* (1964; New York: Vintage, 1995), 26; Movement for Black Lives, "A Vision for Black Lives."

Index